# Eyes Wide Open

Living, Laughing, Loving and Learning
in a Religion-Troubled World

**by George Erickson**

Other books by George Erickson:

*True North: Exploring the Great Wilderness by Bush Plane*

*Time Traveling With Science and the Saints*

*Back to the Barrens: On the Wing With da Vinci & Friends*

The author's website is www.tundracub.com.

Printed and bound in the United States of America

Library of Congress Card Catalog Card Number: 2010925570

ISBN 9780931779176

# Dedication

This book is dedicated with love to my wife, Sally,
the grade-A mother of my two good sons, and my supporter
and partner in the many turns that our lives have taken.

As the old song says:
"When my life is through, and the angels ask me to recall
the thrill of it all, I'll tell them I remember you…"

# Preface

*Eyes Wide Open*, a collection of many of my writings, some new, some previously published, arose from the long-neglected request of a member of the Minnesota Humanists who lived too far from Minneapolis to attend our meetings, but enjoyed the newsletter that I wrote and edited for many years. During that time, I was also vice president of the Minnesota Seaplane Pilots Association, the vice president and president of the Minnesota Humanists, and a board member of the American Humanist Association.

When my friend wrote to suggest this collection, his request was premature. Although I'd written many articles on a wide range of subjects, none of the books listed on the previous page, including my pro-science, adventure/travel bestseller, *True North*, which is based on my thirty eight summers of bush flying in Alaska and Canada, had yet to be conceived.

However, the time has now arrived. Some of these pieces are new. A few have been excerpted and adapted from my books. Others have been published in a wide variety of magazines, newspapers and newsletters. Some are joyful, a few are angry, some are sad. Love, sex, politics, truth, satire, religion, adventure, science, humor, history and opinion fill these pages.

Reviewers wrote that my second book, *Time Traveling with Science and the Saints,*' was incredibly well titled. It is my hope that you will reach the same conclusion well before you have finished *Eyes Wide Open*. You are invited to visit my website: www.tundracub.com.

# Warning

If you are a fundamentalist or a neocon
who can't abide dissent,
or if you are a conservative Catholic
with a pope who's heaven-sent —
**Don't buy this book.**

A few of the tales are fiction;
most of them are true,
but unlike religious stories,
I never confuse the two.

So enough for full disclosure,
it's time to move ahead
with our *Eyes Wide Open*
and a mind that isn't dead.

# Movin' On

I'd become accustomed to the humid warmth of my small — some might say cramped — quarters and to the oscillating rhythms of darkness and ruddy glows that slowly metronomed away my mid-winter days. I'd been there for weeks — no, make that months. How many months, I can't recall, but it seemed like I'd lived there forever. Month after month, the muted sounds of my surroundings had ebbed and flowed tide-like throughout the day.

Whatever I'd wanted had been delivered, as if someone were anticipating my every need. As a consequence, I hadn't felt the slightest desire to leave. In the meantime, I did what little was required of me, which, with eating, sleeping and doing my exercises, consumed my days.

There were, of course, a few distractions — new sounds and odd sensations from time to time. But my life had slumped into sameness as one dull day faded into another. However, if I'd been able to foresee the future, I'd have savored these days, for I was soon to be frightened by the sound of screaming — and the screams would be coming from me!

When another day ran dry with nothing of interest, I turned in early to seek diversion in dreams. Normally, I sleep like a babe, but that night I was terribly restless, prodded by a sense of unease. After shifting and turning for hours, I finally fell asleep, only to abruptly awaken, fully tense and alert — sensing, believing and fearing a premonition that violence was waiting for me.

Suddenly, the calm, familiar sounds that I had always known were overwhelmed by loud, stress-filled voices — one of them fluttering along the edge of hysteria. I listened, trembling as I wondered what was happening. Then a new sound arose, blotting out the others, a persistent, accelerating beat that gained strength as it boomed in my ears. "My heart," I gasped. Never had it pounded like this!

As I fought for control, a Zen-like chant from beyond the walls droned "Ono, Ono, Ono ...." Painful pressures erupted as the walls of my sanctuary seemed to close in. My chest, my shoulders and pelvis, my very skull began to flex as I struggled to escape, but just when I thought I'd be crushed, my room burst open, drenching me with cold, wintry air, and the ruddy glow flared into overwhelming brightness.

Harsh noises buffeted me. I coughed and gasped, trying to breath. Overwhelmed by exploding light, sound and pain, I screamed and screamed and screamed.

I must have fainted, for when I awoke, the lights had dimmed, the pain had vanished and a soft voice had begun to hum a soothing tune. Opening one eye, I surveyed my strange, new surroundings. Warm again, I smiled a contented smile. Laying my tiny hand on a soft, supple breast, I reflected: Being born was a frightful experience, but there might be compensations.

# Water Boy

Envision the bluest of blue July skies, a northern lake surrounding a pine-sheltered cabin, a picnic with laughing children and beer and brats on the grill. Jamie, who is well past two — and is being upstaged by his older sister — picks up a pine cone and quietly toddles away from his parents and their noisy friends. Jamie has decided to make a boat.

Crossing glacier-scarred bedrock, Jamie finds the path that leads to the big, shining thing they call a lake. He pauses to pick a handful of bright, white daisies that line the path, then retrieves his pine cone and continues, stopping briefly beside a hand pump that sits atop a well. Releasing his cone and his flowers, he grasps the pump handle and tries to work it up and down like his father does, but it is heavy and hard to reach. Frustrated, he noisily rattles the handle from side to side, leaves the flowers draped across the pump spout and carefully descends the five, slate steps that end at the pier.

His father's boat is tied to one side of the pier, but the other side is free, so Jamie proceeds, instinctively staying near the center of the dock. When he reaches the end, he turns to look back at the party. No one is looking his way.

Squatting at the end of the dock, Jamie reaches over the side to place his cone on the water, but the water is much too low. He drops to his knees, and then to his stomach, inching forward until his head is over the water.

He has no words for it, but he is surprised to see his face looking upward. He pokes a finger into the water, briefly disturbing his image. As he stares at his face, a minnow swims by. He reaches for it, but the minnow darts away.

Remembering his pine cone, he gently sets it on the water, smiling as it rocks on the ripples, and begins to push it back and forth like a boat while making motoring sounds.

When the minnow returns, Jamie plunges his hand into the water, again to no avail. Aided by a gentle breeze, the pine cone drifts away, just slightly out of reach. Jamie inches forward, his head and shoulders projecting over the water. He can almost reach it. Perhaps one more wriggle, just another inch will do, and it does, but as his hand closes on the cone, he becomes a human teeter totter, his head, chest and arms descending, his legs and feet rising until he suddenly enters a very different world.

Warm, womb-like water enfolds him, and he feels no sense of alarm. Eyes wide open, he discovers a world lit by shimmering shafts of light, of blues and greens and aquamarines. Buoyed by delicious weightlessness, he holds his breath as he paddles along beneath the surface. Briefly captivated by a russet crayfish crawling along the bottom, he reaches for it, only to be distracted by a ribbon-like leech that undulates by. He grabs it, and as the leech squirms within his grasp, Jamie's new world is suddenly shattered by an explosion of sound and light as he is roughly jerked from the depths and heaved up onto the dock.

Jamie looks around in amazement. His new world is gone, and his uncle, who is standing shoulder deep in the lake, is yelling something at him with a voice of alarm. Turning, he sees his mother running toward him. Crying and screaming, "Jamie, Jamie," she pulls him tight — and for the first time in Jamie's short life, Jamie knows fear.

# The Minnesota Trapper

from *True North: Exploring the Great Wilderness by Bush Plane*

Every fall, when the air turns cold and frost fairies etch feathery tableaus upon my window panes, my thoughts drift back through the decades to a boy just barely ten. It's the night of the winter solstice, a time of deep cold and long Northern nights. Under a black sky glittering with the sparks of distant stars, the border country sleeps.

Inside a small cabin, a pale hand slips from beneath a stack of gray woolen blankets and moves from side to side to sense the cold. The hand gropes for a set of wire-rimmed glasses and, having found them, disappears beneath the covers. A moment later, the hand returns to retrieve wool socks, long underwear, Melton pants and a flannel shirt. Beneath the blankets, the occupant curls himself around the clothing, preheating the layers that will have to keep him warm.

A clock strikes seven times. Poking his head from beneath the covers, the boy turns toward a window heavily furred with frost. Seven o' clock and still dark. He considers staying in bed a little longer. I'll wait for the sun, he thinks, but thoughts of his trap line widen his eyes.

He quickly pulls on his clothes, hurrying not because of the waiting riches, but to pile on the layers before they cool. As he turns to leave the room, he runs a finger across the frost-coated window, carving a furrow a quarter-inch deep.

In the darkened living room, a wood burner smiles toothily through rectangular inlets beneath its cast iron door. Feed me, it pleads. The boy gently lays a few pieces of well-split cedar on the coals, then blows across the radiant bed. The oily cedar bursts into flames. Birch follows, and the wood burner springs to life.

His boots, still warm from a night near the fire, exude the tarry aroma of Nor-V-gen boot grease. Bending over, the boy laces rawhide thongs hand over hand through their tall ladders of hooks, then touches the pouch on the side of his boot to be sure that his pocket knife's there. He struggles into a jacket that was loose a year ago, fit last year and now grows tight. Pulling on a woolen cap, he lowers the ear flaps, tugs a pair of leather choppers over brown woolen mittens and quietly slips out the door.

Cold, dry air pinches his nostrils. The metal frames of his glasses bite into his temples and nose. A snow-muffled rumble ruptures the silence as the lake's lens of shore-fast ice contracts, shrinking from the cold until it cracks with the sound of distant thunder.

Guided by the wispy light of a dying aurora, the boy picks his way along a cement-hard trail. Squeaaach, squeaaach, squeaaach — his boots wrench protests from bone-dry snow as he envisions the bicycle that a few more rabbits will buy — a red and white Schwinn with a battery-powered horn and headlight, two rear view mirrors and tasseled handle grips. Stopping beside a rock-hard brook, he marvels at the change a few months can bring, then heads toward the cluster of cedars that tower above his first trap.

The leg hold trap is empty. He carefully walks around it to admit the meager light of the purpling, predawn sky. The trap is set correctly, but nothing has come this way.

The boy has but one leg hold trap. All the rest are snares — supple metal nooses of braided wire that hang a few inches over the trail. A passing rabbit, accustomed to pushing its way through twigs and brush, feels nothing unusual until the noose draws tight around its neck. In the boy's mind, the rabbit dies quickly, aided by the numbing, merciful cold.

His first snare hangs exactly as he left it — a perfect circle, a zero, a delicately frosted cipher hovering just above the trail. Dropping to his knees to examine the pathway, he finds no tracks on its crystalline face.

The second sparkling loop reminds him of his mother's rhinestone-studded choker. "Choker," he thinks, then pulls back from the word with a twinge of regret.

With his first sets empty, his dreams of a bicycle begin to fade. He moves on, wiping his nose on the back of his leather choppers. Paralyzed by the subzero cold, the fine hairs that line his nostrils can no longer sweep back the flow, and the leather slowly hardens beneath a film of mucous ice.

Pushing his way through an alder thicket, the boy carefully approaches his third snare. There, centered in the trail lies the largest rabbit he's ever seen, curled up as if sleeping. Slipping his knife from his boot, the boy slides the blade beneath the noose and pries it open. After making sure that the snare is securely attached to its heavy, club-like stick, he resets the snare, drops the rigid rabbit into a burlap bag and heads for a pine-fringed bog. The sky, now indigo, dyes the snow the deepest blue.

As he nears the edge of the cranberry bog, something moves. He stops, motionless, scanning the trail. A rabbit materializes. Blue-white on blue-white, the animal is almost invisible in the slowly maturing light. The boy waits, not knowing what to do. A minute passes. His unmoving feet protest the cold. Still he waits as winter seeps inward, probing his cuffs and the neck of his jacket. A shiver runs down his body — and the rabbit races down the trail — into a waiting snare.

Yanked off its feet, the rabbit tumbles, dashing blindly back and forth, jerking against the drag as the noose tightens around its neck. The boy stands transfixed. It won't take long, he assures himself as his eyes widen in disbelief at the rabbit's gyrations.

The rabbit plunges on, thrashing violently through one long minute, then two, making frantic but futile attempts to escape. Anguished and hoping to put an end to the animal's misery, the boy drops to his knees, reels in the convulsing animal and jerks the noose tight.

Caught in a ghastly scene of his own making, the horror-stricken boy pulls on the noose as tears yield to sobs of remorse. The rabbit, drawing on unimaginable reserves, twists and turns, striking out with its legs. Appalled at the struggle and thinking to free the rabbit, the boy whips off his mittens and tries to release the snare, but the wire, the strong braided wire, has become so snarled in the animal's fur that release is impossible. Desperate to end the rabbit's pain and his horror, the boy pins the thrashing animal down with one hand and, with the other, raises high the club to which the snare is tied. Surely one blow will end its pain.

The first impact drives the rabbit's head into a cushioning pillow of snow. The second, aimed through tear-flooded lenses, lands more solidly, squirting an eye from its socket in a gush of blood. Still the rabbit thrashes on, fighting for its life. The boy, totally undone and awash with pity, anguish, and a pain he's never known, strikes again and again. Frustrated by the pillowy snow and repelled by the crimson carnage, he pleads for an end to the horror, crying, "Die, DIE, oh please, please diiiieeee."

The rabbit finally quivers and softens beneath his hand, taking with it the fantasy of quick and quiet, painless death. On his knees beside the limp body, the blood-spattered boy sobs while a silent forest watches. Far above, the first breath of dawn brushes frost crystals from the delicate needles of towering Norway pines. Descending, they glitter the air.

With shaking hands steaming in melted snow, the boy wipes his blood-smeared glasses while he tries to regain control. Opening his pocket knife, he saws away at the noose, then lays the limp body beside the trail. Still weeping, he carefully places the frozen rabbit alongside its companion and covers their bodies with snow.

The boy rises, shaking his lowered head as he mourns an innocence lost. Racked with lingering sobs, he walks to the end of his trap line, pulling shut noose after noose after noose. He springs the leg hold trap and leaves it behind to rust. As he trudges back to the cabin, his brow furrows at the thought of his mother, who'll be frightened by his blood-spattered, empty-handed return. When she asks, "Son! What happened? Are you alright?" What will I say? How will I hold back the tears?

# Satan Update

When I was 14, I contracted a serious ankle infection that laid me low for months. Thus restricted, I sought diversion in music and books. One day, while lying on my back with my afflicted leg aloft, I encountered someone whom my peers had been meeting in much more interesting ways. I met the devil.

Were it not for the kindness of a local chemistry professor, my life might not have been enriched at such an early age. But, moved by my plight, he entrusted me with his classical records and with books from his library. And there, in a science fiction anthology, I came upon "Sold to Satan," by Mark Twain, a frequent recipient of fundamentalist scorn.

Because my parents were not very religious, I was ill-informed about supernatural beings, and had considered words like "devil" and "Satan" to be inconsequential terms that occasionally fell from the lips of my churchier friends. But here, in an anthology of great writers, was a masterful piece that put flesh on the devil's bones and finally gave him a voice.

In "Sold to Satan," Twain, who had suffered a decline in his finances, had decided to sell his soul to the devil. He contacted the appropriate agent. A meeting was set, and during a chatty encounter that revealed Satan's composition (pure radium in a polonium sheath), an agreeable price arose and the deal was struck.

In the exchange, Twain became sole owner of a secret radium deposit in a hidden caldera where all of the fireflies of all the ages had gone to die. Because radium was (and still is) expensive, Twain had bucks to burn.

However, in the 20th century, including the pre-Bush years, interest in Satan had waned, and I'd even begun to wonder if the old boy or girl was still around. But when our self-described war president ascended the throne, the devil returned to mind. Remembering Mr. Twain, I decided to give the Prince of Darkness a call. Figuring that I'd start with his last known address, I dialed the basement of one of our largest religious institutions — the Basilica of St. Paul.

"HELL o," a recording responded, "You have reached 666-6666. If you wish to know the future, press 1. If you want to sell your soul, press 2. If you would like to speak to a member of the Moral Majority, press 3. If you want to speak with GWB, he is busy uniting the country and is unavailable. If you wish to speak to His Nibs, press 4. I pressed 4.

"Satan here," came a distant-sounding voice. "I'm in a tiz, so state your biz."

Delighted, I gushed, "Is this really you, Satan? You know — Beelzebub, the Evil One and all that?

"None other," he replied, then abruptly asked. "So what do you want?"

"Well, first of all, I'm sort of surprised that you are still boarding at churches. I thought you'd have gone condo by now."

"No, not me," he replied, "though I gave it some thought a few years back. It's just too comfortable here. Too many old friends. They really can't get on without me, you know. Why, that Voltaire fellow even called me 'the main prop of the church,' and you know what a smart cookie he was! Besides, these folks are my biggest supporters, preachin' about me all the time, keepin' me on everyone's mind. You know, if it weren't for the churches, folks would forget all about me and I'd have to pull a MacArthur and slowly fade away. And believe me, as I go, so goes the religion business, which is why my buddies — guys like the Pope, Robertson, Swaggart and that Palin gal (ain't she a pip!) — keep telling folks I'm real. Let's face it, I heat their buildings and they give me free PR. Call it symbiosis, son."

"I need to ask how I should address you," I apologized. "Mr. Twain called you 'your Excellency' but we're not very big on royalty these days, so what else would you like?"

"Call me Pat," he said. "Good name ... got a couple of buddies in conservative religo-politics who did pretty well by it for a while, although they're kinda down at the moment."

"OK, Pat," I replied, "but you're awfully hard to hear. It's probably just a bad connection, or maybe your cell's going down. Could you beam yourself over here so we could have a face to face?"

Before I could continue, a small voice to my right said, "Well, here I am!"

Turning, I scanned the room.

"Where?"

"Right here — on your printer!"

And there he was, standing on top of my Lexmark Z11 printer, all of ten inches tall — like Ken, of the Barbie doll clan. Dressed as he was in a flowing black robe, he could have passed for mini Darth Vader or even a Catholic priest.

"My goodness, Pat, you're so small," I said. "No wonder I couldn't hear you — and how come no hooves or horns?"

"That's ancient history," he replied. "Got to dress for the times, you know. I dress like a priest when it suits me, but I'm into morphing now. Let me tell you though, times are tough. The latest polls show that less than 50% believe in me. It's not like the old days, when an Inquisition or a Crusade or maybe a good witch hunt could bring in a few thousand souls whenever things got dull.

"But I've had my successes," he continued, puffing up a bit. "There was Jonestown and Waco plus that savings and loan thing, and then Enron and Fannie and Freddie, not to mention Lehman Brothers, AIG and those derivatives that fattened a lot of my friends. Of course, a few got caught, but what the … " sensing my secular nature, he paused … "heck."

"Then there's that nice affair in Yugoslavia that folks called 'ethnic cleansing' although it was mostly another Christian/Muslim war. Now add the Palestine/Israel thing and that trumped-up deal in Iraq. Lots of souls coming my way on that one — over 500,000 now if you count the Iraqis, though no one does. I'm still pretty busy, so what else do you want to know?"

"Is it true that Martin Luther once threw an ink pot at you?"

"It sure is. Missed me, too, and I was a lot bigger then. Good old Marty … never could hit anything smaller than a church door. And speaking of churches, there are way too many these days. Used to be I could sit back and work with just one big set of folks that believed in me. Had 'em scared stiff, too. Then they got to thinkin' on things and dividin' and next thing you know there are more denominations than ticks on a dog, and they all have the "truth" but can't agree. It's hard, I tell you, keeping track of what I'm supposed to be, and who's where and doin' what to whom. Not simple like in the good old, church-run Dark Ages. Nowadays a Rolodex just can't hack it. Had to computerize years back. Matter of fact, that's how I got here today. Just zipped in on the modem.

"But," he continued, "you have to admit that I'm a great guy to have around when folks feel like steppin' out of line. Geraldine, that friend of Flip Wilson, had it right. She did whatever she pleased and figured on me to make it good. Many times I've heard her cry, 'The devil made me do it' — cleared her conscience just fine."

"But, Pat," I asked. "Aren't you pushing some major projects — something spectacular, like a horrific earthquake or an asteroid whacking us? What about that tsunami in Indonesia or Hurricane Katrina? You must have had a hand in them."

"Sorry," he said. "I prefer to see folks do themselves in. It's less tiring and way more interesting, and besides, I'm always surprised at how inventive you humans can be, especially when you have a hundred or so different-but-true religions to stir things up.

"Listen son," he said, suddenly turning serious, "You've probably guessed that most of this religion stuff is myth and legend, but at one time there really was a Garden of Eden, and it was a lot bigger than folks think. There was plenty for all because there weren't many people. Then folks began to dream up gods in their own image, both proud and vain — including a god that demanded praise and appeasement. But they needed a scapegoat for when they did wrong, and that's when they dreamed up me.

"I started out pulling the usual pranks, but after a few hundred years, I got bored. And that's when I had my great idea, my masterpiece. 'Make lots of babies,' I told them, 'Make boatloads of babies, for, like you, they are made in the image of your God, and it pleases him."

"Only a fool would believe that the garden could feed and shelter without limit, but they did, and some still do, so WANT arrived, followed by GREED and WAR. Now, with the population still climbing, the pot is beginning to boil — the same pot under which I once lit a tiny flame.

My buddies who oppose contraception and sex education have caused so many deaths from AIDS and unwanted pregnancies that I can hardly keep up. Just wait and see — bad as it is, the overcrowding is going to get worse. People will pray for miracles and demand that science save the day. Given the choice to use their heads now or risk disaster later, how do you think they'll choose?"

"Not well," I replied.

He heaved a sigh, and over a sagging shoulder, gave me a sidelong glance.

"Want to sell your soul?"

"I don't see how I can," I replied. "First, I'm not so sure there is such a thing, and if there isn't, it wouldn't be fair to you. And second, if there is, which I doubt, why should I sell it to you instead of using eBay?"

"Well, that's OK," he said. "Price is way down anyway. Supply and demand, you know. Lots of poverty; lots of souls. Kids selling out for a pair of Nikes and their folks cashin' in for a line of coke."

Straightening up, he leaned a little closer, squinted at me and asked, "You're one of those rational types, aren't you?"

"That's right," I replied.

"Humanist?"

"Of course."

"Atheist?" he asked.

"Why not?" I replied.

"Oh, lordy," he cried, "No wonder I'm feeling so weak. So just what **do** you believe in?"

"I believe in things that make sense and in ideas that can survive being questioned — not in self-styled patriots or zealots who yell 'traitor' or 'heretic' whenever they're challenged."

He let out a cry of anguish, and like the wicked witch from the Wizard of Oz, began to melt within his dark black robes. When he was no taller than a shot glass, he glared up at me, and with a tiny, fear-filled voice inquired: "Are there others out there like you?"

Before I could answer, Old Nick had shrunk to the size of an ember. Like the final spark of a dying fire, he flickered and disappeared, leaving behind an empty room to receive my reply: "You'd be surprised, Patty baby, you'd be very, very surprised."

# Dear Patient

Thank you for visiting West Memorial Cardiac Center.

Several weeks ago we supplied you with a monitor that you could activate if you experienced further fainting spells. The recordings that you subsequently made have been quite helpful, and we can now offer a diagnosis. It appears that you are suffering from what we call an episodic, atrioventricular block, which we refer to as an A/V block, a condition that must be taken seriously. If left untreated, an A/V block can cause death.

In normal hearts, the two upper chambers, the atria, which we once called auricles, work in harmony with the two lower chambers, the ventricles. However, when an A/V block occurs, the atria and the ventricles lose synchronization. Blood pressure falls, and the patient faints. To allow you to understand more precisely what is happening without becoming too technical, we offer the following analogy.

First, you must understand that A/V blocking provides an example of our androgynous nature, the word "androgynous" referring to the fact that all individuals have, in varying proportions, some of the characteristics of both sexes. This is also true of their individual organs, including the heart.

In normal hearts, the two ventricles, which are analogous to the male portions, listen or try to listen to the two atria — the female portions — which jabber incessantly, as in many male/female relationships. As the years pass, some ventricles become hard of hearing. Others become weary of the incessant din and begin to tune it out, turning instead to thoughts of comely waitresses in low-cut blouses whose lovely appurtenances almost tumbled into the day dreamer's calamari at the Wildcat Bar and Grill.

As you might expect, ventricular inattention infuriates the atria, who yell, "OK, if your little mind must wander, I'll just quit talking to you," and the whole damn works comes crashing down. Things end up on the floor and, as usual, it's all his fault.

There's nothing like crashing to the floor to get one's attention, so the poor ventricles leap back to the present and quickly ask, "What did you say?" And because it is their nature, the atria usually forgive the wayward ventricles and begin to chatter again. Unfortunately, being male and therefore inclined to meditate on great thoughts, the ventricle's minds eventually wander again, and as the bumps and bruises accumulate, the loving couple is compelled to decide between wearing a helmet and foam rubber clothing or installing a pacemaker, which is really a misspelling of the word "peacemaker."

Once equipped with the new PaceMakerSupreme, Ms. Atrium's powerful helper can deliver a bazillion-volt shock to the dullard ventricles when their wandering minds turn to football or nubile women with eye-catching buns. Thanks to this electronic marvel, which our skilled surgeons can implant at your convenience, your life can again be normal, and you will no longer need to worry that an atrio-ventricular dispute will send you crashing to the floor.

# Crystals Lite

When Public Television broadcast "Healing and the Mind," Bill Moyers' thoughtful foray into alternative medicine, I thought of my Auntie Kay, who believed in the power of crystals. Convinced that her crystals could cure a host of afflictions, she kept her home sparkling from pantry to porch. However, her lovely collection now graces my shelves, for her gems proved useless against the staph infection that wrote an end to my Auntie Kay.

These converts to New Age holistics include seekers like Marie, who sports a sliver of barite in the inflamed flesh of her pierced nostril, and her boyfriend, Keith, who is hooked on malachite. Marie and Keith are the New Age version of the folks who still ignore Mr. Barnum's warning — "There's a sucker born every minute."

Although I, too, love their color, their glitter and shine, and admire gems for their beauty alone, I prefer a science that calmly says 'pyrite' to a fraud that promises GOLD! What, then, does science say about gems, and how does New Age respond? Well, since some savant has declared it the stone of my birth, let's consider aquamarine.

Science, with its rational, analytical approach, informs us that aquamarine is beryllium aluminum silicate, and that some of its siblings are emerald, morganite and heliodor. It reveals that the beryl children run from deep blue-green to yellow, and can be brown or purple or clear, depending on how much sodium or cesium lies in their crystalline cores. It reports that aquamarine is softer than corundum but harder than quartz, and that its hexagonal crystals line the pegmatites of North Carolina, Colorado and Vermont.

Science has a great deal more to say, but having sampled its approach, let's examine the New Age view, where reality wavers twixt here and there, and truth is whatever one says.

Our leap vaults us from the bedrock of science to a makeshift raft propelled by wandering currents while opposed by a countering wind. Its occupants are most remarkable, for they are captains all. Using various charms and a flexible course, they sail on a spiritual sea.

Our raft, which is a part of the New Age fleet, has chosen its cargo well, carrying implications, promises and religions anew — an ideal cargo: so light, yet so profitable.

The home port of our New Age raft is the typical store/sanctuary found in your town, in her town and mine. In its windows and cases lie eye-popping gems and crystals that prompt sighs and aaahhhhs. Stepping inside, I say to myself, *"this is my kind of store,"* as I gawk at its pyrites, its calcites and its bounty of baubulous delights. In a soothing touch, a gentle nocturne stirs the earth-scented air. How pleasant; how relaxing. And then I notice the little messages, a different one for each display.

"Calcite," one proclaims, "will enhance mental balance and alertness." (I could use a tad of calcite.) Citrine is pledged to "help unblock congestion on emotional and physical levels." (Nothing needed there.) As for my birthstone and her siblings, this emporium stocks only emerald and aquamarine, which is, as I'd expected, an *absolute marvel.*

Aquamarine, *my* birthstone, not only treats "ailments of the head, neck and throat," it offers "protection for sensitive people" and should be worn to "calm fears, ease anxiety and to ensure a good night's sleep."

I am truly impressed! Once again, I can stroll the streets in safety, protected by just a bit of aquamarine, my pockets freed from stun guns and mace. And for a good night's sleep, I'll simply slip a crystal or two beneath my pillow and remove the old .38 — no more anxiety, no more fear, and no more "Smith & Wesson" embossed upon my morning cheeks.

Suddenly, my skeptical mind revives. "Would a more expensive stone be more effective?" I ask.

"Oh, yes!"

"And at what velocity must I throw this stone to protect myself?" I pleasantly inquire.

The clerk's smile fades, replaced by a look of battleship gray.

Sensing our dwindling rapport, I offer thanks for her time, pick up a pamphlet on the *"Uses of Gemstones and Minerals for Personal Transformation"* and head for home. "What a shame," I muse. Perhaps she should revise her chakra stone layout for increased harmony, or wear a pound or two of ... What's this? No crystal to "liberate laughter," no gem to "expand one's sense of humor?" Here, indeed, is a niche to fill, a void that seeks my soul.

And so, to repair this gap in crystal holistics and to bolster the humor impaired, I now offer Menckenite. Distilled from the essence of snicker, Menckenite is synthesized in a secret lab in Smiley, Minnesota, population 666. Menckenite is reasonably priced at $1,200 per carat, and is absolutely guaranteed to enhance one's sense of humor and pleasant nature, as it has my own, ensuring that with every purchase you will receive not only a friendly smile, but a pat on the wallet, er, back, as well.

One caution: Overuse of Menckenite has been known to cause a serious complication called PMS or Post-Menckenite Syndrome, also known as "skepticism," the intensity of the symptoms being proportionate to the amount of Menckenite purchased. We therefore urge our customers to limit their expenditures to modest sums, perhaps three or four hundred dollars per week.

Those who follow our advice will be spared a depressing revelation concerning the New Age, or any age. It's about a system known to Las Vegas, to psychics and religions as well. A few spot it quickly; others never catch on. Known as the FIRST LAW OF REALITY, it goes like this: "YOU GIVE ME MONEY; I TAKE IT."

*"I will believe the most preposterous claim, but the more preposterous it is, the better the proof must be!"* — Isaac Asimov

# Working Girl

There is no way to describe the state of Carol Cyder's mind when they lowered the $1,000,000 certified check into her nicked and trembling hands.

They had called her straight from the boning line, her arms still smeared with chicken fat, the same fat that stained her semi-white uniform and her dull gray, rundown shoes. And she was scared. Oh God, was she scared.

Twenty four years on the boning line watching others being summoned to Personnel — on their way to getting canned — and now it was her turn.

The company nurse tried to reassure her. "They only want to talk to you," she said, but it sounded like a lie.

"They just don't want a scene," thought Carol.

"How could they?" she wondered as she struggled up the slippery iron stairs, and by the time she'd reached the second flight, she was winded and gasping for air.

"I'm a little heavy," she apologized. In fact, she was sixty pounds long — a lot for a five-foot-four.

As she neared the top of the final flight, she saw herself slowly climbing her high school stairs — overweight, awkward and plain. Someone was yelling "Cyder the cipher, Cyder the cipher," and though she missed the meaning, she understood their intent. Years later, when she'd asked her foreman what "cipher" meant, he told her it meant "zero" — the same as nothing.

When she arrived at personnel, they told her to take a seat until the manager was free. As she waited, her eyes began to mist. "Twenty four years, hardly ever sick, and what about the two-week vacation they owe me?" Then she remembered that they'd call you in if a relative died, but she had no one, so it had to be the ax.

When she looked up, she saw not only the personnel manager, but the plant manager as well, and she burst into tears, sinking into a well of despair so deep that it took almost five minutes to calm her down, to explain that she had won the million-dollar plant lottery, that she was not being fired, and that if she did things right, her boning line days would be over.

Again, she began to cry. Great sobs of relief rolled through her, rising and falling like ocean swells until, by the time she recovered, the nurse, the entire office staff and both of the managers were almost as tearful as she.

As she lay in bed that night, listening to the clicking of billiard balls from the pool hall below, she finally admitted what everyone knew — that her life had finally changed and that from now on Carol Cyder would be calling the shots.

Suddenly Carol had friends. She sensed that they came with the money, and would go with the money, but it was nice to have friends no matter who paid the bills. And besides, her friends were so helpful.

They helped her find a big new apartment with pale blue walls, a big Jacuzzi and a nice view of the interstate, and they invited Carol to join their monthly trips to the casino. They helped her select a salmon-colored, turbocharged, quadrophoniced Trans Am with fat, white-lettered tires, a moon roof and soft leather seats, and they dined every night at restaurants that were worlds apart from White Castle or Burger King. And Elaine, the girl who knew everyone but had always ignored her, hooked her up with a financial guy from a firm that promised a hefty 9%, tax-free return.

She took a liking to blackjack, the only game she almost understood, and for a while stayed ahead of the game, but as the months passed, her luck disappeared. Her bonds, however, kept their 9% promise, but they weren't tax exempt. "Carol," he said, "That was just a misunderstanding."

Thinking ahead for the first time in her life, Carol enrolled in the community college to become an LPN, but one day, as she hurried to class, she failed to see a stop sign and T-boned a luxury car. The Trans Am was totaled. She was not badly hurt. He was. A lawsuit followed — and

Carol had forgotten to add the Trans Am to her insurance policy. Yielding to fear and remorse, she agreed to an out-of-court settlement that carried off her bonds.

Toward the end of the month, on the day that the first snow began to fall, Carol went through her mail, listening again to the click of the pool balls while throwing out the "Occupant mail" and paying bill after bill until her bank balance read $289.43.

In the back of her closet, she found her semi-white uniform, her dull gray shoes and her torn hair net. Her uniform, now two sizes too small, would never fit, but they'd let her buy a new one on time at the company store. As she jammed her feet into her sneakers, her brow furrowed at the sight of the varicosities that webbed her legs. They seemed larger and darker than they were just a few months ago, but she pushed the thought from her mind.

She had kept her '69 Chevy when she bought the new Trans Am, so she still could get to the plant, which was fortunate because she sensed it would take a while before she'd be invited to car pool with the other boning line workers.

A week after a solitary Thanksgiving dinner at Denny's, Carol returned to Personnel. The receptionist was new. They had trouble finding her file, and no one remembered her. When they asked for her name, she haltingly replied, "Carol, Carol Cyder."

They eventually found her folder buried in a file labeled "Medical risk! Do not rehire," somehow misspelled as Cipher, Carolyn C.

# Of Alder Brush and Army Worms

I've been chain sawing steadily for hours, brushing several acres of lakeshore that nature has left in a tangled heap of deadfalls and rotting logs. The sun, the blast and heat of the engine and the shimmering, purple exhaust have finally worn me down. Sliding to the ground, I rest my back against the broad, slanting trunk of a lofty Norway pine.

The thicket of alder brush that obscured a magnificent view of Lake Vermilion lies flattened. Above the debris, a dragonfly begins to patrol beneath the pine, finally alighting on a nearby aspen where a slim tent caterpillar, the vanguard of the hoard due to arrive next year, struggles upward in search of succulent leaves.

Ten years ago, the worm population exploded, stripping the aspens almost bare before shifting to the less delectable birch and maple. Moving from grove to grove, the caterpillar carpets spun speeding cars out of control on worm-slicked highways, and on a few occasions, even locomotive wheels whirred uselessly in the fluids of wormy excess.

The following summer brought a corresponding boom of the caterpillars' natural enemy. I call them "friendly" flies, for although they're deadly to worms, they never nibble on humans. This worm, however, is safe, for the flies are a year away, and as the green-striped worm inches higher, intent on finding a meal that will allow it to perpetuate the multi-year cycle of wormy boom and bust, it occurs to me that we and the worms have an important trait in common.

Humans, too, have often bred to the point where nature could no longer provide. Without predators to limit our numbers, some have starved and some have turned against their neighbors in a desperate fight for food. The worms can be forgiven, for they have no frontal lobes that give them the power to reason – but humans lack that excuse.

Like my little grandson, we keep demanding "mo, mo, mo!" of whatever we like, with little concern for the consequence. It takes no genius, not even a high IQ, to understand that a limited Earth will require a limited population. We see as much in our gardens, for like the worms, plants also live in a world of push and shove. Worse yet, they lack the power to change: When un-thinned carrots compete in crowded soil, scrawny plants result. But with proper spacing to allow sufficient soil and moisture, each plant can ascend as high as its DNA allows.

Now, with most of the smothering alder flattened and the balsam thickets thinned, young maples, birch and poplar will no longer need to grow sideways in a desperate search for a sunlit sky.

When the caterpillar begins to dine, I think of the farmer hailed by a motorist who needed directions. After admiring the fine stand of oats, the tall rows of corn and the massive stone fence that rimmed the field, the motorist exclaimed "God surely gave you a marvelous farm."

"That may be," replied the farmer, "but you should have seen this place before I helped him out."

Like the farmers who care for their fields, we need to take charge of our lives and our numbers. We need to promote *effective* birth control and oppose those who would keep women pregnant regardless of their circumstances. With world populations approaching 7 billion — a level that our planet *cannot* sustain — we must not leave family "planning" to a god that controls population with famine, plagues and war.

Led by people like G. W. Bush, the puppet of the religious right who vowed that "no one will ever out-Bible me," these believers risk the health and happiness of every child.

In the Northern woods, it's quiet — still far from the "madding" crowd. Tilting my head back, I admire the cool, green canopy of the towering Norway pine. I think back a century to the day when the loggers came, cutting, trampling and thinning, but leaving behind this struggling evergreen and others that were just too small. These trees had a head start. Uncrowded, with abundant nutrients, they soared skyward, becoming giants of strength and grace.

What nature can do for trees, we can also do for ourselves if we become wise enough to limit our numbers and curb pollution. If not, life will surely continue, but the standard of living we enjoy today will degrade from a pleasant fact to a treasured memory.

# Going for the Gold

It's a gray September morning. Outside, a chilling rain slants through the long-needled spruce trees that shelter my home. Snug inside, with a mug of coffee close at hand, I lean back, prop my feet on my desk and survey my surroundings.

The wall to my left displays maps of Canada, Alaska and Australia. Along either side of the maps run rows of photographs: an immense herd of caribou fording the Thelon River, fourteen sturdy musk oxen circled around their calves — horned heads down and ready, and a seaplane whose pilot overshot a landing, standing his Cub on its nose and float tips at the edge of an arctic lake.

Gracing the wall to my right are an eclectic assortment of books that include the nutty humor of Dave Barry, Jacob Bronowski's *The Ascent of Man* and Hugo's *Les Miserables*, plus books by Sagan, London, Abbey, Leopold and McPhee. At the end of the lowest shelf sits a gleaming clump of crystals — a cluster of iron pyrites from Arkansas that is also called Fool's Gold.

Arkansas, besides being stocked with an endless variety of homespun churches (lacking only my favorite, Flip Wilson's "Church of Where It's At Now, Brother") is also a rock hound's dream, and one year, just a few miles from Hot Springs Village, I chanced upon a shop called "The Rockery" that easily topped them all.

I have always been a sucker for pretty bits of glass, crystals and beads. Like the Australian bowerbird that decorates his gracefully-arched bower with pieces of glass and plastic to attract a mate, colors also call to me. Had the Dutch come to me for Manhattan, they'd have gotten a better deal.

After drooling over crystals of amethyst, tourmaline, calcite and quartz, I purchased a brassy clump of pyrite with a hundred shining faces, and when it winks at me from high on its shelf, and whispers thoughts of gold, I think of Martin Frobisher, and a lesson that should never grow old.

In 1576, Sir Martin returned to England from the north end of Hudson Bay. Having failed to find the Northwest Passage, he'd filled his hold with glittering stones that his men believed held gold. Chemists declared them worthless, but Michael Lok, one of the expedition's sponsors, kept searching for an alchemist who would claim to find traces of gold. When Lok asked that alchemist how he managed to find gold where others had failed, he replied that the secret lay in knowing "how to flatter nature."

Aided by the alchemist's claim, Frobisher easily found backers for a second voyage, which also failed to find the passage, but returned triumphant with 200 tons of mica and pyrite-flecked rocks — the gold of fools. Those who claimed that the ore held gold outvoted the chemists who resolutely disagreed, and the following spring, fifteen ships and 41 miners sailed again for the Arctic, there to explore Baffin Island and to mine 1,300 tons of identically worthless ore.

Evidence finally conquered belief, but only after lives had been lost and investors ruined. And as a result of the expeditions, one of Frobisher's captains penned a maxim we still find useful today: "All that glistereth is not gold."

In today's world we test almost everything. Consumer magazines evaluate products, chemists analyze for content, accountants count, and stores take inventory. We skeptically examine gas mileage claims and candidates for office, saying, "Show me the proof." Today, just saying that something is true no longer suffices — except for religion.

While the real world is subject to truth in advertising laws, product liability and money back guarantees, religion still peddles pyrites, promising rewards tomorrow for your money, your credulity and your obedience today. "Gold," it cries, "Heaven, miracles and bliss can be yours, just for the asking!"

Some of us are like the realists of Frobisher's day. When we try to reason with those who see gold, most of them turn away. The truly devoted scorn us and pity our lack of faith while refusing to test their own against evidence they choose to ignore.

Some — the Christian Scientists and other faith "healers" bet the lives of their children on the mythical gold. Many contribute heavily, and sometimes ruinously, to support the voyage and their visionary clergy-captains who promise a better world. Like Frobisher's men, some die along the way. A few change their minds, but most sail on for the rest of their lives, cruising a self-centered sea.

I once sailed as an officer on just such a ship — the S. S. Presbyterian. Like most spiritual ships, the vessel rarely sailed serious waters, the crew being too busy singing hymns and burnishing brass to tend to the pressing needs they'd see whenever they went ashore.

One year, when our wealthier officers began to pressure the crew to pledge even more to embellish our splendid vessel, I decided to escape, and late one evening, when we passed abeam the Rational Islands, I slipped across the gunwale and quietly swam to shore.

Forty years later, I sit in my study, my eyes wandering over the assortment of maps and books and photos as I recall the adventures and knowledge those decades have brought. I share my experiences with groups of all ages through science and nature programs that span the globe from the Arctic to Australia, and by funding college scholarships with the money that once helped maintain the large and expensive ship.

Others persist. Misled by an ancient, erroneous map, they search for the mythical port, while from high on my shelf, my crystalline "ore" still sparkles and whispers its lie: "Gold, GOLD!," it calls to me.

"Frobisher," I reply.

# No Fear of Flying

As long as I can remember, I've dreamed that I could fly — at first, gliding a foot above the ground with effortless, block-long strides. While others plugged along, I'd float gracefully from step to step, immune to all but a tiny part of gravity's pervasive pull. Half realizing that I was dreaming as I glided from jeté to jeté, I'd tell myself — This is so *EASY! THIS* time I'll remember how it's done when I'm back in the light of day.

As the years progressed, I soared higher, flying prone like Superman while holding a board in my hands that I'd angle to direct my flight to familiar cities and plains, and to lands that no others have seen. There was always a slight sense of danger, but I soared through the nights for year after year, and I never fell from the skies.

More recently, I'm drawn to a ramshackle hangar and a dust-covered aircraft that I sold many years ago, my sleek and sensuous Beechcraft Bonanza, which, in my dreams, I still own. As my hand wipes away the layers of grime that mask her gleaming red and white paint, I'm embarrassed by my neglect and resolve to return for a wash and wax, and to fly her once again.

A few years ago, I began to dream that I'm a passenger in a 747 approaching Minneapolis at the end of a long winter flight. As in the endless series of *Airport* films, the voice of a distraught flight attendant leaps from the cabin speakers: "Something has happened to our flight crew. Please — please! We need a pilot!"

Walter Mitty-like, I stride to the empty flight deck. Slipping gracefully into the pilot's seat, I slide my feet onto the rudder pedals, grasp the control yoke and calmly reach for the mike.

"Minneapolis Center, this is Northwest 747 inbound from Honolulu. We have an emergency. The flight crew has disappeared. However, we'll be landing as planned."

"Northwest 747, this is Minneapolis Center. Minneapolis is below minimums. Try Chicago."

Low on fuel, I can't make Chicago. Instead, I turn to the north, ease back the power and begin a long descent toward a huge, ice-coated lake called Lake Mille Lacs, the Voyageurs' Lake of a Thousand Lakes.

With less than 20 minutes to touchdown, I tell Minneapolis Center to have the radio and TV stations warn ice fisherman off of the lake, then advise my anxious passengers that everything's cool, that they shouldn't worry while I check out the Boeing's controls. Arcing the 747 through roller coaster turns, I quickly discover that the big old girl flies exactly like my Cub.

Crossing the town of Milaca, I'm down to a thousand feet, heading into a ten-knot wind with the big lake dead ahead. Gear down, flaps to 20 degrees, power at 70%, nose up just a tad. It occurs to me that the wheels of the heavy Boeing might break through the lake's three-foot lens of ice, so I add a touch of power to spool up the jets while the gear retracts, then ease it back again.

As the 747 thunders over Onamia, I'm a little too low. Powered up to slow the Boeing's descent, her jets and wing tip vortices rip shingles from snow-dusted roofs just a hundred feet below. Ahead, pickup trucks and snowmobiles race across the lake, scattering before the onrushing jet. Raising the Boeing's nose a trifle, I keep the 747 airborne while she bleeds off speed. The wide-body's engines touch the ice with feathery grace as I pull back the throttles, deploy the thrust reversers and throttle up into thundering, full reverse.

An ancient airspeed indicator as big as a dinner plate reports 160 miles per hour as the roaring engines fill the sky with snow. The jet slows to 140, then 130. At 120, the Boeing rams a six-foot-high pressure ridge, ripping the jets from her wings. Belly-flopped, she careens at a hundred and ten toward an ice fishing shack with a big TV antenna one hundred yards ahead. I stamp on the left rudder pedal, sloughing the plane to avoid the shack, which looms ever larger as the jet begins to turn. Time slows. The fuselage will miss it, but the wing will reduce it to kindling.

Suddenly, the door pops open and a fisherman emerges, momentarily transfixed by the hurtling jet. As if denying reality, he ducks back into his shack, slamming the door behind him. The fishing shack, struck by the Boeing's massive wing, explodes, sending the antenna twirling into the sky. Skating on, the giant aircraft finally slides to a stop.

In the background, surrounded by the splintered remains of his shack, the fisherman suddenly pops out of his bathtub-sized ice fishing hole, gasping for breath. Leaping to his feet, he shakes a fist at the wayward Boeing and runs to the nearest car.

In the final scene, the crew has miraculously reappeared, and the passengers, indifferent to the cold, have gathered on the ice. As the captain shakes my hand and offers his heartfelt thanks, he asks where I learned my skills. The crowd stills, awaiting my response. Backed by the sound of wailing sirens, I carefully phrase my reply: "As long as I can remember, I've dreamed that I could fly ..."

# Of Boeings, Banyans and Foolish Beliefs

Except for the muted roar of the powerful engines that propel my jet through the sky, I can hardly believe I am moving. I am the midnight occupant of seat 19J, coach class, on a Northwest Airlines 747 that has caught the core of the jet stream on a flight from Hawaii to Minneapolis, where the temperature has finally risen to ten below.

The "how-goes-it" chart on the cabin video ticks off a mile every ten seconds, reports that we are cruising at 37,000 feet, and makes Minneapolis seem temperate by listing an outside air temperature of minus 75. As we speed through the sky at heights where unassisted life cannot survive, we are cocooned by technologies that provide safety and warmth while we enjoy peanuts, Coke, and passable meals with a rust-colored beverage called "orange juice" that could easily eat through glass.

Sagging back in my seat, I stare into the night. As our wing-tip strobes blink their tiny warnings, I slip into semi-sleep, returning to the Big Island's Kona coast, where the setting sun bounces bronze light across Kailua Bay and splashes boughs of bougainvillea with dappled evening light.

I am at the busiest intersection of the Kona Coast, at Palani Court and Alii Drive, but as the Hondas, mopeds, and Jaguars motor by, I am almost invisible, for I am seated within the buttressing, wall-like roots of a giant banyan tree.

The banyan's immense roots have been scarred by knife-wielding idiots, some of them spurred by passion ("Kimo loves Marie"), one by wit ("Stop Plate Tectonics") and some by a mindless form of environmentalism ("Keep Kona Green") — its letters still oozing sap. Disgusted, I tilt my eyes upward past roots that ascend into the banyan's round-leaved canopy, and I wonder how anyone could deface a tree that brings thoughts of Gautama Buddha and Confucius, the source of the Golden Rule.

Sheltered between its partitioning roots, I begin to examine three very different publications: a flier advertising "KONA'S ECLECTIC PSYCHIC FAIR," "The Bathroom Digest," (my concession to philosophy), and "Hawaiian Superstitions."

The "PSYCHIC FAIR" offers "hypnosis, life-renewal, astrology, palmistry, massage, tarot reading and crystal visioning. It even promises DIVINITY, mine just for the asking, not to mention numerology, clairvoyance, aromatherapy and hand writing analysis plus a free lecture — "Admission just $2.50!" However, my personal clairvoyance, which resides in the House of Horse Sense, is skeptical of their ability to deliver divinity, predicts that "aromatherapy" refers to the scent of money, and warns that they intend to massage my wallet.

There will also be a demonstration of Egyptian Magic, which sounds interesting, but I am much too eager to plumb the depths of "The Bathroom Digest" to be distracted by sleight of hand.

I had skimmed the Bathroom Digest, so I knew I had quite a find. Intended for those who like to ruminate as they evacuate, it's a compendium of little known facts plus early quotes from flegling authors like Poe, Twain, Kipling, Bierce and London.

The Bathroom Digest begins by listing some of the big names (like LBJ and W.C. Fields) who commonly read in the bathroom, then proceeds to offer trivia: "a newborn panda is smaller than a mouse," and "the motto on the first coin officially minted by the U.S. was MIND YOUR BUSINESS." (This practical motto displeased many believers, who, during a period of post-World War II, anti-communist passion, persuaded vote-conscious politicians to adopt "In God We Trust.")

The Digest claims that a ten-gallon hat holds three gallons, that the Babylonians of 3000 BCE had waste-water plumbing, and that Patrick Henry, who said "Give me liberty or give me death," owned 65 slaves when he died.

Continuing with history, it reveals that the next two people who tried Franklin's kite experiment were killed by lightning and informs us that the Olympic flame was conceived for the 1936 games by Adolf Hitler. Finally, it suggests that "Death is nature's way of telling you to slow down."

As I turn to "Hawaiian Beliefs," I wonder if the author will include the current big three religions but, as usual, they're given a pass.

Pele, the goddess of fire, is the best known of the Hawaiian deities, and although she is just an "aumakua"— a lesser god — her followers have convinced superstitious tourists that taking a tad of lava from the islands will bring bad luck. However, I have a cigar box full of lava chips in my basement (doesn't everyone?) and Pele and I are still the best of friends.

Some older Hawaiians believe that disturbing the bones of the dead will bring bad luck, and that your enemies can work magic against you with just a strand of your hair or a fingernail clipping. Others claim that those who anger Pele will be turned to stone, and as proof, they point to the hollow columns of lava that hardened around tree trunks which quickly burned away.

The old beliefs are dying, but they're being replaced by other fantasies. At a dinner party, I was told by a delightful, intelligent Japanese-American lady that one should never move in January because it would bring bad luck. She also claimed that a woman who leaves her house within six weeks of childbirth will bring more bad luck, then added, "Of course, I don't know if this is true, but my mother told me it was, so I tell everyone just in case." And so it goes — and goes — and goes.

By the time I finish reading "Hawaiian Superstitions" the sun has begun to sink beneath Kailua Bay. It shrinks to a tiny point of light, winks out, and then reappears as the wing-tip strobe blinking "See me…. See me…..See me….." into the vast Pacific night.

Thirty minutes later the "how-goes-it" display reveals that we will soon be crossing the mainland near Santa Barbara, its bejeweled coastline aglow with shimmering light all the way to San Diego.

I've been four hours aloft, with three yet to pass before my 747, a magnificent product of science, technology, logic, skill, conscience and dedication to perfection, comes thundering out of the dawn to land on a frozen runway. I'll be exhausted, and while I wait for my baggage, I'll join my fellow passengers who'll be checking the local papers, some for the news; some for astrological or theological advice on how to manage their day.

While our four thundering blowtorches propel our Boeing eastward,

I ponder this technological marvel that owes nothing to spinning prayer wheels, to rattling beads or to revelations. Despite a takeoff weight of 300 tons, we rose from Oahu like a rocket, caught a favorable jet stream and will span the 5,000 miles to Minnesota in less than seven hours.

As we fly leap the Pacific beneath star-studded skies, I think of the tides — the endless, oceanic respirations that rise and fall two times a day. I press my face to the window and lift my jacket over my head to shutter the cabin's light. Far below, the undulating reflections of a half-moon waver across the darkened face of the ocean, its rhythms revealed by moonlight shifting along the slow roll of its undulating swells. Hunched over, nose flattened to the window, I sit transfixed.

In every flash of moonlight on every rhythmic swell, I sense the pulse of the tireless heart that beats in every sea. Evolved from the ocean, with the salt of its seas in my veins, I smile and blink back the saline film that suddenly mists my eyes. Six miles above her billows and brine, I am one with the sea. And though some will say that's not divine, it's good enough for me. Divinity at last!

# Lady Liberty and the Population Bomb

I've snorkeled the Barrier Reef of Belize, crossed the Australian Outback and camped on the Arctic Coast, but I've never stood at the foot of our symbol of freedom, the Statue of Liberty.

The idea to build the statue came from a Frenchman named Edouard de Laboulaye during the centennial celebration of our Declaration of Independence. New Yorkers were skeptical, so the famous sculptor, one Frederic Bartholdi, courted Philadelphia, which agreed to exhibit Liberty's upraised arm and its torch at the city's World's Fair.

After returning the arm and torch to Paris, Bartholdi finished the statue, using a quarter million dollars donated by the people of France. (The head, it was said, was that of his mother — and the body that of his mistress.) He then had it disassembled, packed into 214 crates and shipped to New York in 1875 for assembly on Bedloe's Island, now Liberty Island.

Unfortunately, we Americans had not raised our quarter million dollars for Lady Liberty's pedestal, which is almost as tall as the statue. Accepting the challenge, Joseph Pulitzer criticized the tightfisted rich and promised to print the name of everyone who contributed a dollar or more. Thus, most of the funds for Liberty's pedestal came from ordinary folks, a dollar or two at a time.

When the Statue of Liberty was dedicated, the Times of London sniffed, "We question why Liberty should be sent from France, which has too little, to America, which has too much." Not surprisingly, some American clergy protested the erection of this "pagan god on our soil." Significantly, no one mentioned immigration at the dedication, neither those who presented the gift nor those who accepted it. That idea came later, in 1903, from the pen of Emma Lazarus.

Lazarus had the statue in mind when she wrote *The New Colossus*. "... Keep ancient lands, your storied pomp. ...Give me your tired, your poor, your huddled masses yearning to breathe free. The wretched refuse of your teeming shore. Send these, the homeless, tempest-tost to me, I lift my lamp beside the golden door."

In 1903, when *The New Colossus* was attached to Liberty's base, the United States was relatively empty. We numbered just 78 million — about a fourth of our current population, but now, a century later, our situation has drastically changed.

Across the globe nearly a billion persons are added each decade while millions die from starvation — the result of overpopulation. Those who survive look to other nations, chiefly America, to fill their bellies or take them in. They arrive in decrepit freighters. They risk their lives in makeshift rafts to escape from Haiti, presenting us with the difficult choice of taking them in or turning them back.

In one six month period, with corporations downsizing and millions of Americans unemployed, our federal government issued 829,000 work permits to foreign nationals. In 2009, during a deepening recession that raised the unemployment rate to 10%, Hewlett Packard dumped some 15,000 American workers while building eight software "universities" in India, and Honeywell chose to spend $50 million on a research facility in India rather than build it here and employ Americans.

In 1994, Californians, swamped with illegals who openly run past border guards, promoted Proposition 187, a measure designed to bar illegals from public schools, from all but emergency health care and from social services. Predictably, California's Cardinal Roger Mahoney called Proposition 187 a "devastating assault on human dignity." In so doing, he parroted the Pope's claim that the United States has no right to limit immigration and his rejection of the concept of national sovereignty. Tell me, isn't the Vatican a sovereign nation (thanks to Ronald Reagan), and shouldn't they be setting an example by packing in these people whom their Vatican Roulette birth control policy has created?

Shortsighted churches have sponsored Hmong and Kurdish immigrants even though their responsibility for those immigrants ends after thirty days, causing school and welfare crises in Wausau, Wisconsin and Fargo, North Dakota. In Fargo, Lutheran and Episcopal churches have refused to halt their resettlement programs. In New York, the descendants of one Rodriguez family consume a million dollars per year in welfare benefits, and in Sacramento, Russian Pentecostal immigrants with double digit families have strained the welfare budget.

There are solutions: illegals encountered at sea should be turned back unless they are escaping persecution likely to result in death — as in the famous 1939 U.S. rejection of the St. Louis, a German ship loaded with Jewish refugees who were fleeing the Nazis. When demanding to be admitted becomes unsuccessful, the intrusions will stop.

Illegals and their offspring should be deported. Mexicans should not be returned to the border, but to Mexico City, making it less convenient to return while taking the problem to the seat of the Mexican government.

Those who *knowingly* employ, import or hide illegals should be fined, perhaps jailed, AND made to pay for the cost of deportation.

So what about Emma Lazarus and her "golden doors?" Given our quadrupled population and our growing ranks of unemployed, their jobs shipped abroad, would Emma want to admit refugees from Pakistan, where the average grandparent has FORTY grandchildren? And what about the magnificent Lady of Liberty? If she truly represents freedom, that surely must include the freedom to decide whom we will and will not admit.

Why shouldn't it include the freedom to require immigrants to learn functional English within three years or provide their own interpreters? Why shouldn't it mean the freedom to require sponsors of immigrants to be responsible for ALL of their needs for two years, including health care and legal representation?

In spite of her solid appearance, the figure that raises her torch above Bedloe's Island is just an empty shell, her copper skin hiding an erector set of steel. Any definition of freedom that allows unlimited immigration will please the shortsighted, but it will be as empty as the lady herself, for Liberty is a symbol, not a rock-solid guarantee.

Her symbolism should not be intended just for America, but for the all of the world. Her promise must no longer mean that we will accept all who want to come, but that we will assist those who want to control their populations, dump their despots and raise meaningful Liberty statues that they can call their own.

# From Atop the Campanile

Venice in the early days of fall, 1609. Beyond the lagoon that separates the mud islands of the great city from the coast of Italy, an ochre autumn has begun to touch the hills, soon to set the lagoon aglow with a colorful palette of leaves dispensed by the Po and the Piave Rivers.

Above the square, in St. Mark's lofty Campanile, a squarish man topped with a shock of russet hair is holding forth before a group of dignitaries. The Senators of Venice are respectfully attentive, for the red-headed one is Galileo Galilei, scientist, physician, and inventor - and, as history has noted, father to more children than a bachelor should have.

Close below lies the Grand Canal, its waters rippled bronze by the wake of gondolas and a declining sun. To one side is the palace of the Doge; to the other, St. Mark's Cathedral. But it's to the south that Galileo raises his arm as he speaks.

"Honored Senators, allow me to direct your attention to the far horizon. Shield your eyes, that your vision will be most acute. There, as if emerging from the Adriatic, just in line with the Canal of the Glass Workers, see you a ship, a caravel, sails straining in a contrary wind?"

In spite of the shielding and squinting, there is only the ocean, and skepticism—not sails— fills their eyes. With furrowed brows and uneasy grumbles, they turn their gaze on Galileo.

"And now Senators, look you through my spyglass which I have fixed upon the spot."

Silence, then cries of astonishment, as one senator after another crowds to the lens tube, each quickly setting surprise aside to ponder the value of such a device.

Galileo continues. "The vessel is the Santa Rosa, long overdue and thought to have been lost at sea. One hears that her owners are eager to sell their shares of her cargo to anyone foolish enough to gamble upon her return. Carrying full sail, 12 hours will pass before the public learns of her, time enough for a purchase and a profit. This, gentlemen, is but one use for an instrument that can render an object fifty miles distant as if it were five."

But Galileo's words bring no response, for the senators have departed, market bound.

Galileo, now alone, immersed in fading light and the waning sounds of Venice, lifts his spyglass from its mount and swings it to the west, toward the mountains that obscure Padua and the university where he once thrived. He slowly turns to the southwest, bringing into focus the mountains that separate him from the culture and security of Florence. Finally, almost reluctantly, he directs his marvelous instrument south, as if to probe the haze beyond the Apennines in contemplation of distant, disturbing Rome.

Does he envision himself kneeling before the Inquisition like his fellow scientist, Giordano Bruno, now 17 years dead, who was tortured and burned to death for holding the same beliefs? Does he recognize the cloister of Santa Maria Sopra Minerva where he will someday stand accused? Does he see the red-hatted ranks of cardinals who will confront him, all Dominicans, with many related to the Pope? And does he somehow sense that he will survive after being forced to recant and to live a life of house arrest, going blind from studying the sun spots that the Vatican says don't exist?

Heaving a sigh, Galileo clutches his spyglass to his chest, closes his eyes and drifts into thought, seeing himself in his final days, bedridden and blind, his once-dazzling candle diminished to a feeble flame that flutters, flickers and dies. And then, from a tiny ember at the base of the wick, a bright flame suddenly leaps to life.

When Galileo descends from the bell tower with his precious looking glass cradled in his arms, he seems content. I've had a vision, he thinks. My work will not perish. My light will die, but my torch will be passed. It was.

Some say that when Galileo died, his spirit sought refuge in the womb of an Englishwoman far from the tyrants of Rome, there to await a rebirth that would fall on Christmas Day. His mother would name him Isaac, but the world would call him NEWTON.

Galileo died in 1642, the year of Newton's birth.

# Philosophical Geometry – Solid, man!

A freethinker's like a rubber ball,
ready to roll, unafraid to fall.
We can stop if we like and pause for a rest,
but movin' on's what we like the best.

Like the balls so round, we like to go,
to find out what the other balls know.
Our roaming takes us far and wide,
to customs and thoughts that some deride.

The religious cones have a different bent.
Compared to the balls, they've hardly went.
The cones always orbit a preconception,
that limits their scope as well as perception.
For roll as they might, as sure as they've parted,
the cones end up right back where they started.

Pat Robertson's noisy, conservative rubes,
I offer as unmoving cubes,
unlike the balls that freely roam,
or even the cones that orbit their home.
Firm in their faith but afraid of a fall,
their minds stay put, going nowhere at all.

And yet there's hope, for cubes can bend,
the mind can mend, and then ascend,
from cube to cone, from cone to ball,
from fearful stance to growing tall.

And if you need a reason, dear,
for squares going round, becoming spheres,
we'll borrow a thought that religions revere:
Perhaps there's a MIRACLE working here!

On the other hand, I must confess,
on rare occasions, balls regress.
Under press of events or mental decline,
a few of the balls have been known to resign.

But all in all, I'll have you know,
there's more that ascend than head below.

# And a Little Mouse Shall Lead Them

The literalist beliefs of the Southern Baptists who have boycotted Disney for refusing to discriminate against gays brings to mind Galileo, who said that humankind is composed of two types: " ... those apt at inventing fables and those disposed to believe them." He's still right, but, unlike the religionists whose exhortations and complaints clutter airwaves, I side with the millions of Americans who are attuned to realists and educators like Roddenberry, Asimov, Edison and Twain — and to pleasant characters like Mickey Mouse.

Early Christians didn't like education much, some of their various saints having declared it irrelevant, vain and distracting. Would that they had been content to merely ignore education, rather than oppose it, for they persecuted or killed dissenters. And when secular governments finally made that impossible, they retarded science and education for centuries, opposing Copernicus, Galileo, Newton and Darwin and all the great minds who have repeatedly proved them wrong.

In murdering Michael Servetus, the spiritual source for Unitarianism, early Christian leaders set a precedent that would bury millions more during the Crusades, the Inquisition, the European witch hysteria, the Thirty Years War and the ghastly Holocaust, when German Lutherans and German Catholics murdered German Jews. "But," you say, "that was then, and this is *now*."

Look, then, to Ireland, where Protestants have clashed with Catholics. In the Middle East it's Shiites against Sunnies, who both hate Jews. In India it's Hindus vs. Muslims vs. Sikhs. In the former Yugoslavia, Muslims warred against Orthodox Christians and Roman Catholics, who, when not fighting Muslims, warred against each other. Religion-inspired zealots bombed the World Trade Center, go gunning for Planned Parenthood doctors, withhold medical care from their children, decree death sentences on authors, sexually, mentally and physically abuse children, preach against population control, fleece the gullible and give special meaning to once-ordinary places like Jonestown, Waco and Rancho Santa Fe, California, site of the Heaven's Gate cult suicide.

In the United States, these extremists fight science, seeking public funds for church schools where science can be replaced by creationism, where contraception can be a dirty word, and where books and ideas can be banned.

And yet, I will say that none of this is the fault of the man they call the Prince of Peace, for their zealots have chosen to follow his path in name, but not in deed.

Fortunately, there are still a few havens from the schemers and proselytizers. One, believe it or not, is located in the Deep South, on an island of secularity near Orlando, Florida. They call it Disney World, and I call it wonderful.

The Magic Kingdom makes no attempt to pass off fantasy as fact or to convert delight to devotion. At Epcot, where imagination and humanity are emphasized, no evangelists hold forth.

Every morning, thousands of fun and knowledge-seekers like my wife, my grandchildren and me pour through the gates of Disney World to laugh at the horseplay of the Diamond Jubilee Revue, and to scare ourselves when confronted by the wicked Queen and Snow White's luscious, lethal, blood-red apple. Wherever we went, we laughed and learned.

As we strolled the sidewalks between China's impressive exhibit and Norway's Akershus restaurant, people of all origins and religions bustled past, all intent on those marvelous secular pastimes of learning and enjoying their lives.

At MGM we gaped at stunt scenes from Indiana Jones, sat riveted to the trials of the Little Mermaid, and were dazzled by a stage show of "The Beauty and the Beast." At Epcot's The Land, we found nutrition and sustenance. Across the way, we smiled at "The Making of Me," a factual, humorous movie about the source of babies.

We watched stunning films of France's Alps and the Eiffel Tower, of Norway's fiords and of Canada's beauty, from Newfoundland to the Arctic to Vancouver. And at the close of each day, with the street lights dimmed, we enjoyed IllumiNations, a spectacular fireworks/laser/fountain display highlighting the many nations of Epcot, its brilliant conclusion accompanied by the thunder of Beethoven's 1812 overture. Never have I seen so many people so relaxed, so happy. And all without a single, intrusive, "Have you been saved?"

We each had our favorite Disney character. My wife was taken with the Muppets, and my granddaughter became fascinated with Figment, a character from the Journey Through Imagination show, which she had to see FIVE times.

As for me, I'm one of the kids who will always love Mickey. Like the vast majority of Disney characters (don't forget Grumpy) he has a smile and an embrace for everyone. Just being a friend is his religion. Not surprisingly, Mickey's tolerance and secularity rankles the haters in the Southern Baptists.

Misled by literal belief in an ancient, erroneous book that's interpreted many ways, the Southern Baptists seek to injure those they dislike with new laws and economic pressure, which makes me wonder if their Jesus, their holy child-grown-to-man, would support their unloving discrimination. I doubt it.

Given a choice between Mickey, who embodies Peace on Earth and Good Will to All, and the Southern Baptists, who enthusiastically support our addled president's war, I'm convinced that the Prince of Peace would happily don a Mickey Mouse shirt and sport a Mickey Mouse watch. In response to the Southern Baptists, I think I'll buy three Mickey Mouse ties — one for Mickey, one for me, and one for the Prince of Peace.

# It Ain't Necessarily So

When my wife and I moved to a suburb of St. Paul, we considered buying a house across the street from a church with a large billboard that boasted a miraculous event. I suggested that we should buy the house and then erect an equally large sign proclaiming, "It ain't necessarily so."

Those words come to mind whenever I encounter people who relate stories that are obviously suspect or even patently wrong — the modern version of those who believed in a flat Earth despite the curved shadow it cast upon the moon. To be wrong or misinformed is no great transgression, but it's regrettable that so many people repeat a story even though their common sense must be shouting, "Something's fishy here."

Consider the nice fellow I met in Missouri recently while I was en route to watch a night launch of the space shuttle Columbia (FANTASTIC). A pleasant fellow, he was manning a booth in an arts and crafts festival, answering questions behind tables stacked with crystals and rock formations. Before long, we got to talking about geodes, which are roughly spherical, hollow rocks that looks like trash on the outside, but are often lined with crystals of quartz, calcite, amethyst or a host of other minerals. Geodes form when a cavity in rock fully or partially fills with crystals that precipitate from the mineral-saturated fluids that enter the void.

"These all come from fruit, you know," he said. "That's why they're hollow —'cause the insides dry out and the minerals change to crystals. Why, I've seen geodes bigger than a man." (There are some very large geodes). "And some are flat on the bottom 'cause the fruit squashes a little before it dries out." He was wrong, of course, but, not being inclined to dispute him, I went on to other matters. He had a great display. His prices were right. But he was wrong, and he should have known it, had he listened to his common sense.

Georgia now. While I fill up with regular, a black man standing on the curb at the stop sign harangues motorists, "witlessing" for the "only true religion" while ignoring the dilemma created by the existence of the other "only true religions." Inside the station I am greeted by an enormous white woman adorned with a huge cross, her fingers constricted by multiple rings that pinch each digit into little sausages, each terminated with an unbelievably long, blaze-red, fake fingernail.

"Mornin' honey," she greets me. "Cash or credit?" As the transaction proceeds, she queries, "You been saved?"

"From what?" I reply, playing dumb.

"From the fires of eternal damnation," she replies, looking at me as if wondering where I had been for the last 2,000 years.

"Well," I reply, "religion doesn't make much sense to me ... too many contradictions."

"Don't have to make sense, honey," she counters. Then, as I sign for the gas and turn for the door she concludes with, "Better think it over. Judgment day's a comin' an' hell's forever ... HAVE A NICE DAY!"

And I did have a nice day ... a great day really, as we drove on through the beautiful hills north of Atlanta. Then, while coming down one of the steeper grades, I remembered a similar road, one that followed the Mississippi River Valley into a quiet Minnesota town.

It was early summer, and as I slid onto the vinyl-covered restaurant stool I suddenly realized that I had apparently stumbled upon the monthly meeting of the Liars Club. It was the season of the mayfly, the J. Edgar Hoover of the bug kingdom — an insect everyone recognizes but few understand.

To begin with, the mayfly has a surplus of names. Some call them dayflies, others say "shadflies." Some prefer fish flies, lake flies, willow bugs or twenty-four-hour bugs. Along the American side of the Great Lakes they were once mockingly called Canadian Soldiers, in reference to their fragile nature. Not surprisingly, on the Canadian side, they became Yankee Soldiers for the same reason.

The fellow on my right claimed they developed from unfertilized fish eggs. Another said they rose from dead fish along the shoreline, while a third maintained that regardless of how they formed, they all came from Canada, carried south by the wind. Another piece of wisdom, refuted by the swarms of mayflies constantly landing and departing from the window sill, was "once they land, they never fly again!"

All agreed, however, that they hatched, mated and died within twenty four hours, and all of them were wrong — wrong about the mayfly's beginnings and wrong about its life. Had they checked with the Web or a library, they would have discovered that the life of the mayfly is more fascinating than any blend of stories and myths.

The mayflies that halo our street lights and grease lighted bridges with their bodies have already lived for two years in the muddy bottoms of nearby lakes and rivers. During those years as nymphs, they shed their skins some thirty times and, having eaten for the last time, rise from the waters on lacelike wings, now 'imagoes.' After several hours they do what no other insects do, once again shedding their coverings, leaving their delicate molts behind. Adult imagoes now, they abandon the ash-grey husks of youth and launch their pale, shining bodies into the mayfly cloud in search of their mates.

Some are soon successful, with others persisting until the following day. Once coupled, they slowly descend, sometimes rising and falling back. Others spiral higher and higher until lost from sight. Into the waters of the lakes, ponds and rivers, each fertilized female ejects some 1,500 eggs, which fall to the bottom and hatch as tiny, gilled nymphs.

In two years, as adults, these delicate insects, whose ancestors fluttered among the dinosaurs, will unfold their gauzy wings and perform, once again, the mating dance of the skies.

These good folks who pass on stories without question, never consulting Wikipedia or striding through library doors, are missing something. They are missing one of the comforting and unifying facts of life: that given enough information, THINGS MAKE SENSE. They are missing the fun of having an inquiring mind, a mind that weighs and evaluates whatever is offered — a mind that is free to say "It ain't necessarily so."

# Rhythm & Blues (and Babies)

There was an old woman who lived in a shoe,
Who had so many children, she knew not what to do.

She asked her husband, who talked to the priest,
Who spoke with the bishop, who said, "At the least,
I'll ask the cardinal to query the pope,
When it comes to babies, he knows all the dope."

The pope reviewed the Holy Writ
of previous popes who had happened to sit,
in judgment of the means of prevention,
that humans employ to avoid conception.

From pope to cardinal, from bishop to priest,
from husband to wife (on this scale, the least)
The "word" from on high was "Don't be upset.
Just stick with the game called Vatican Roulette."

Dressed up to sound modern and ready to use,
it taps out the beat of rhythm and blues.
But you'd best be adroit to avoid the bad news:
Just once miss the rhythm, and here come the blues.

In the Western Hemisphere, the nations with the worst poverty, the worst education and the highest birth rates are south of our border. And what anti-birth control, pro-procreation religion has dominated their cultures for centuries? Catholicism!

When countries with different population ethics and standards of living attempt to restrict illegal immigration they are labeled xenophobic, just as those who criticize the Roman Catholic Church are called "Catholic bashers" by a church that prefers to call names rather than address the issues.

Restricting (not eliminating) immigration is NOT xenophobic. It is COMMON SENSE. France, which once accepted anyone, began deporting illegal immigrants in the '90s when France determined to become a zero immigration country.

My feelings mirror those of the Federation for Immigration Reform, which opposes the moralistic argument that we are (endlessly) our brother's keeper: "Must we subdivide and distribute our assets (and our children's assets and their children's assets) among the children of the world. Americans are already outnumbered 20 - 1 by the rest of the world. Our grandchildren will be outnumbered even worse. Must we condemn them to the poverty of an equal distribution because others will not reduce their birth rates? How would that benefit them or the descendants of others?"

These are appropriate questions, but they fail to affix blame on those responsible: religions that fight contraception and abortion and governments that yield to their pressures. Propelled by hormones and the procreation-pushing dogmas of reactionary religions, the Catholic and pro-reproduction, abstinence-only Protestant segments of our population will continue to increase. So be it — but the members of the religions whose policies cause these excesses should be responsible for these people.

As long as our doors are open, we will be sought out by the offspring of the prolific who find it easier to dilute the wealth, quality of life and sanity of the developed countries than to stay at home and work for education and family planning. Just as we restrict the size of our own families to levels we can afford to decently support and educate, why shouldn't other nations do the same? We must restrict — not eliminate — immigration. We must also help those who are willing to work for change in their own countries.

By 2050 the Earth will need to feed and support ANOTHER 6 billion people — with 95% of that increase occurring in poor countries. Immense shanty cities will dwarf the present day slums of Calcutta, Mexico City, Sao Paulo and Bombay, becoming centers of mass poverty, disease and social collapse. The population density of Lagos is already five times that of New York, and in Kenya, fully half the population is soon to become sexually mature.

By 2025 the U.S. population is expected to increase 29%. Guatemala is likely to grow more than 60%, with the Mexican population expanding twice that rapidly at 135%, with many of them eager to head north.

Some look to industrial development for an answer, but development cannot keep pace. What it will do, however, is pollute the Earth and line the pockets of politicians and factory owners.

Somehow, nations must begin to think and act like responsible parents who plan how many mouths they can feed because that planning, not chance, must determine the standard of living that they will be able to maintain. We need to limit the numbers that would come to our table. We need to learn how and when to say NO.

# Dancing in the Branches
# of the Humanist Tree

"To a natural philosopher[scientist], there is no natural object
unimportant or trifling… a soap bubble… an apple… a pebble.
He walks in the midst of wonders." John Hershel

Back in the eighties, the State of Minnesota finally realized that too
many dentists, having switched from text books to Golf Digest after
graduating, were skipping continuing education courses and were, as a
consequence, practicing antique dentistry. I'm pleased to say that I was not
one of them, so it made no difference to me when continuing education
courses became compulsory.

Actually, I was pleased that those recluses would have to share the
pain or boredom (it varied) that some of the lectures produced. In my
view, good speakers should be able to communicate, have no distracting
quirks and deliver material relevant to their subject. And since we often
paid big bucks to attend, it seemed reasonable to expect speakers to fulfill
these requirements.

Consequently, after several years of hearing presentations that were
one-third jokes, or presented by speakers who constantly toyed with the
mike cord, which generated annoying rumbles and clicks, I began sending
them a critique of their performance, listing their pluses and minuses as I
saw them with suggestions for improvement. I also mentioned that I was
sending a copy to the sponsors of the seminar. I was the feisty old gal in
the Wendy's commercial who looked in her burger and cried, "Where's
the beef?"

Several years later, speaker evaluation forms began to appear, the quality of our sessions went up — and I retired.

Consider, then, the apprehension with which I paid my fees to attend the seventh annual Humanist Weekend, sponsored by the North American Committee for Humanism (NACH). In the back of my mind lurked memories of the old issues of *The Humanist* magazine, issues long on nuance and short on resolve, with page after page of what I considered to be philosophical froth. I worried that here I was, plunking down big bucks and a chunk of my valuable time to be bored by a bunch of graying philosophers.

On the bright side, perhaps I'd meet Fred Edwords, the editor of *The Humanist* magazine, and I pictured myself nudging him awake and speaking into his ear trumpet.

The program for the first evening involved a discussion between two speakers from the University of Minnesota, with one presenting the modernist viewpoint regarding our present state of affairs, and the other presenting the view of the postmodernists — "modernism" being the conviction that since the Enlightenment, society has quite effectively relied on science, independence, individual initiative and a belief that truths can be determined and progress achieved, while the postmodernists assert that we have abandoned the spiritual and the subjective, and that the capitalism derived from science and technology initiatives has been damaging to the environment and to humanity as well.

Furthermore, the more radical postmodernists argued that the search for truth in objective knowledge ignores the "truths within us," and that truth is what each individual wishes it to be — or that there might be no such thing as truth or reality.

As it happens, I am a "roots" humanist who usually grubs around the base of the humanist tree, poking through the soil with my comrades, sending nourishment to support those who occupy the limbs above. My formal education has been primarily scientific. What literary and philosophical background I have acquired has been gathered on my own, and judging by the questions from the audience, I was somewhere near the midrange of philosophical sophistication, being able to follow, but sometimes only with effort.

The first gentleman, the modernist, hadn't lost sight of plain English, relying on it quite often. However, he absolutely could not manage without an occasional "zeitgeist" or "gestalt." Nevertheless, I and most of the audience, were able to understand him.

The second speaker, the postmodernist, was either an embodiment of his philosophy or a mighty fine actor, presenting the most subjective appearance, opinions, and surprising assertions that I have encountered since the invention of trickle-down economics. In spite of his use of plain language, complete sentences and a rational tone, he left many of us scratching our heads, much like an audience that had just viewed 2001, "A Space Odyssey."

During his talk, and in the questioning that followed, it became obvious that many postmodernists use science as their favorite whipping boy. It also became apparent that I was not the only one who'd been straining to read the noodles in the soup when one questioner began by saying, "I almost hate to say this, but am I the only one who doesn't have a clue as to what you are talking about?"

He wasn't alone. Had the speakers dropped the "zeitgeists" and considered the diverse background of the audience, they wouldn't have left so many behind.

During the question period that followed the evening session, I patiently waited my turn, eager to question those who scapegoat science and technology while remembering that the meeting was scheduled to end at 10 pm. Suddenly, at 9:45, the moderator called for the last question, not mine, and I left the meeting disappointed that a response to the critics of science and technology had not been made.

On my way home, I debated the propriety of printing copies of a defense of science to be distributed the following morning. Would it be inappropriate, too pushy? Perhaps out of bounds? Dare I leave my precious roots, ascend the trunk and decorate its lofty limbs with my rebuttal?

I decided that if Humanism really advocates the free and open exchange of ideas, my input was not only appropriate, it was required. Besides, I reminded myself, these folks are not ogres. I saw no chips on their shoulders and, as the saying goes, they put on their pants (or panty hose) one leg at a time.

That night, I wrote "In Defense of Science and Technology," printed 100 copies and fell into bed at 1:45 am. When the morning session opened, I distributed copies to all. Later, many sought me out to express agreement, and one of the speakers took time from his presentation to express his thanks and support.

## "IN DEFENSE OF SCIENCE AND TECHNOLOGY"

During yesterday's airing of modernist/postmodernist viewpoints, science and technology were criticized directly by some and indirectly by others. Love Canal and nuclear weapons were given as examples, as they frequently are. While science and technology are fair game, it is unfortunate that time was not available to rise in their defense. What many forget is that SCIENCE IS THE SEARCH FOR KNOWLEDGE, and TECHNOLOGY is the SUM OF THE WAYS THAT SOCIETY USES THAT KNOWLEDGE TO PROVIDE THE COMFORTS AND CONVENIENCES OF CIVILIZATION.

To portray science or technology as the villain ignores our role in determining how their fruits are used. Science and technology have not failed; they have been phenomenally successful. The fault lies not with scientists, who are not insensitive to the fragrance and the radiance of a rose, and to imply that they are insensitive is extremely prejudicial. Many people of science are deeply attuned to the aesthetic nature of the world in general and the subjects of their study in particular. To cast blame on science or technology is to join ranks with the hard core religionists, the fundamentalists in particular, against whom science has fought a long and unrelenting battle, frequently at great cost.

Science is not at fault, nor is technology. The fault is ours. It belongs to those of us who treasure opinion more than knowledge. It belongs to those who use technology to garner profits regardless of the human and environmental costs. It belongs to churches that preach love but tolerate greed and bigotry, and to the ignorant and indolent who only read the sports pages and comics, and rely on astrology tables, churches or science-ignorant politicians or commentators to lead the way.

The famous physicist, Leo Szilard, fought against use of the atom bomb, cabling and sending memoranda to President Roosevelt, urging an international demonstration so that the Japanese could witness its power. But others, not scientists, determined that the bomb should be used for effect — and not as a mere demonstration.

As I looked about our meeting room, noting the average age of the participants, I calculated that were it not for science, many would not be here. Most of the remainder, assailed with an assortment of pock marks, uncorrected vision, hearing loss and perhaps the occasional missing limb, would find it difficult to communicate their disdain for science, speaking, as we most certainly would, through the gaps left by missing teeth.

Jacob Bronowski, a humanist and scientist, will always be fondly remembered by those who saw him in the stunning BBC series, "The Ascent of Man." Near the end of the series he addressed the criticism that many so wrongly make of science: that it is dehumanizing; that it is responsible for our ills.

In that scene, Bronowski slowly walked into an Auschwitz pond until the water overlapped the tops of his well polished shoes. Bending over, he reached into the pond and brought up a fist full of verdant, sodden grass. Then, looking up into the camera, he began: "It is said that science will dehumanize people and turn them into numbers. That is false, tragically false. Look for yourself. This is the concentration camp and crematorium at Auschwitz. THIS is where people were turned into numbers. Into this pond were flushed the ashes of some four million people. And that was not done by gas. It was done by ARROGANCE. It was done by DOGMA. It was done by IGNORANCE. When people believe that they have absolute knowledge, WITH NO TEST IN REALITY, this is how they behave."

There were eight presentations that morning, including those of our AHA President, Suzanne Paul, and the managing editor of *The Humanist* magazine, Fred Edwords. Without naming names, and while admitting my bias, let me say that the presentations ranged from the eminently rational to one that, if equated with food, would have supplied the nutritional value of a cube of celery. Most speeches ranked somewhere in between, their value to the audience determined largely by the speaker's ability to communicate without relying on jargon.

When the talks had ended, the audience divided into groups, each group meeting with a speaker of their choice. Though it was tempting to meet with those I agreed with, it seemed unproductive. And since I did not really care to disrupt those of the celery persuasion, I chose the middle road, and met with Fred Edwords.

I had three reasons for choosing Mr. Edwords: First, he gave a bright, rational, witty talk regarding myths and symbols, and how Humanism might benefit by adopting some "religious" practices, such as storytelling, to promote our message. Second, the idea of using stories and songs was in contrast to my usual analytical approach. And third, Mr. Edwords not only managed quite well without an ear trumpet, he was younger than I and seemed quite alert. So while other groups pondered subjects like Science and Spirituality, Economic Justice, Feminism, etc., we reviewed meaningful stories, recommended movies and books, and told a few jokes. As usual, my story about the Catholic kittens brought down the house.

Nevertheless, like one of Garrison Keillor's Lake Woebegone Lutherans, I suspected that under the guise of deliberating, we had been guilty of having too much fun, that somehow we had been playing hooky while others labored on. Still, there were lessons -- lessons like "lighten up." But, as we will see, "lightening up," can be hard to do.

So, like the song that asks "What it's all about, Alfie," I'd sum it up by saying that if the last several centuries have taught us anything, it is that we must continue to apply skepticism to those who claim to have absolute truth, and to be equally wary of postmodernists who cannot find any at all.

The conference and its surroundings inadvertently revealed a concern that's with me every day. It shadowed me during the speeches, the receptions and during one speaker's thoughts on Candide. As we dined, discussed and disputed, resplendent in well-tailored suits, others were tending their business fourteen floors below. There, in the main lobby restrooms, street people quietly slipped in and out, some seeking heat, some for a wash and a quick change of clothes.

The conference, much like this report, was a little enlightening, a little amusing, and it offered a chance to meet good people who are trying to find a better way. But the street people also spoke with their quick glances and their silence. They reminded me that Humanism will mean more to the world when we act on the needs of the many as eagerly as we bend the ears of our few.

# Michael Bristor

In the Minneapolis public school system, bigotry survives, thanks to a negligent, insensitive school board and a Catholic teacher – a teacher who began her classes with prayer and made a pariah of Michael Bristor, a child from a freethinking family that resisted her efforts. Parental protests to the principal proved useless, as did appeals to the school board. Only when Mrs. Bristor contacted the Minnesota Civil Liberties Union via the Minnesota Atheists did they begin to pay attention. In the meantime, the behavior of Michael's schoolmates and a loss of honor at the school caused the Bristors to move to Wisconsin.

When the Minnesota Civil Rights Department found in favor of the Bristors, who had sued the school board, the Twin Cities Reader published an article concerning the Bristors' school board conflict.

In support of Michael and his parents, I attended the next meeting of the board to read the following letter.

> As a friend of public education and the President of the Humanist Association of Minneapolis and St. Paul, I am here to protest the board's indifference to the practices of Michael Bristor's first grade teacher, Ms. Asuncion, and to the damage she has done. I do so with regret, for the public education system has benefited me enormously, and I find it repugnant that I need to criticize a public school system already under siege by book banners and those who would ruin the public schools with a voucher system. Let me add that I would be here testifying on behalf of any child, whether a Muslim, a Buddhist or a child from any minority point of view.

If the allegations against Ms. Asuncion are accurate, and if principal Azell and the board have failed to correct the offenses, the Bristors have been wronged. Let me ask the board if they would have delayed if the teacher had been promoting the Muslim doctrine or the teachings of the Rev. Sun Yung Moon? Would the protest of Christian parents have been ignored? Would their children have been required to show submission and shame by putting their heads down on the desk, and would they have been denied academic awards? I doubt it.

Instead, the board has chosen to ignore the law, coercing little Michael to conform to the will of the majority. By making him a pariah and withholding honors, they operated from, and advanced, the bigoted assumption that religious people know better — in fact ARE better, than those who manage just fine without leaning on a supernatural belief.

Teacher Asuncion typifies those whose concept of freedom of religion is that the religious are free to say whatever they want, and rest of us are free to shut up and listen. Furthermore, the board was apparently more concerned over the costs of terminating Ms. Asuncion than in ending her abuses.

While the Bristors will find vocal support from every nonreligious group, the majority of caring, mainline Christians would also side with Michael if they were asked. They would never have put Michael and his family through the anguish they have suffered.

If the allegations are true, the Board should admit its errors, correct them and settle with the Bristors. That would be mature, honest, simple and honorable thing to do. Or it can do what is often done: deny, delay, and eventually lose in court. If this route is chosen, I believe that the district will not only lose, it will lose BIG. And it will deserve it!

# On the Road Again

It's spring again
      And birds on the wing again,
            Start to sing again,
                  Go to Texas

Every spring, my wife and I head south to visit relatives who live near San Antonio in a town called Fredericksburg. As the miles flow by, there is a noticeable change of season — and of reason. And by the time we reach the full-blown spring of Texas, we appreciate the rationality of two of Texas' eminent women, the writer Molly Ivins and former Governor Ann Richards, who opined "Poor George (G. W. Bush), can't help it, he was born with a silver foot in his mouth!"

Iowa, as most folks know, is not that different from southern Minnesota, although politically, as well as geographically, it's a lot more square. But after setting aside jokes about Iowegians and Minnesnowtans, I have to admit that Iowa serves two marvelous purposes: It houses Iowa City's Betty McCollister and her enclave of humanists, and it accepts the spring floods of the Des Moines River, (what choice have they?) which arise in the tiled fields and streams of southwestern Minnesota.

On this trip, computer business compelled a westerly detour through Nebraska, and though the country looked much like southern Minnesota, the sounds were changed. WCCO, the most popular of the secular Twin Cities radio stations, had faded away, public radio had become a feeble voice, and there was a slow but steady increase in the WORD OF GOD. Nevertheless, the computer folks in Lincoln knew their business and sent us down the road in less time than it takes to say Microsoft.

It was late evening when we crossed the Kansas border while thinking pleasant thoughts of Dorothy, Auntie Em' and the beautiful Yellow Brick Road. We pulled into the Sunrise Motel and asked for a non-smoking room. The clerk looked momentarily puzzled, then said, "Don't have any." Ah, yes, I thought to myself, if you want to sample a time machine, just head for the conservative hustings of Smilin' Bob Dole.

After settling in, a short walk brought us to Lennie's Restaurant, where things began to look up, for they had a no-smoking section: two small tables in one corner, representing a whole ten percent of their seating. As I scanned the menu, a gaggle of 60-ish women surged in, all amply supplied with girth, mirth and dangling crosses — and accompanied by a nun with a baby that looked like Walter Matthau.

As Dave Barry says, "Trust me folks, I'm not making this stuff up."

When my chicken fried steak arrived, it was excellent, so I chalked one up for Kansas.

The next morning, we headed south to Wichita past roadsides aglow with blooming redbud trees. And though Kansas gets by without the "purple mountain majesties," its greening winter wheat promised to yield the "amber waves of grain," upon which so many of us depend.

Hours later we pulled into Oklahoma City's beautiful Cowboy Hall of Fame and Western Heritage Center, which features works of Charles Russell and Frederick Remington.

I've always like Russell. His realism is superb, his colors often vivid, yet muted when appropriate. His scenes, whether bristling with action or lazing along the trail, are believable, as are the characters that populate them. But I have two more reasons for admiring Russell: He was a kind, generous gentleman, and only quietly religious (if at all) for he had little or no use for preachers.

The "*Charles M Russell Book*" that I bought years ago is a treasure for the art it contains and for the man it portrays. Unlike some of his contemporaries who painted the West from their eastern studios, Russell painted the cowboy's life as he lived it.

His letters, however, revealed the man within — thoughtful and sensitive, even touching at times. Despite little schooling and imperfect spelling, he wrote letters that could thaw a snow queen's heart, and he decorated their margins with sketches of life on the range. Some of his letters are reproduced in my book. The museum, however, had a larger volume, "*The Letters of Charles M. Russell*" — only $100 per copy. What a shame that the sentiments of such a thoughtful man should be priced out of reach for all but a few.

South of Oklahoma City, I-35 cuts through the Arbuckle Range, exposing layer upon layer of sedimentary rock. In a nearby scenic park, a display identifies the layers, giving the age of each in millions of years. As I examined the display, I wondered how fundamentalists, when confronted with such obvious evidence of an ancient Earth, can preach that the Earth is less than 10,000 years old.

In Texas, the red-tailed hawks of the central and northern plains gave way to turkey buzzards and, in a similar progression, the only newspaper I could find that gives a fair shake to Hillary Clinton was USA Today. In it, columnist Barbara Reynolds asked why those who pillory Hillary failed to criticize Neil Bush, who played the commodities market with money borrowed from a friend at Silverado S & L, which went belly up. When Neil's friend failed to pay the S & L, we taxpayers made good the loss, yet few publications said a word.

Even the bumper stickers revealed the conservative shift: "Impeach The President — and Mr. Clinton, Too!" Our car radio brimmed with the rantings of Rush Limbaugh and a new one to me — the Phyllis Schlafly Report. Yet outside my window, nature offered a flood of blue bonnets that filled the ditches and flowed into the fields, there to mingle with Indian paint brush and snow-white poppies.

Texas has not escaped the economic trials of the other states that are joined by I-35. Villages with hopeful names like Rising Star and Promise are shriveling into ghost towns, their people and businesses gone to brighter lights, leaving perhaps one operating gas station and, with luck, a shabby general store patrolled by a scruffy looking dog.

Texas, with more miles of Mexican border than New Mexico, Arizona and California combined, revealed the porosity of its border everywhere I turned. Road crews — Mexican-American. Workers stripping and painting aircraft at the Fredericksburg airport — Mexican-American. Even the Hunan Chinese Restaurant in Kerrville employed a largely Mexican-American staff.

And just as omnipresent are the fruits of the Catholic Church: stair step children herded by young, cross-bearing, pregnant Latino mothers who seem oblivious to population problems, being the products of a religion that promotes procreation while opposing effective birth control and abortion.

Worse yet, a San Antonio Express News columnist named Don Feder actually promotes religion as THE ANSWER, taking swings at "condom-happy Planned Parenthood" in the process. Deriding the "thirty year secular jihad" that he claims has swept aside religious influence, he argues that it's all the fault of "Secular humanist ideologues — they're the ones in charge." Should I laugh or cry?

Even so, bright lights still sometimes shine. Lights like Catherine Fahringer and her friends, who picketed a San Antonio Catholic Church with signs reading "The Pope is Not Infallible: He Isn't Even Reasonable" and "OverPOPEulation — a Clear and Present DANGER."

Although conservatives control most of the Southern press and airwaves, Fahringer is not alone. Witness the woman I followed six blocks out of my way in order to read the bumper stickers that covered the back of her car. Stickers like "A woman without a man is like a fish without a bicycle" and "If you don't like abortion, don't have one."

Back in Fredericksburg, a decidedly German town, I found two unexpected treats. The first, a concert featuring the music of Dvorak, Bach and Beethoven played by visiting musicians from England. The second, a visual diversion to accompany the concert. Enter "Birgit" and "Brunhilda," two blond, braided, beaming 40-ish valkyries, undoubtedly sisters, who arrived as the concert began.

Round-nosed, round-cheeked, roundly-contoured women — substantial, yet not fat — the long braids of one were coiled upon her head, the braids of the other descended almost to her waist. In a word, they were Rubenesque, with nary a straight line in sight. They knew they were striking, but in their hushed conversation and glances, I detected no hint of pride, only an abundance of pleasant self-assurance.

Accompanied by the strains of Beethoven, I admired their innovative dress, their pleasure in each other and in themselves, and their obvious delight at hearing great music, well-played. And I marveled that I should have encountered Brunhilda and Birgit with Beethoven and Bach while deep in the heart of Texas.

Our aunt will soon leave Texas, having decided to move to Minnesota, the place of her birth, so we won't be making our semiannual trek to the South again. I'll miss the redbuds, the blue bonnets, the blushing fields of primrose and even the chicken fried steak. But like my old friend, Charlie Russell, I won't miss the pompous preachers — or the Phyllis Schlafly Report.

# Perspective

The morning traffic on I-35 oscillated between five and 15 miles per hour, then sludged to a halt, leaving me facing an array of antigovernment stickers on the rusting pickup ahead. On its tailgate, a multitude of redundant stickers proclaimed the owner's love of Jesus and his willingness to die for the right to own an AK 47. A nearby antiabortion slogan nestled up to a sticker reading "I hate fags."

Tossing a cigarette butt out of his window, Mr. Sweetness and Light inched ahead, revealing a bumper spanned by a half-dozen "READ THE BOOK" stickers. Disgusted, I envisioned my response: a windshield panel urging "Read MANY books" printed in reverse for the benefit of the guy up front.

The space ahead widened. We moved, then stopped, then moved again, lurching down the highway like inchworms. Thank heavens I wasn't driving our stick shift car. Clutch — shift — clutch — shift. That's all I'd need — another irritant to add to my woes.

In the past few months, I'd had a major investment go down the drain and had sold my home and business during a down market to the only interested buyers. The professional movers were all booked up, so we endured our adventure in moving in an asthmatic rental truck on a fine August day that hit 102 degrees. It felt like 102 *Centigrade*.

A few months later, our son announced a divorce which would again involve us with his wealthy Scrooge-in-laws. Worse yet, all of my trials had occurred while I was suffering from a thyroid gone wild that stripped away 25 pounds, pushed my pulse to 130, inhibited sleep and demanded that everything be done *right now*.

Finally, with my thyroid neutered and replaced by a pill, my pulse had returned to normal. Still, as I sat fidgeting behind Mr. Morality, I wasn't happy because I was running very late.

I was en route to the University Hospital to learn about cystic fibrosis so I could help the child of some friends who would soon be moving to town. Because his parents were working full time, I had offered to give them a hand.

Edith McLane, the hospital's respiratory therapist, brushed aside my tardiness. Smiling but businesslike, she explained that cystic fibrosis produces mucous within the lungs, restricting the flow of air, and that the disease can damage other organs. Unless the mucus is loosened with periodic chest pummeling and coughed up, it clogs the lungs, eventually bringing death.

Thinking that hand pummeling would be too time consuming, and perhaps even boring, I asked, "Why not give the patient some sort of electric pummeler? Something that would vibrate like an orbital sander or a padded saber saw?"

"We do," she replied. "We have several devices for use here and at home, but even with the machines, our patients still need help. And, there are many areas they can't reach very well, especially when they're tilted head down to assist the drainage. Besides, all of our patients like the therapist much more than any of the machines."

As we headed down the corridor toward the treatment rooms, I asked Edith why some call cystic fibrosis an acquired disease while others say it's inherited.

"That's easy," she said. "It's both. Although CF is acquired, it's also genetic. You inherit a susceptibility to it. From then on it's like shooting dice. As long as you roll sevens you avoid the disease, but if you toss snake eyes, you don't. With early testing and regular treatment, we try to keep our patients rolling sevens.

"This morning," she said, "six patients will be getting treatments. Every one of them agreed to let you watch, but Kathy spoke up first, so she'll be your volunteer.

"Kathy was about five years old when she first came to us. She's ten now, and she's back for what we call a tune-up. We try to get her in the best possible shape so she can go home for a month or more. Then we'll see her about every other month for as long as she stays stable."

Realizing that Kathy might soon arrive, I quickly asked why none of the leaflets I had been given said anything about life expectancy.

"It's really hard to know," said Ellen. "The lucky ones see forty years. Some don't make it to twenty. But with the help of genetic testing and gene splicing, we hope to find a new treatment, or maybe even a cure."

As I pondered her response, the treatment room door swung slowly inward and Kathy entered, propelling an IV stand in front of herself like an icon-laden scepter, as if the stand, with its swaying bag and squeaking wheel, would somehow hold the disease at bay.

"Hello, Kathy," I began, choosing my words with care. "Thanks for helping me watch this pummeling thing. There's a boy your age who'll be needing my help with home care."

"Oh, that's OK," she replied, smiling slightly as she pulled her terry cloth robe around her thin frame,with fingers that seemed swollen — an indication that one or more of those "other organs" had already become involved. Climbing onto the table while carefully supporting her IV, she assumed the first of the many positions that are needed to allow the mucous to drain from her lungs. And the pummeling began.

Wop, wop, wop, wop, wop, wop — the therapist's cupped hands beat a jolting rhythm on her side, not hard enough to hurt, but enough to jar, rapidly metronoming along at 200 beats per minute — about three or four strokes per second. Then finally, a pause, some coughing and clearing of mucous — and the next position.

As Ellen worked, we talked, with Kathy putting in a few words whenever she changed positions. Thirty minutes later, when they were only half done, I left, smiling back at Kathy, whose gangly, Norman Rockwellish body continued to vibrate beneath the therapist's hands as she returned my gentle wave.

When I stopped at the office to thank the therapists for the literature they'd provided, I sensed a change of mood.

"What's wrong?" I asked.

Turning away, the attendant pointed to a five-word notice reading "Mary Tremble died last night."

At first, the name didn't register. But then I remembered. As the recipient of a heart-lung transplant made necessary by the CF she'd been fighting for years, Mary Tremble had been front-page news and a longtime patient at the "U." Married and a mother of two, she had run out of sevens when she was only 28.

As I walked to my car, the cold winter air needled my lungs and pinched my nostrils. Sliding behind the steering wheel, I shoved the key in the ignition, and sat for a moment, blinking back tears. What about Kathy? I wondered. How many years remained for her, and what sort of years would they be? Could she go to college? Would she live to marry? Would she have children? Would she ever be able to travel, to wander awestruck through canyon cathedrals or paddle an emerald lake with snow-capped peaks attending?

With Kathy's smile still filling my mind, and with my ancient Plymouth running and warm, I drove down Washington Avenue and onto the interstate, where the traffic, like my problems, had all but disappeared.

# Grace Under Fire:

## What to Say When You Haven't Got a Prayer

A few years ago, one of my friends and his family set aside a few days to visit his sister-in-law, a gracious and friendly hostess named Dorothy, and, as usual, the visit went quite well. At mealtimes, as was her habit, Dorothy always said "grace" and crossed herself before serving. One day, although she knew quite well that my friends had rejected religion, Dorothy turned abruptly to their ten-year-old son and said, "I think it would be nice if someone else said the prayer! Would you do this, Lee?"

Lee, caught by surprise, consented, and, as Dorothy bowed her head, he turned toward her and earnestly began to speak.

"I would like to thank you, Aunt Dorothy, for this wonderful meal and for letting us visit you this summer. This is a really keen place. I played golf and tennis and fished and did all sorts of fun things."

Then, turning to address his parents, he said, "Mom and Dad, thanks for bringing us to Aunt Dorothy's. It's lots of fun and the Olson's dog, Shep, remembered me again this year."

Lee thought for a moment and continued, "I'd like to thank the farmers who grew our food, and the workers in the factories and the truck drivers who bring the food to the stores and the people in the stores who sell it to us."

He paused again, and then resumed, "And then there's those chickens. I'd like to thank those chickens who gave their lives so that ..."

"That's quite enough, Lee," interrupted Dorothy.

Later, my friends praised their son's response, complimenting him for so accurately reflecting the ideals that they had tried to instill in their children.

In my book, Lee's offering had far more value than a memorized grace, a spinning prayer wheel or an offer of thanks to an unseen deity who no one can prove exists. Besides, whatever happened to Matthew 6:8, the Bible passage that warns believers against reciting the same prayer again and again? And what about Matthew 6:6, which frowns on public piety and advises the supplicant to pray within one's closet?

# Strike the Harp and Join the Folly

Having endured an unending litany of Christmas music since well before Thanksgiving, when the eager merchants could no longer restrain themselves, you might wonder how I have the nerve to prolong the process with talk of holiday music, good or bad.

Knowing my disdain for mysticism, you might also be tempted to wager a twenty that I'll take a Scrooge-eye view of music that glorifies gods. But save your bucks, ducks, because beneath my gray cerebrum, where our primitive urges dwell, those carols still get me 'cause I'm a sucker for a song.

Most of us grew up with "Silent Night" and "Joy to the World" — some in families that found the message in the music or in others that looked to the words. Nevertheless, the carols are fixed in our heritage, and though we reject the words, we can never shed the song.

Joined later by the moving music of "Oh Holy Night" and the less inspirational "Twelve Days of Christmas" (the holiday equivalent of "99 Bottles of Beer"), the realm of Christmas music runs from A (Antiquarian) to B (Beautiful) to C (Commercial). Some songs leave me cold, while others, like "I Heard the Bells on Christmas Day," will move me every time.

It's always been there, this emotional response to music, even from my grade school days when I was moved to tears by Brahms' First Symphony and its soaring, singing sounds. And so it has been with Roger Whittaker's, "Why," with "The Age of Aquarius" from "HAIR," with parts of "Jonathan Livingston Seagull," and with the marvelous piece from "Fiddler on the Roof" that no parent ever forgets — "Sunrise, Sunset."

Still, I prefer the secular Christmas songs. Beautiful as they are, the religious carols have messages that exclude me, messages that would make me a hypocrite were I to join in song. So I shy away from singing carols and hymns. And when there is no escape, I hope that those around me will understand that they, too, would remain silent if asked to sing in praise of the great god Vishnu.

As a result, I am a whiz at "Chestnuts Roasting on an Open Fire." I delight at "Jingle Bells" and I can out-Bing Mr. Crosby when "White Christmas" comes along. Perhaps that's just what's needed — to join in the songs, refraining when our heads say, "No," but belting out our best when the message suits our hearts.

# Ban Those Books

Taking a page from the Catholics' index of prohibited books, Pat Robertson and Friends have gathered up some horrible books to place on the fundamentalist's hit list. I've read all but two, but thanks to Pat, I'll be reading that last pair soon.

These titles, now available for freethinking wear, have been printed on T-shirts, and beneath the admonition to "Read a Banned Book," you will find *Little House on the Prairie, Tom Sawyer, Sleeping Beauty, Where's Waldo?, The Catcher in the Rye, The Color Purple, Lord of the Flies, Of Mice and Men* and *I Know Why the Caged Bird Sings*.

If your chest yearns for the attention heaped on Dolly Parton, just slip into one of these. People will stop you just to read the titles, and the conversation takes off from there.

As a fashion alternative, consider a T-shirt or sweat shirt from the Minnesota Public Radio catalogue, Wireless. Mine says "CELEBRATE FREEDOM: READ A BANNED BOOK," and then lists these terrible titles: *1984, Flowers for Algernon, Gone With the Wind, One Flew Over The Cuckoo's Nest, Ordinary People, Huckleberry Finn, The Diary of Ann Frank, The Great Gatsby, The Martian Chronicles, To Kill A Mockingbird* and *Uncle Tom's Cabin*. If the church doesn't like them, they must be good!

# The Truth About Tackle

I once thought that pet owners were the nuttiest people on earth. They baby-talk to their animals, they buy them toys and treats, and the names they come up with are wild. Sasha, my pet Sheltie, although sired by "Stormy Weather's Thunderbolt" and birthed by "Bonnie Blue Bell of the Lochs," never rose to showdog status. In fact, I should have named her "Bonnie Big Butt" because of her most prominent feature.

Running a close second in the nuttiest people category are the wine lovers, the cork sniffers who lecture about "beads" and rhapsodize over the wine's delicate "nose" while swirling it in ever higher circles, demonstrating that the wine may be sloshed, but they are not.

In third place and rising fast are the fishermen, soon to eclipse the lovers of Pérignon and pets. These poor innocents, indoctrinated since childhood by monthly doses of "Field and Stream," "Sports Afield" and "Outdoor Life," actually BELIEVE all those stories and will buy anything that looks like a lure. As a consequence, boats that could once support a guide, three guests and their gear, are now overburdened with one guide, one guest and his outrageous tackle box.

Consider my friend, Phil, who will buy anything that has hooks and eyes, with the possible exception of ladies' undergarments. If you tell Phil "This lure can catch whales in the Gobi desert," the deal's as good as done. Only $47.50? He'll take two as insurance against one being left behind on a dawdling dromedary.

Because of folks like Phil, guides who routinely trot five mile portages with a canoe on each shoulder have suffered fractures when they lift his benign-looking box, only to discover that it has the mass of a neutron star. Needless to say, this challenge has thinned their ranks. Some choose early retirement, while others have turned to less honorable work, such as writing articles about other peoples' idiosyncrasies. As a consequence, poor Phil now transports his own box by disassembling it when he reaches land and then portaging the individual trays.

On countless lakes across the fish-filled North, a thousand Phils set forth each day. When the CHOSEN SPOT is finally gained, the serious work begins. What a sight these fishermen are: They flip the latch of the tackle box and slowly raise the top, their eyes reflecting the beautifully contoured, enameled, porcelained, bejeweled, feathered and luminescent lures within, all made by machine and priced by Midas.

Which lure to choose? There are 93 in the top drawer alone, all of them thoroughly tangled. As if in a trance, our fisherman sorts through the trays, caressing each lure as the sun arcs high.

A selection is finally made. The chosen lure is disengaged from its rivals and anointed with Big Dollar fish scent. While rinsing the residue from his fingers, our sportsman is suddenly galvanized with pain, and jerks his hand from the water ... along with an equally surprised pike. Our fisherman, who has been adrift for forty-five minutes and has yet to wet a line, has caught a pike on his fingertips, and he suddenly realizes, as I once did, that he'd brought along too much rigging while also missing the boat.

A few years ago, when monstrous subarctic trout (or maybe rocks) had pirated the last of my largest lures, I was compelled to improvise when smaller spoons failed to produce a bite. And then I got to thinking ... for thousands of years the natives survived with no more than bone hooks and sinew. Yet here I was, the typical modern fisherman, carting around an endless variety of expensive hardware in country where standing too close to the water risks being attacked by hungry trout.

I vowed to reform. Like Vilhjalmar Stefansson, the famous Arctic explorer, I decided to adopt the ways of the natives and abandon my high-tech box. My lures, like those of old, would be made from common materials, of items from everyday life — a beer can opener, the old, removable pull tabs from pop cans and battered teaspoons.

The church key was the toughest. It already had a hole in the handle, but the business end needed drilling for the eye of the treble hook, and that church key steel is HARD!

The pop can tabs were a breeze. After punching a hole in the end of the tab for the treble hook and clipping the leader through the finger hole, I bent a slight curve in the tab to provide just the right action.

For extra strength, I use three tabs stacked one on top of another. These are my Triple Tab Sonic Vibrator models that retail for $34.95, plus only $12 for shipping and handling. Northern pike simply love them.

But the most fun, in the water and out, is the teaspoon. How I love to sit at fishing camp tables, watching anglers argue the relative merits of Rapalas and Daredevils, their fervor and volume even transcending important philosophical arguments like "Less filling! Tastes great!"

Holding forth my stainless steel spoon with a gleaming treble hook dangling from its lip, I casually maneuver between the debaters. Silence reigns. They gawk and stare. Then smiles break out and they begin to laugh.

"What in heaven's name is THAT?" they ask.

"A soup spoon for your mother-in-law?" one ventures, and laughter follows.

"No," I reply, "but it's great for catching fish."

"You must be kidding," they say. So I bring out the pictures of a Snare River grayling that came to dine on my spoon, and the lunker northern that found its undulations irresistible. My spoons sell briskly because they're COLLECTOR'S ITEMS, modestly priced at $28.00 — for a limited time only.

Then I break out my church key — the Northern Guide model — with its sides artificially scarred and worn, implying years of productive use. At only $49.65, they disappear like Big Macs at a high school picnic.

So folks, just scrap your two-ton tackle box and buy these three fine lures. In the Quetico, the Caribbean or the Arctic, they're all you'll ever need. Some say that fish strike these lures so hard that their scales fall off — and you don't even have to clean 'em.

These three lures will do you just fine, but for the truly discriminating sportsman (and woman) we now offer our newest model, the top of the line, state-of-the-art Bassomatic Buzz Bomb. It's part Sony and part shoehorn with a little... Well, you've just got to see it to BELIEVE IT! Price available on request.

# Trust Me

These two simple words can oil troubled waters or ring bells of alarm. Sometimes they warn of Barnum's observation: "There's a sucker born every minute." Again and again, the proselytizers, the maligned used car salesmen and the telephone solicitors strain our credulity. And when all else fails, the universal plea emerges — "Trust me."

When industry, politicians and government make the same request, we often acquiesce. For decades, and especially during the '70s, those sirens sweet-talked us with lyrics from "Jesus Christ, Superstar": "Everything's all right, everything's fine ... and we want you to sleep well tonight ... close your eyes, just relax, think of nothing tonigghhhhtttt..."

We trusted them; we went along. Led by the Reagan/Bush I and II trio, we restricted abortion and family planning both here and abroad. We reduced per capita spending on education, gutted OSHA, ignored environmental issues, and cut the taxes of the rich.

Allied with the Catholic Church, the fundamentalists and the conservative corps for consumption, conservative administrations have endorsed a policy of "buy and breed." For a while we had a serious environmentalist vice president, and now environmental issues are finally deemed substantive, as if millions had just awakened to the need. These millions must also realize is that we will not solve our environmental problems until we address their causes, and the largest is overpopulation.

We were warned. There was Malthus, accompanied by a host of detractors. And though science has delayed his predicted crisis, we are still riding the rails he foresaw, heading towards the same destination, though on an accelerating timetable.

George Perkins, one of our first environmentalists, warned us a century ago that "by our tree cutting and swamp drainage we are breaking up the floor ... and window frames of our dwelling for fuel to warm our bodies." Later came Paul Ehrlich and *The Population Bomb*, the Club of Rome's *Limits to Growth* and the work of the Zero Population Growth movement.

Then Bill McKibben wrote a very grim book titled *The End of Nature*. As the title implies, unless we change our ways, and change them soon, the "end of nature" is waiting in the wings.

"Nature," says McKibben, "takes forever." With eternity on its side, it has had all the ages past, and more to come. For eons, it has experimented, revised and remodeled at a patient, sub-glacial pace. Things proceeded slowly — until man.

Unlike the Bristlecone pines and the lichens that cling to outcroppings of frost-shattered rocks, we live but a speck of time. But in the 2,000-year life span of a single sequoia, man creates one hundred generations, making tiny steps along the path of evolution. Because we are curious folks and can leave nothing alone, science develops, and with it, technology.

However, because knowledge grows faster than wisdom, we switched from adapting to nature to shaping nature to suit our needs. We turned the Earth inside out in search of wealth, spreading tailings and dross over meadows and stream. We clear cut rainforests that absorb carbon dioxide and release oxygen. In just thirty years we have raised atmospheric $CO_2$ levels by 10%. Every year, our cars pump their own weight in carbon into the atmosphere, and millions of Chinese, Indians and Russians are waiting to buy cars, eager to hit the road. To quote Mr. McKibben, what we are doing is like "taking a one-week fling, and in the process, contracting a horrible disease."

As a greenhouse gas, methane is twenty times more harmful than $CO_2$. Our stockyards, the termites that thrive in the debris of trashed rainforests, and the rice paddies of the world all generate methane — but they make a "light" methane. An even greater threat is the "heavy" methane that lies locked in the frozen tundra and in the mud of the continental shelves. And here, says McKibben, "the story begins to get scary."

Let me put it simply. The greenhouse effect, which is already intensifying, warms air, land and sea, releasing heavy methane, which accelerates the effect. As temperatures rise, the air absorbs more water vapor, which is also a greenhouse gas. As a result, Nature, our patient, resilient benefactor is facing an assault like none before, though it will certainly survive in altered form, although we may not. But forget, for the moment, the greenhouse gases, and consider the forests that we water with acid rain.

As temperatures rise, the tree zones (and deserts) will move north forty miles for every degree. Whole forests will die, for our Northern soils are far less fertile than Southern loams. Their oxygen production and their carbon dioxide consumption will stop. When NASA's James Hansen attempted to warn Congress of the "definite dangers of future drought," the Reagan White House tried to change his testimony — and Reagan's response to changes in the ozone layer was to recommend that we "wear caps and sunglasses."

George Will chided Senator Gore for being concerned about environmental issues "that are, in the eyes of the electorate, not even peripheral." People devoted to profit motive have laughed at those with a planet motive as they continue to prod nature further from its providential role.

Where shall we house the displaced millions when the ice caps melt and the oceans rise? In your house? In mine? Or in the homes of those whose religions, greed and politics have pushed populations and pollution so high? Twenty percent of Bangladesh will disappear. The Nile delta, where most Egyptians reside, will submerge. Consider the Netherlands, our Gulf States and the near certainty that a hotter atmosphere and warmer oceans will produce storms that will make hurricanes like Katrina routine.

Inland, as the dry Southwest expands north and east, the already endangered Ogallala aquifer, unreplenished by dwindling rains, will be sucked dry. The flow of the Colorado River, already a trickle where it enters Mexico, will drop by a third. The Great Lakes will slowly warm and green with oxygen-depleting algae. Fish will die.

There are those who argue that increased rainfall near the poles will stop the warming, ushering in an early ice age instead. What a marvelous alternative! Crop losses would still be extreme, and their alternative scenario only emphasizes the need to adopt sensible environmental and population policies now.

Consider the ozone layer that filters out excessive ultraviolet radiation, the layer George Bush Sr. trivialized by calling Senator Gore Mr. Ozone. Studies show that the resultant increase in UV radiation limits leaf growth, cuts crop yields and even reduces plankton, the basis of the ocean's great food chain. As plankton decrease, so do the tiny shrimp (krill) and all the higher forms: the tuna, the mackerel, the sardines, cod and whales. At this moment, about half of the world's protein needs are filled from the ocean. How shall we manage with more people and fewer fish? A miracle, perhaps?

Worse yet, a decrease in $CO_2$-consuming plankton will accelerate the greenhouse effect. Then, in the words of G W Bush's senior science advisor, Arnold Schwarzenegger, it will be "Hasta la vista, baby!" Some will claim that God will provide, that science will save us, or that more people will mean more minds to find a solution. Others take the Gaia hypothesis to the extreme, claiming that the planet is a living entity, capable of healing itself and providing for life. However, how do we know that nature will react in a way that will suit our needs? We must choose between those who urge a change in course, and those who love — and profit from — the status quo.

For me, it's a simple choice. I prefer cod and crustaceans to 400-horsepower Corvettes. I prefer contraception to Calcutta. I would dim Las Vegas' lights and mandate a change to energy-efficient bulbs. I would restrict immigration to levels that balance emigration. I would limit free trade to countries with a stable population and comparable, ENFORCED environmental laws, and I would legislate trade barriers against those without.

Consider the environmental and population changes that have already degraded our Earth and the lives of so many. Isn't our planet precious enough to safeguard with strong legislation? Will we act soon and sensibly or will we heed those who would have us cancel the sober cab? "Party on," they say, with music intended to soothe: "Don't worry ... Be happy ... TRUST ME!"

# Noah in the 21st Century

The following is based on a right-wing Internet piece intended
to ridicule liberals — author unknown.
Being one of those liberals, I revised it,
and it now sings a different tune.

In the year 2020, the Lord came unto Noah, who had moved to the United States to escape the endless Arab/Israeli conflict, and said, "Once again, the Earth has become wicked and overpopulated thanks to the Islamic and Catholic opposition to contraception, and I foresee the end of all flesh. Build me another ark and save two of every living thing along with a few good humans."

He gave Noah the blueprints, telling him, "You have six months to build the ark before I will begin to rain for, let's see — how about 40 days and 40 nights."

Six months later, the Lord returned and saw Noah weeping in his yard — but no ark was in sight.

"Noah!" he roared, "I'm about to start the rain! The clouds are brimming, but where is the ark?"

"Forgive me, Lord," begged Noah. "But things have changed. I applied for a building permit, and I've been arguing with the inspector about the need for a sprinkler system. My neighbors claim that I've violated the zoning laws by building the ark in my yard and exceeding the height limitations."

"Well," said God, "I can see that a sprinkler system would be a good idea, especially with all of those methane-producing critters in close quarters, and since I, too, appreciate the Golden Rule, which is common to so many religions — that one should treat others as he'd wish to be treated — I can sympathize with your neighbors. And zoning laws make sense. Without them, you couldn't keep heaven out of hell, and what a mess that would be."

Then Noah wailed, "The Department of Transportation demanded that I post a bond to cover the cost of moving power lines so the ark can reach the sea. I argued that the sea would be coming to us, but they would hear none of it."

"I can understand that," said God. "We've had crackpots predicting the end of the world for centuries, and they've always been wrong, so I'm not surprised that they didn't believe you."

Noah continued. "Getting the wood was also a problem. There's a ban on cutting trees because, well, they're pretty rare now since we've cut so many forests to make homes for the 25 billion people, not to mention junk mail, and because we just can't get the government and corporations to use both sides of a sheet of paper."

"Oh, dear," said God, "I had no idea that trees were scarce. Maybe I'd better pay more attention to earthly things, but I've been so distracted by the millions of silly, right-wing prayers who want things that aren't good for them."

"When I started gathering the animals," said Noah, "I got sued by an animal rights group that didn't want me to confine animals against their will. They argued the accommodations were too restrictive and it was cruel and inhumane to put so many animals in a confined space."

"You know," said God, "I never thought of that. Maybe some of these humans are more advanced than I thought."

"Then," said Noah, "The EPA ruled that I couldn't build the ark until they'd conducted an environmental impact study on your proposed flood, and I'm still trying to resolve a complaint with the Human Rights Commission on how many minorities I'm supposed to hire for my building crew."

"Well, why not," said God. "I wouldn't want an ark to be built by people who weren't getting a fair wage, even though I am going to drown them. After all, it's the unions that stood up to the industrialists to get the workers decent pay. Those tightwads will never pass through the eye of a needle, if you know what I mean."

"And," Noah said, "To make matters worse, the IRS seized all my assets, claiming that I'm trying to leave the country illegally with endangered species."

"You know," said God, "I think they learned that trick from the churches. Get the money. Make all sorts of promises. All I wanted was for folks to be good, but they've turned my religion into a megabucks business. Get the money and build big asset-consuming cathedrals and crystal palaces. Oh sure, spend a small part on good works for PR, but get the money. Promise pie in the sky, but above all, get the money — that's what these guys have done.

Maybe now you'll understand why I'm tempted to turn on the big faucet in the sky. It's too bad, though, that all those other people and critters will die. But what really puzzles me is why so many of those good folks you chose to be saved because they served others so well turned out to be atheists. That's just so weird! It makes me wonder if I'm getting senile."

Finally Noah said, "You know, God, what about that commandment not to kill people? If you do this, won't you be setting a bad example?"

And God sat there, thinking slowly — like an overloaded computer — then heaved his shoulders (gods have shoulders) and said, "You know, Noah, it's just too much. You do whatever you think is right, but ask those atheists for advice. I checked them out, and they're not perfect, but they're a lot better than those nuts who've been fighting science for 2000 years. I'll give you one more chance. Maybe 100 years. By then you'll have solved your problems or done yourselves in, and it won't be on my hands." (gods have hands, too.)

# Bismallah

The Muslim world includes much of Africa and virtually all of Arabia, extending to the east as far as the Himalayas and south to the Gulf of Siam and much of Indonesia.

Every day in that world, whether engaged in commerce or retribution, alms-giving or sexual intercourse, millions of Muslim males will utter *"Bismallah."* (It is for Allah.) That phrase contains the essence of a religion called Islam that began in the early 600s when an Arab merchant named Muhammad Ibn Abdullah endured an experience that would change the course of the Arab world.

Muhammad's once-nomadic tribe settled in Mecca, where they entered the merchant class. As hard times fell behind, replaced by wealth for Muhammad's tribe, the old tribal values of concern for the poor soon fell away as capitalism blossomed. Troubled by what he saw, Muhammad sought a new ideology to counter the economic changes that had made a religion of money.

The Arabs of Muhammad's time had never been deeply involved in religion, although they had an assortment of deities, including al-Lat plus a number of shrines, the most significant being a large, black stone in Mecca called the Kaaba. With no mythology of an afterlife, they believed that one's destiny lay nestled in the hands of fate.

Around 620 CE, during the holy season now known as Ramadan, Muhammad and his family made a pilgrimage to Mt. Hira, where he claimed that the angel Gabriel, an emissary from the God of Moses, compelled him to recite a new scripture, beginning a process of revelation that continued for more than two decades and produced the Qur'an (Koran) — the Recitation.

Muhammad made no claim to being the author of a new universal religion — only that he was to be a messenger to his people, who already believed al-Lat to be the same God worshipped by Jews and Christians. In time the new religion became known as Islam, a term for the surrender that each (Muslim) believer made to al-Lat.

Islam taught that Muslims had a duty to further justice and to create an equitable society where the poor are fed and sheltered. It proclaimed that is it wrong to build personal wealth and ignore the poor, and made proper alms-giving a requirement. Muhammad preached an ethic that many would have called socialism, much like the precepts of early Christianity.

Unlike Christianity, Islam was not doctrinal. It neither required nor encouraged speculation about the nature of God, nor did it even suggest the need to set aside one's reason. Instead, Muslims were expected to examine the world attentively and with curiosity, a practice that helped to develop an early and accurate science — a science whose practitioners never endured the pain and scorn that Western scientists received from Christianity for more than 16 centuries.

Unlike Christians, Muslims dismiss theological speculation as *"zanna"* — self-centered guesswork about the unknowable. And unlike Christian literalists, they believed that the stories of the Last Supper, the prophets, and of heaven are merely parables that should not be taken literally.

Muhammad's new religion grew rapidly, but suffered severe losses when he began to condemn worship of the traditional gods other than al-Lat. By 622 most of his followers had defected, and the Muslims had become a despised minority, finally seeking refuge in the northern city of Medina. It is from this flight to Medina (the Hegira) that the Muslim calendar begins. There, the Muslims fought for their lives against the dominant Meccans and local opponents, developing the theology of a just, defensive war. However, counter to the Western stereotype, there is evidence that Muslims forced no one to convert, for the Koran states that, "There is to be no compulsion in religion."

Eight years passed before Muhammad was able to return to Mecca, where he began the Islamic tradition of making a pilgrimage to the Kaaba. With perseverance and political skill, he brought most of the Arab tribes to Islam before his death in 632.

The following thirteen centuries have seen conquerors, rulers and colonialists come and go throughout Arabia, yet Islam has survived. Now, pious Muslims, like pious Christians and many Humanists, have become convinced that the capitalist world lacks heart, having adopted the god of greed instead of a moral philosophy. Yet Muslims share the same "preach versus practice" gap that many Christians face.

Islam opposes alcohol and drugs, yet millions of Muslims cannot manage without their daily, mind-numbing chew of quat. Muslim leaders own mansions around the globe, but they fail to feed and clothe the poor.

For the most part, the preaching of Islam and Christianity falls on deaf ears. Those inclined to treat others fairly and humanely do so. Those not so inclined continue to preach and pray anyway, becoming paragons of hypocrisy who damage not only the common good, but the religion they proclaim as well.

As a result, humanity muddles along, proselytized by an endless supply of charlatans who claim to know the way, yet encourage violence against their opponents, amass arsenals and dupe believers, even as they fight among themselves. The Muslims, in spite of the Koran's emphasis on brotherhood, spend millions to war against each other while ignoring the poverty of their poor.

Finally, we have the much-persecuted Jews, who (like the "select" Baptists) claim to be the chosen ones, a claim that implies superiority, which nets them anger and scorn.

These three similar-yet-different religions are bound by common threads: much preaching of tolerance, brotherhood and charity but inadequate practice, fanatic fundamentalist fringes that constantly destroy any chance of harmony, and holy texts that still encourage procreation at a time when the Earth cries out for less — not more.

# In Praise of Water

from *Back to the Barrens: On the Wing With da Vinci & Friends*

Heaping the fire with driftwood to speed my post-swim warming, I strip off my clothes and head for the lake. The sun has set, leaving a pinking sky to light my way. With my float for a laundry table, I begin the old rub-a-dub while pine-scented, forest-cooled air flows out from the woods and onto the lake.

As I finish washing my shirt, tiny, prickling sensations begin to tickle my legs. Bending over in the half-light of dusk, I discover a school of minnows nibbling away at a myriad of tiny air bubbles trapped in the hairs of my legs. That's weird, I say to myself, but it's not as odd as the ultra thin, yard-long, horsehair worms that swim like snakes through fresh water lakes, or the caddis fly larvae that crawl along the bottom, their sides and back covered with debris to disguise them from predators.

The minnows dart from gleaming bubble to bubble, gulping them down as if they're delicacies. They've discovered the ultimate diet food — lots of eating but zero calories. As they feast on nothing, I begin to feel guilty — like a sentient television set that regrets ensnaring minds with worthless fluff.

"OK, minnies," I say to the throng, "fantasy time is over," and swim away, surging through invigorating, July-warmed water. I'm glad that I passed up Cree Lake.

The Cub's wing struts become my laundry lines, and as I wring out my clothes, sending ripples far into the lake, I reflect on one of my favorite subjects — water.

What a marvelous thing is water. It covers 70% of the earth, distributing and moderating arctic cold and tropical heat. Even 15% of dust is water. We humans are 60% water; tomatoes — 95%. Our blood chemistry is similar to that of the oceans from whence we evolved. Lose 2% of your water, and you become thirsty, lose 5% and you'll soon go out of your mind, but a 12% drop is lethal.

Most liquids contract as they cool, as does water, but only water changes its mind and begins to expand when it reaches 39 degrees Fahrenheit (4 Celsius). Thus, as lakes and oceans cool, the coldest water lies on top, where it freezes, sheltering the water below from frigid winds that could freeze to the core all but the deepest of lakes.

Almost all chemicals are acids or bases, but water can be either. It's an almost perfect solvent. It can act as a catalyst, enabling chemical reactions like a cheering section that doesn't take part in the game. Water carries nutrients through all living matter and removes metabolic waste. It has the highest surface tension of all room temperature liquids except mercury, which is why it can support a magnetized needle to make a primitive compass. Despite its surface tension, water exhibits capillarity, which lets it invade its surroundings and even flow uphill. Water transmits sound five times faster than air, which is why, when you hit two rocks together while you're underwater, you hear a clink, not a clunk.

Water is essential to life, but if you make it from Hydrogen 1 instead of $H^2$, you get heavy water, which looks the same but behaves quite badly. Seeds will not germinate in heavy water. If you drink it, you die.

Thanks to the Gulf Stream, which carries more heat north in one hour than all of the warmth produced by coal in a year, tropical plants can flourish in southern Ireland. Early American ship captains who understood the Gulf Stream (thanks largely to Benjamin Franklin) knew why sailing from America to Britain took two weeks less than the return trip, but the British didn't, so they often sailed against the Stream, which put them at a disadvantage.

Contrary to popular belief, water is slightly compressible. Were it not, the oceans would rise enough to submerge ten million square miles of lowlands that include Florida, the Netherlands and a big chunk of India. Most North Americans have an abundance of water, but much of the world does not. About 97% of the world's fresh water is locked away in ice, leaving us just 3%, most of which comes from wells with falling water levels caused by a world population that has quadrupled in the last 100 years.

When I bend beneath the water to rinse the soap from my hair, the baptism scene from *Oh Brother, Where Art Thou* fills my mind. The Coen brothers treated the subject lightly, but baptism has ancient roots, arising first from Confucian custom, but also from the Hindu ritual of bathing in the Ganges, and from the rituals of Egyptians who revered the Nile.

Among the first of the gods were the water gods. The Babylonians believed that water came from deep in the Earth, delivered by Enki, the god of springs and rivers. The Incans worshipped Wiracocha, who arose from the water to create the sun, the moon and the stars. The Apache and Blackfoot believed that nothing moved until the Old Man floated past on a raft and commanded the world into existence. And in two beliefs echoing Moses, Sargon, the founder of Babylon, is rescued from the reeds by Akki, the water carrier. Karna, the subject of an Indian story, is found floating on the Ganges, each to be later abandoned, Noah-like, to a flood.

In North America, an adaptation of the water source is popular — the belief that humans were created from mud, a mixture of the biblical dust and water. The ancient Chinese, however, believed that a lonely goddess fashioned the first humans from yellow mud, just as the Greeks proclaimed that Prometheus used mud to make the first man, whom Athena breathed into life. Oddly enough, the process of evolution also depends on water, relying in part on evidence that life first arose in the oceans billions of years ago, and then evolved during the multimillion generations that followed.

With paintings, photographs and fountains we have honored water. Frederick Handel's Water Music is played all around the world, and Claude Debussy, who understood that water could batter or soothe, gave musical voice to the wave, the spray and the mist in a work he named "La Mer."

Nevertheless, many societies, especially ours, are incredibly wasteful of water. In so doing, we running the oft-stated risk of not missing the water until the well has run dry – and running dry, many are, which is why corporations in the India, France, the U.S. and elsewhere around the world are buying up water rights. If they continue unchecked, these corporations will, with aggressive pricing, finally make us truly appreciate the value of the life-giving fluid called water.

# Thou Shalt Not Steal

## (But If You Steal, I Will Help You Spend It)

Remember situation ethics, the concept that upsets biblical literalists who love rigid rules and the constancy of the Ten Commandments? Well, according to the Associated Press and *Freethought Today*, the Roman Catholic Church must be willing to make exceptions (special dispensations to themselves, let us say) when it works to their advantage.

In Mexico, Vicar Rodolfo Silva argues that the church should take donations from drug dealers to aid in "their salvation," and because the church can use the money. (If the bank raises an eyebrow at the white powder on the bills, they'll just say it came from Rosa's Bakery.)

The Vicar elaborated, "Here we take money from anybody. If a narco-trafficker comes and offers a lot of money, what can I say but, 'Give it to me.' " Then, spreading a wider net, he indicated that the church would accept money from thieves and prostitutes.

Ah, yes. The CHURCH — the self-appointed source of ethics and morality. Know it by the company it SEEKS.

# Under the Covers

There's a *Fifties* restaurant not far from my home. The food is great, and the walls feature posters from films like Picnic, High Noon and Psycho plus ads for cars that were loaded with chrome. Better yet, the background music sparks memories of Elvis and the birth of rock and roll.

When our waitress, complete with bobby sox, saddle shoes and a poodle skirt, has taken our order, I flip through the pages of the booth's juke box and drop in a nickel. As Kiss of Fire tries to inflame our hearts, my wife and I begin to scan the titles, playing again the titillating game of adding "under the covers" to titles like The Happy Wanderer, All Shook Up and, hilariously, On Top of Old Smoky!

When I tack the phrase onto Lovin' You, I recall a series of events involving me and my sons and topic S — for sex.

My wife and I have two sons, but no daughters, so I knew that the subject of sex would someday fall to me.

That day came earlier than I'd expected. I was carrying three-year-old Chris to bed when he pressed his hand against my chest and asked with childlike directness, "Papa, how come you're so flat and Mom's so floppy?"

"Well," I brilliantly replied, "That's just how ladies are."

A year later, after Chris had loudly and very pointedly noticed a pregnant woman in the supermarket, I quietly explained that she was big because she was going to have a baby. And as we left the store, he whispered, "Papa?"

"What?" I replied.

"How does the baby get out?"

Always preferring to go with the facts, I told him that ladies have a small opening that gets bigger when it's time for the baby to be born.

He thought for a moment and then asked, "Does Mom have one?"

"Yeeeeeeeeeeeesssss…"

"Can I see it?"

As I groped for an answer, the god of all fathers smiled down on me, and the best answer imaginable popped into my head:

"Ask your mother."

A few months passed, and then one evening, when we had finished reading Dr. Seuss, Chris crawled into my lap.

"Papa," he asked, "where do babies come from?"

Well — this time I was ready for him. I had decided that when the time arrived, I would keep my response factual, brief and cool — unlike some parents who become flustered and overreact, often providing too much detail, which can cause a child to lose interest.

Let me tell you, I was soooo cool — and factual — and reasonably brief.

I began with falling in love and getting married, followed by some vague anatomy — plus more being in love — then ended with the nine-month gestation period and a routine birth — and then more love stuff.

"And that's how it is," I concluded. "Now — do you have any questions?"

"Uh, huh," he said.

I was thrilled. I had piqued his interest, just as I'd planned.

"What else do you want to know?" I asked.

He paused, as if framing a critical question, then looked up at me and asked, "Why are there nine holes in a golf course?"

Years passed, a few too many, I must admit, and when Chris was ten and his brother, Lars, was eight, I sat them down on the sofa one evening. With one on each side of me, and with a very nice picture book, I set out to do what I should have done before.

The book, with colorful artwork, laid it all on the line as we turned from page to page. The love and marriage part took perhaps eight pages, but by the time we arrived at the illustration of the loving couple embracing beneath the covers, I suddenly realized that Chris had turned to stone, becoming the very image of an Easter Island statue, while Lars, being younger and always more likely to reveal his emotions, had gone limp, sagging toward the edge of the sofa like a Salvador Dali clock that's oozing toward the floor.

Fighting back laughter, I made it to the end of the book, at which time Lars, who had recovered, loudly exclaimed, "Wow, at least they let you get under the covers!"

Having done my job, I left the matter to the school and to nature, confident that time and hormones would remove any desire to hide beneath the covers, or for that matter, to even want a bed.

# Texas – and Trees?

I often share Willie Nelson's eagerness to get "On the Road Again," but whenever I return from a car trip to Texas, home looks pretty good. As expected, our spring journey from Minnesota to Texas delivered fields carpeted with blue bonnets, prickly poppies and primrose, but it also provoked an argument against the absolutists who oppose situation ethics, claiming that lying is NEVER justified.

In the Hill Country near Fredericksburg, Texas, they say that during the pioneer days, the Indians and settlers once found themselves at odds, with an Indian attack in the making. It was Easter time, and when the settlers' children became alarmed at the host of Indian campfires flickering in the hills, they were told it was only the Easter bunnies dyeing their eggs. Now that's a lie, but I can't imagine anyone preferring to frighten a child by, in this case, telling them the truth. As it happened, the attack failed to happen and, at least for the duration, peace prevailed.

Our travels took us past groves of gorgeous redbud trees with violet blossoms dancing to the tips of every branch, and it revealed another species with the most delicate shade of pale, yellow-green, budding leaves, misting every tree in a haze of accumulating chlorophyll. I finally realized that these lovely trees and bushes were the lowly mesquite, a species not highly valued on the Texoma plains. Yet its springtime splendor started me thinking of the debt we owe to trees.

From the lovely tamarack (larch) of the North, the only conifer to go for the gold in the fall, to the stilted mangroves of the southern coasts, they shade and shelter us and make the oxygen that supports our lives. We build our homes from them, shred them and press their pulp into sheets of paper to communicate our thoughts and retain our ideas. Their blossoms perfume our air. Their forms delight the eye.

We are indebted to them all; to the dwarf willow of the Far North, to the ghost gums and bottle trees of Australia, and to the graceful sea pines and rainbow-barked Eucalyptus trees that adorn the Pacific Rim.

Their seeds and blossoms feed the animals of the forest floor and sustain the birds. And in their old age, lightning-struck, with limbs torn away and a rotting core, they become home to all manner of climbing and flying creatures that need these hollowed spires for homes.

And yet, we self-centered humans continue to cut clear entire forests, replanting a single species, replacing formerly diversified forests with monocultures. Wildlife suffers. If increasing amounts of timber are harvested prior to old age due to decreasing commercial value, where will the animals go that require hollows for nesting? Where will birds find the insects that live under rotting bark? And where will humans go to lean against a tree that is unbelievably large and humbling? Where will they go to see a living thing that is older than their ancestors, something their arms cannot begin to enclose?

In the tropics alone, an area larger than Iowa is stripped of trees each year. On the West Coast of the United States, loggers are seeking to cut into some of the oldest stands of trees on the public lands of our continent. They claim that they must cut the trees, that jobs will be lost if they are not logged. Yet, when these trees are gone, won't those jobs be lost?

While they cry about jobs, the logging companies continue to ship logs to Japan where they are processed into finished products, employing Japanese workers instead of American. These men are not foresters, they are miners, clear cutting ancient forests like miners strip-mine coal.

As one by one these ancients fall, we lose more than trees, and more than cellulose pulp. We lose homes for living creatures and yet another chance to reach out and touch something majestic. We lose the opportunity to raise our eyes into their highest branches and feel a sense of awe.

# Of Cookie Trees and Bubble Balls

Christmas is over; the days are short, and now that the season's binary stars (Santa Claus and you know who) have set, I am moved to reveal how I introduced my grandchildren to the unbelievable in a way that *should* profit them.

It is a summery day at a modest cabin set amid native grasses, hawk-weed, buttercups and daisies. A bubbling three-year-old named Kirsten ambles from blossom to blossom adding one after another to the bouquet she clutches in her chubby hand. Behind her, an adult patiently follows, listening to her chatter. Though he looks MUCH TOO YOUNG to be a grandparent, he is her grandfather.

"Kirsten," he says. "When you've finished picking flowers, we should pick a tree for you." Her eyes widen at the thought of picking a tree as he continues. "We'll go back in the woods and look for two little Norway Pines that will be easy to dig — one for you and one for your brother. Then we'll plant them near the cabin."

One hundred feet into the woods they come upon just the right trees, two frail saplings that began life in a few inches of soil in a cleft in the rough granite slope. Although just two feet tall, their roots have fanned out laterally, binding the soil and moss into a carpet that peels away from the rock like a throw rug lifts from the floor.

As they carry the trees to the cabin, he tells her that they should plant the trees within a few feet of the brook, so they will always have water. Then he adds, "And because you helped me get these trees, they will always belong to you and your brother, Brian.

Better yet, these trees will become special trees called Cookie Trees that grow a cookie every night. But you must pick the cookie every morning because the birds and the squirrels like cookies too."

Sure enough, the following morning, nestled in the long, green needles of the little Norway Pine, a cookie waits. It looks exactly like an animal cookie, a hippopotamus, in fact, but that makes no difference. Though two years pass, the Cookie Trees faithfully produce cookies whenever Kirsten and Brian arrive.

When we look again, Kirsten is almost six and Brian is three. She has noticed that the cookie is an animal cookie, and mentions it with an inquiring look in her eyes. "Kirsten," her grandfather asks, "Do you really believe that trees can grow cookies?" She hesitates, then answers, "No."

"Then how do you suppose it got there?" he asks. She stands there fingering the cookie as she thinks it over, then slowly raises a hand and points a finger at her grandfather. "You're right," he says, "but don't tell your brother for another year or two so that he, too, can have the satisfaction of finding it out."

We again see Kirsten and her grandfather after another year has passed. In his hands he cradles a beautiful, champagne-colored, crystalline sphere as large as a bowling ball. Within it lie cascades of bubbles. Trapped within the glass as it cooled, they catch the rays of the autumn sun and beguile the eye. With her nose almost touching the glass, she asks, "Where did you get this, Grandpa?"

"It came from a rock shop in Arkansas," he replies. "This Bubble Ball is a very special ball, because every bubble stands for someone who is very important to me. That one over there is for Brian and this one — he points — is for you. Whenever I want to know what you or Brian are doing, all I have to do is take off my glasses so that I can get very close and look into your bubble — and there you are."

She stands there speechless, not knowing what to think. Her eyes shift back and forth while her mind pursues the possibilities. Then he asks her, "Kirsten, do you think that's really true, or is it just a nice story?"

A smile springs to her face as she heaves a sigh of relief. "Just a story," she replies.

The Bubble Ball and the Cookie Tree long ago became passé, but they haven't lost their purpose. If my grandkids someday talk of heavens and hells and of virgin births or water becoming wine, I'll remind them of the cookie tree and the eye-catching bubbles in the wondrous Bubble Ball.

Postscript

I would like to report that my efforts at positive, rational thinking bore fruit, but Kirsten, unlike her brother, eventually became such a "loving," teenage Christian that she took pains to avoid all contact with her *nearby*, non-believing grandparents. Oh, well, she's only nineteen and still has a lot to learn.

# Death as a Fact of Life

All cultures have their peculiarities, and the more repressive the culture, the more frequent and severe those peculiarities often become. In certain Polynesian and African cultures with warm climates, going "topless" was the norm, but in cooler climates, where clothing was needed for at least part of the year, some cultures went beyond need to dictate propriety: Catholics have required women to cover their heads in church; male Hasidic Jews don a skullcap yarmulke from "dawn to dusk," while fundamentalist Muslims require female members to veil themselves in public.

The Inuit (Eskimo) tolerance for the pranks and misbehavior of their children surprised the first explorers, who had experienced the opposite ethic of "spare the rod and spoil the child." And while a Humanist would smile tolerantly if threatened with a curse, the same curse could undermine those who believe in voodoo spells. All these customs are interesting, but the events of 9-11 remind me that the customs surrounding death are most compelling. I refer not to the myriad of ways in which we preserve, decorate, and dispose of our dead, but of the needless void into which some survivors fall when a body cannot be found.

Over the centuries, we have come to revere the body as much as, or more than, the memory of the deceased, demanding a *habeas corpus* in every case. But when a body cannot be produced, our culture leads many to believe that their grieving will be incomplete, and that they will be denied the "closure" that many think they need.

This debatable need to recover the body has nowhere been more painfully and interminably obvious than in Southeast Asia, where some still search for the MIAs, in Oklahoma City, where right-wing extremists shredded buildings and bodies in a split-second blast, and after the assault on the World Trade Center by religious fundamentalists. In the latter two, the search for bodies was eventually stopped, leaving a few mourners with nothing to bury — no ashes to scatter.

If I were able, I would remind these unfortunate mourners of the thousands lost at sea in peacetime and during war, their bodies gone forever. Their survivors managed, partly because they had to, and partly because the idea of needing a body for "closure" had not yet arrived. But now that it has, closure has become a cultural concept that cuts two ways, aiding those who find the remains and hindering those who don't. And while I would not criticize those burdened with grief, I hope that society will come to see our bodies as living factories, with a mind that can say good words and hands that can do good works. Good words and works endure. Honor them. Forget about closure.

"Why should I fear death? If I am, death is not.
If death is, I am not.
Why should I fear that which cannot exist when I do?"

— Epicurus

# Into the Looking Glass

from *Water Flying*

"That thing is just like a mirror," said Jack, as he pushed the nose of his Cessna down until he was flying just 15 feet above Ouichita Lake. Weaving back and forth between a scattering of boats, he hot dogged down the long Arkansas waterway. His low flying was, of course, illegal, but worse yet, Jack was toying with a deadly hazard called glassy water that seaplane pilots are warned to respect. Buoyed by the fact that he'd recently made three *simulated* glassy water landings with ease, Jack continued his reckless flight — and then inadvertently descended a little too low.

Nose low, the floats touched the water, simultaneously digging two brief but beautiful furrows through the lake's surface as Newton's laws took charge. In an instant, the floats dug in, the tail rose and the speeding Skyhawk somersaulted into the water in a fountain of spray. Subjected to forces beyond its strength, Jack's seatbelt tore loose from its moorings.

The Cessna stayed afloat long enough for boaters to pull Jack from the wreckage. Two months later, he's walking again, but he's blind in one eye. His license is gone, and he'll never fly again. His passenger died.

Jack's story is make believe, told to prove a point, but what happened to Jack was benign compared to what really happened to two very different pilots who ignored the old pilot's warning: "Be careful near the edge of the air."

All seaplane pilots are aware of the hazards of glassy water landings and takeoffs. With no ripples to guide them, it is truly impossible to judge one's height above the water. Time and again, pilots have taken off, only to fly back into a surface they cannot see. Faced with a glassy water takeoff, pros take care to maintain a positive rate of climb.

Some, while landing, have leveled off fifty feet above the surface. Thinking they were about to touch, they stalled into the water in a nose-dropping crash. Still others, believing they are still high, fail to raise the nose in time and, like Jack, suddenly find themselves stunned and struggling inside a flooding, inverted airplane. And that is exactly what really happened to a Minnesota pilot who, after declining a check ride, set up to land his newly-purchased Cessna 180. Had he maintained a partial power, nose high attitude until his aircraft touched the water, he would still be flying today — but he didn't.

The bows of the slightly nose-low floats dug in, followed instantly by the screech of ripping metal as both floats snapped like bananas just ahead of the front spreader bar. The Cessna flipped, slamming it into the water upside down. Despite his multiple ratings and thick log book, the pilot died.

Another pilot, Captain Robert Madison, had a much more costly crash. Captain Madison was a World War II combat pilot; the plane he was flying was an Air Force B-29 named Beetle Bomb, and the crash site was Nevada's deep and lengthy Lake Mead!

On July 21, 1948, Madison and his crew of four left California behind as they climbed eastward to study variations in solar radiation at different altitudes as part of the Upper Air Research Project. As reported in the Las Vegas newspapers, "The mission called for runs from 'as low as possible' to 30,000 feet and back. … On their final run of the day, the crew began their descent," leveling off over Lake Mead's deserted thirty-mile-long Overton Arm.

As the huge plane roared down Lake Mead at 250 mph, Scientist John Simeroth watched his instruments while Captain Madison described the sight: "Just look at that lake," he said. "There's not a ripple on it anywhere. *That thing is just a mirror!*" And then, as one crewmember later put it, "All hell broke loose."

When the B-29 brushed the water, engines 2, 3, and 4 were torn from the plane, and engine 1 caught fire. With a severely damaged horizontal stabilizer and left wing, Beetle Bomb bounced into the air, staggering along briefly as the stunned crew scrambled to get ready to ditch.

Within seconds, Beetle Bomb crashed tail-first (fortunately) into the water. All five men survived, but Sgt. Frank Rico suffered a broken arm.

As the B-29 settled into Lake Mead, the crew scrambled into two life rafts to await rescue, which arrived five hours later, thanks to an alert C-47 pilot who spotted a dye marker the survivors deployed.

Fifty three years later, in 2001, a dive team led by Greg Mikolasek and Melody Gritz located Beetle Bomb 300 feet below Lake Mead's sparkling surface with the aid of side-scan radar, then later dove down to the wreckage. "When my eyes adjusted," said Mikolasek, "I realized we had come down right on the bomber's cockpit. The first thing I saw and touched was the pilot-side hatch through which the crew had escaped. The feeling was just incredible."

The crash site is still off limits while the National Park Service and the Air Force try to work out the details. In the meantime, the unseen Beetle Bomb provides a reminder to all those who would fly low over rivers and lakes: The air can be quite forgiving, but the edge of the water can be exceedingly hard.

# Eggs and Bunnies, Birds and Birth

## Letter to a grandchild

Where did Easter come from, you ask, and why does it fall on a different day every year? Well, here's the answer, dear.

Easter can come as early as March 22 or as late as April 25 because it's based upon a Jewish holiday called Passover, which is tied to the first full moon after the spring (March 22) equinox, when day and night are both 12 hours long. Got that?

According to an English monk named Bede, the Sunday that celebrates the alleged resurrection of a man called Jesus was called Easter because it became associated with a spring holiday for the goddess Eostre, who was believed to bring new life and light. Got that, too?

So what does Eostre (and Easter) have to do with bunnies and Easter eggs? According to her worshipers, Eostre saved a bird whose wings had been frozen by a harsh winter by turning it into a magical rabbit that could lay eggs. And because rabbits reproduce rapidly, they are associated with fertility, so the connection between rabbits and eggs, which are the means by which many birds reproduce, and Eostre, who represented new life and fertility, rings true. Still with me?

Other cultures that had never heard of Eostre also associated eggs with spring and fertility. Before eating their hard-boiled eggs, some people tap them against another's, believing that the person who cracks the other's egg will have good luck, and the British custom of egg rolling gave rise to the modern search for Easter eggs on the White House lawn.

A few Christians still refuse to celebrate holidays that arose from non-Christian customs. As a result, they don't get to party very much because most of the Christian holidays are connected to pre-Christian celebrations that include Halloween, Easter, Christmas and harvest holidays like Thanksgiving.

The Roman Catholic Church, which was the first (and most powerful) of the many Christian denominations, realized that if it accepted symbols like the Christmas tree, the Easter egg and the harvest table, it would grow more quickly, and although Christians still celebrate the mythical resurrection of a teacher named Jesus, millions of others are just happy to welcome spring.

As you might expect, the world's Buddhists, Shintos and Hindus don't celebrate Easter, nor do Jews, Muslims or the millions of people who don't accept supernatural beliefs, and who consider Jesus a teacher. Unfortunately, sweetie, the Jews' refusal to agree about the divinity of Jesus brought them centuries of persecution from Christians.

So what should an intelligent person do about Easter? Well, until you are grown up, you should probably go along with it when you are with people who like to believe these stories. However, when you're not with them, just enjoy the Easter egg hunt and the hidden treats, for spring is a wonderful season, and every day of your life is a good day to open your eyes, to put a smile in your heart, and to keep superstition out of your mind.

# Night Flight

When George Lucas opened *Star Wars* with "A long time ago, in a galaxy far, far away ...", he reached for the hearts of those who yearn for faraway places with strange sounding names. Some of us, the lucky ones, have flown those distant shores, soared above their deserts and danced between their peaks. And though I belong to that fortunate group, the flight I'll always treasure is the one I made one night in July, when I went to visit the stars.

I was sitting alone on my front porch steps beneath a fading primrose sky, when I heard my Beechcraft call. I'd flown at night many times before, but never just for fun, so I headed out to the darkened field, and as the airport beacon painted the hangar white, then green, then white, then green, I pushed open its heavy doors. Flipping on the hangar lights, I climbed into my Bonanza, settled into its comfortable seat, and relaxed while savoring its singular scents, its solidity and latent speed. Prompted by a voice that urged, "Let's fly, let's fly," I rolled the Bonanza out of its hangar and performed a leisurely pre-flight check while a nearby owl queried the indigo night, asking who - who, who; who – who, who?

Accelerating quickly, the lightly loaded Bonanza climbed into the tranquil sky. With nowhere to go, we spiraled upward while the streetlights dimmed and the horizons widened into a panorama of firefly lights.

At 11,000 feet, I throttled back to economy cruise and trimmed for level flight. With my hands in my lap, I ruddered the Beech through mile-wide, figure-eight turns, twisting beneath the Milky Way as the glow below turned slowly, first this way, then that.

Radiating outward from Sioux Falls like the glittering spokes of a Ferris wheel, the highways, illuminated by the dots and dashes of headlights, became flickering strips of Morse code. To the north, small explosions of light rode one spoke to Del Rapids, Brookings and Watertown; to the west sparkled Mitchell and Chamberlain; to the south, Vermillion and Sioux City. Heading east, a string of vehicles crawled like luminous procession caterpillars toward the beacons of Luverne and Worthington before turning northeast to a valley town called Mankato, and on to the dim and distant sunrise glow of Minneapolis and St. Paul.

While a gibbous moon glinted off lakes and ponds, the earth, as if mirroring the stars, flickered with hundreds of modern campfires — the yard lights of the farms that persuaded Premier Khrushchev to soften his cold war stance following an impressive night flight over a country gleaming with industrial light.

When lightning began to brighten the western sky, I turned on my radio. A line of Dakota thunderstorms was mauling Pierre, some two hundred miles to the west. But with hours to burn 'til the storms could arrive, I settled back and wove through the silky sky while rain poured down on the prairies, and my strobes winked back at the white-hot rivets that bonded the patchwork sky. Jerked alert by a sudden *CRACK*, I reached for my flashlight, and discovered the shattered body of a June bug pasted onto my windshield. What a shame, I thought. Was this humble creature carried aloft by the distant storms, then swept along by the jet stream just to fall through my Beech's prop? Or was he a flier like me, propelled by his genes to reach for the moon on the final flight of his life?

The thunderstorms, lit by their own internal strobes, drew closer, and the once-smooth air became restless, rolling like ocean swells upraised by a distant storm. Throttled back, the Beech began a long descent, arcing through swan-like turns as we spiraled back to earth.

Gear down, flaps to twenty, prop at high rpm. Pillowed in cool night air, we turned on base and settled onto final. The approach lights flashed past as the nose-high Beech descended, its wheels reaching for the ground like the feet of a Canadian goose as we entered the tunnel of light.

When I parked the Beech in the hangar, I left the doors open wide, shut off the lights and felt my way back to the cockpit. Settling into the Bonanza's commodious seat, I closed my eyes and, accompanied by the metronomic tick, tick, tick of the cooling engine, slid into the arms of night.

When the marmalade shades of morning probed my east-facing eyes, I yawned myself awake. From the peak of the hangar, the tireless owl now questioned the dawn. The Bonanza, its engine cold and silent, seemed not to have moved an inch. For a moment, I wondered — was my orbiting flight just a hangar-bound dream, a fantasy flight while the stars shown bright? And then it began to rain.

# Lost Over Australia

*from Back to the Barrens: On the Wing With da Vinci & Friends*

When people ask if I've ever been lost on my flights through the Far North, I explain that the Cub can carry eight hundred miles of fuel. "I can't get lost," I say, as I pull out my pocket map and drop a finger into the center of the Northwest Territories' "Zone of Inaccessibility."

"Head north and you run into the Arctic Ocean; fly east and there's Hudson Bay; to the west you'll hit the Mackenzie River; head south and you'll find — corn." Still, despite my bravado, the truth is that long ago I got lost in Australia while accompanied by my flying friend, Wesley Miller.

Some travelers visit Australia to dive the Great Barrier Reef, some to brown their bodies on the Gold Coast beaches of Queensland and New South Wales, and some to cast aside a former life.

Wes and I, having signed up for a fly-it-yourself tour in rented Cessnas, were there for the wildlife, eager to photograph emus, bower birds, wallabies and kangaroos. But most of all, we wanted to visit central Australia's Mecca, the massive 230 million-year-old sandstone tortoise shell they call Ayers Rock — the ochre pupil of the desert's awesome eye.

In Australia's Red Center, as in the Arctic, the countryside dominates the people and colors their language: the Dry, the Wet, the Burn, salt bush, ghost gums and the gibbers (stones) of the Gibber Plains. There, aborigines cook emus in pits with the head exposed, knowing that when steam issues from the birds' nostrils, the flesh is done. And there, not far from the Rock, I met a suntanned eight-year-old who had never felt rain.

After checking out in the Cessna Skylanes in Melbourne (pronounced "Melbin" by proper Aussies), we began a two-week circuit that included stops at Broken Hill, Andamooka, Ayers Rock, Alice Springs, Mount Isa, the Gulf of Carpenteria, Cairns, Townsville and Charlieville.

On the first legs of the tour, abundant landmarks made navigation by map alone a breeze. However, on leaving Broken Hill as the eighth aircraft in a ten-plane flight, our takeoff was delayed to allow another aircraft to land, and we lost sight of the plane we were supposed to follow. After takeoff, we quickly discovered the futility of trying to correlate a map to what had become a featureless plain below.

Our Cessna was equipped with an antique ADF (automatic direction finder) that may have guided us to the next airport, but neither Wes nor I had ever used one, so on we flew, trying vainly to locate ourselves over the blank-faced outback with a map that may as well have depicted the ocean. Riding in the cool air a few thousand feet above the realities of the desert, Wes and I began to consider our limited options.

When the lead planes radioed that they had reached the airport and were landing, we still had nothing in sight. Trailed by the two aircraft that had followed us, we finally stumbled upon a gravel runway that our tour leader had told us to avoid except in an emergency because it was restricted to those who had business on an Aborigine reservation. However, having come closer to an emergency than we wanted, we radioed the tour leader and landed. Fifteen minutes later, he arrived to lead us back to the fold.

That night, Wes and I got out the manual for the ADF, having learned that navigating by finger-on-the-map, which had worked so well in the abundantly landmarked Arctic, was a wonderful way to get lost over Australia's unadorned outback plains.

If nothing else, our brief disorientation taught us to avoid relying on the other guy's navigation and to have a little charity when a worried voice reaches out on the party line of the airways to ask a fellow traveler, "Where in the hell are we?" Fortunately, whenever I've heard those words in my headset, they've always sorted it out, slowly refining "about here" to "Oh yaa, here we are."

# Dining Out

"We would like the corner table by the window, please."

It was still early, not quite five o' clock, so the supper club was almost empty. The window would provide a diversion for our two sons, ages five and six, who were unaccustomed to first class restaurants, and they were obviously impressed with their first exposure to soft lights, candles, quiet music, big menus, ice water in goblets and cloth napkins.

As the meal progressed, I noticed a gentleman — perhaps in his sixties — who was seated three tables away. At first when our casual glances met, it was "de nada," of no consequence. But I slowly realized that he was watching us with more than casual interest, averting his eyes whenever I turned his way.

When I spotted a small part of the man's face in a wall mirror, I began watching him. He was not observing my wife or me, he was staring at our sons.

As or meal progressed his face softened, even becoming wistful, and my annoyance began to fade. Did I see his eyes glisten? And was it a cold or perhaps a tear that called for his handkerchief?

When I looked up again, he was conversing with the waiter, who had delivered a sheet of paper and an envelope. He began writing, pausing occasionally to glance at the boys before continuing.

Before long he rose and spoke briefly with the hostess, to whom he handed the envelope, then paid his bill and left.

I was still mulling over the incident when the hostess approached, handed me an envelope and explained it was from the gentleman who had just left.

"Dear folks," he began. Many years ago, my wife and I had two nice, well behaved young sons just like your two little boys. They were as good as good could be and rarely needed discipline.

"One evening, when they were about kindergarten age, my wife and I decided to take them to the best steak house in town. When we were nearly finished, an older couple nearby motioned to me, indicating they would like to speak with me privately. 'Your sons, they said, are so well behaved. They remind me of the sons we once had. Would you mind if we gave each of them a dollar for being such good boys?'

"I thought about it and politely declined, feeling that we shouldn't pay them to be good, but I promised to tell them that the other customers appreciated their behavior. Now my sons are grown and gone and this encounter tonight has brought such wonderful memories. I should have given them the money; it wouldn't have done any harm. It's too late now for my sons, but perhaps you will let me give these to yours."

Inside the envelope were two one dollar bills. I ran out the door, hoping to catch him, but he was gone. He could have joined us, perhaps for dessert.

That evening, when we returned home, I read my boys the letter, gave them the money, told them they were great and hugged them and hugged them and hugged them.

# St. George's Commandments

Because of my contacts in the education community, I occasionally speak to high school and college students about religion and its freethought alternatives. In response to a frequently asked question about the Ten Commandments, I say that freethinkers don't have much use for most of them because they primarily deal with a vain and insecure God. I then offer the following list, explaining that it is probably incomplete, but it provides an example of how most freethinkers operate.

1. Use your head — think critically. Use your hands — be helpful. Use your heart — be caring.

2. Remember, everyone needs to be loved.

3. Leave thoughts of gods and miracles, heavens and hells to those who invented them. Many people believe they need religion to make them be good — we do well without.

4. Be at least as good as your parents. If they weren't very good, you have an easy job. If they were great, you're lucky. If everyone did this, the human race would rapidly improve.

5. Get an education. It might be expensive, but ignorance costs more.

6. Support democracy. It's not perfect, but it's the best system running.

7. Support science. All of your comforts and conveniences derive from science.

8. Make today a little better for someone else, and today will be better for you.

9. Be tolerant. Why should others consider your viewpoint if you won't consider theirs?

10. When you screw up, admit it — and apologize.

11. Appreciate and protect the planet that feeds you. Recycle. Don't pollute.

12. Be good to your body. Why damage something that took millions of years to evolve?

13. Practice safe sex and family planning. The Earth is getting crowded. Malls, factories and parking lots are expanding at the expense of the forests and farms that sustain us.

Remember, religion is like alcohol. Most people can take a little without apparent harm, but for some, it's a mind altering drug, which is why the gullible can be fleeced again and again, why true believers die in Wacos and Jonestowns and Heaven's Gate fantasies — and why one fanatic climbed into a lion's den at a Japanese zoo to bring the lion to Jesus. (Here, kitty, kitty.) He was mauled.

It also explains why a New Hampshire couple intended to sacrifice their three children on the church's altar, but were stopped just in time. Yes, we humans have evolved, but some have evolved a lot more than others.

# Humor Is a Funny Thing

Contrary to popular belief, the "age of independence" is not a state that males acquire with time. Instead, they are born into it, celebrating their free will until infected with the most dreaded of the childhood maladies — puberty. Then their independence, eroded by hormonal tides, slowly slips away, to be replaced with zits and a brilliant revelation: the purpose of life is PLEASING GIRLS. (Divorced females will find this concept hilarious.)

Nevertheless, this is how I once came to agree to do the humor column for our high school newspaper. The girls had said I was funny (?) so I agreed. Taking jokes from here and sayings from there, I put them in my column, discovering the meaning of "plagiarism " in the early months of tenth grade when I learned that they wanted ORIGINAL stuff.

I was as inept as a novice comedian who's asked to "say something funny!" Fortunately, a serious, six-month illness intervened, during which I entertained physicians instead. Given the alternative of writing a regular humor column or enduring the illness again, I would probably react like Jack Benny who, when commanded by a robber, "Your money or your life!" took plenty of time to decide.

Humor infects us all, from the severely stricken to the almost immune. Some of us are incorrigible, finding (and stifling) giggles at the grave. Others "just don't get it," and the more we explain the more the humor fades.

Regardless of its form, (puns, hyperbole, satire, slapstick, mimicry, etc.) most humor has a purpose. Jack Benny used humor in its "purest" form, just to entertain, poking fun at himself and his miserly ways, rarely to ridicule or criticize others. However, as long as we have snickered and roared, our laughter has usually been directed at, guess who — the other guy.

Ambrose Bierce used his wonderful wit to spear everything in sight, with much of his best found in the "Devil's Dictionary":

SAINT .. a dead sinner revised and edited.

RELIGION .. the daughter of Hope and Fear, explaining to Ignorance the nature of the Unknowable.

CONSERVATIVE .. One who is enamored of existing evils, as distinguished from a LIBERAL, who wishes to replace them with others.

And CABBAGE .. a vegetable about as large and wise as a man's head.

Unfortunately, Ambrose disappeared during a trip to Mexico in 1914, perhaps stricken not by Montezuma, but by some Mexican Ayatollahs who were not amused. This brings us to religion, the one area where most of us don't know whether to laugh or cry... except for columnist Dave Barry.

According to Dave, when one religion considers the beliefs and practices of another, they say to themselves, "These people have the brains of a trout."

Dave observes that we have eliminated the old multiple-god system, arriving at belief "... in just one God, and he never turns people into toads or anything, unless you count Spiro Agnew." He then examines the broadcast preachers (Copeland comes to mind) who endlessly interpret scripture: "And so we can see it was BEZEL who told SHAM to go to Begorrah.... Now people ask me, they say, "Brother Ray Bob Tom, what do you mean it was BEZEL who told SHAM?" And I say, "What I mean is that when we're talking about who told who to go to Begorrah.... "

Dave concludes, "It can take upwards of a week to get through an entire sentence, which is why you often have to send in a Love Offering to get cassettes so you'll remember what it is that God wants you to do."

Garrison Keillor's touch is more gentle, describing in "Lake Wobegone" the boredom of his small church's humorless life, the interminable hours of Bible study, and how he envied the Catholics' colorful, noisy displays and seemingly endless celebrations.

To the credit of my Catholic friends, no one can match the stories they tell on themselves, many of them quite barbed. Just recently, my neighbor, Pat, told of the parish priest who, while taking his morning stroll, came across a little girl cuddling some kittens. He stooped down and asked her, "And what sort of kittens might these be, little lady?"

"Catholic kittens, father," she replied.

"Well, isn't that wonderful," he exclaimed.

Some days later he returned, this time with the bishop in tow, and as he had hoped, came upon the little girl, who was again playing with her kittens. Knowing the answer, he winked at the bishop and asked once again, "What kind of kittens did you say these are, my dear?"

To his great surprise, she answered, "Atheist kittens, father."

"Wh-what?" he stammered, "Didn't you tell me just a week ago that they're Catholic kittens?"

"Yes, father," the little girl replied, "but their eyes are open now."

As for ethnic jokes, I fear they will never end, and recommend that if you find one irresistible, do as I do and tell them on yourself. In fact, I usually preface them with a comment about my discomfort with ethnic jokes. I then explain that since I'm unable to resist, I will tell the story about a Norwegian because that's the bulk of my ancestry.

In the search for humor, some folks did an Internet survey asking people to submit jokes and to vote for the Best Joke Ever. There were thousands of submissions, bringing clever tales like the turtle who was mugged by two snails while crossing the road. When the police arrived and asked what happened, the turtle replied, "I don't know, everything happened too fast."

The trophy, however, went to the story of two hunters. As they trudge through the woods, one of them collapses. He's not breathing and his pupils are dilated. The other guy whips out his cell phone and dials 911. "I think my friend is dead," he yells. "What can I do?"

The operator says, "Calm down, first, let's make sure he's dead."

There's a silence, then a shot.

Back on the phone, the guy asks, "OK, now what?"

Psychologists think that one reason people become psychotic when deprived of dreams is that our nutty dreams are what keep us from going round the bend — that dreams let out the junk that would otherwise impair our days.

Perhaps the same thing is true of humor; that being able to joke about all of the idiocy, pain and adversity enables us to carry on. In fact, physicians have even demonstrated that laughter improves their patients' well-being and shortens hospital stays. That's easy for them to say, for they can leave when they want. But what about us patients? We're stuck in there, and "ouch" back *there*, and also with the bill.

# Wonders of the World

Because the ancient Romans and Greeks admired travel, statues and great buildings, Antipater of Sidon decided (some two thousand years ago) to compile a list of wondrous sights. He settled on VII (this was before Arabic numerals, folks) as a reasonable number. Besides, the number VII was believed to have special powers.

Copycats offered their choices, but Antipater's list survived them all. With apologies to Antipater, I confess that I could remember only two of his seven selections, one being the Pyramids, and the other, the Colossus at Rhodes, the 105-foot statue of the sun god Helios that overlooked the harbor of Rhodes.

That leaves five: the Hanging Gardens of Babylon (which I should have remembered), the Statue of Zeus — destroyed in 476 CE (anyone want to research who did it in?), the Temple of Diana, the Mausoleum at Halicarnassus and finally, the 400-foot Pharos Lighthouse at Alexandria, Egypt, the most practical and functional of them all, guiding sailors into port with its lofty flames for 1,500 years.

Sometime in the last century, travelers who appreciated nature more than bricks and mortar developed a different list: the Seven Natural Wonders. And although they had the whole world to select from, their list was almost as parochial as Antipater's: six of their seven reside within the United States, the exception being South Africa's Victoria Falls.

All the rest, I have seen: Rainbow Natural Bridge in Utah, the Sequoia trees of California, the Grand Canyon, Washington's Crater Lake and Wizard Island, Yellowstone Park, and New Mexico's Carlsbad Caverns.

So what sort of list would a 21st century Humanist create? As for me, selecting seven from a starting list of dozens proved too restrictive, so I now offer my Ten Natural Wonders, which is followed by my list of Twelve Human-produced Wonders.

## Erickson's Ten Natural Wonders of the World

I favor three of those already named in the Seven Natural Wonders: the Grand Canyon, Yellowstone Park and the Giant Sequoias.

For the next three, you'll need hiking boots, because number four is Africa's Serengeti Plain and the wildlife it shelters. Five is Russia's endangered Lake Baikal, so large and deep that it contains a fifth of the world's fresh water. Six is Canada's Thelon Sanctuary, through which the placid Thelon River flows, its 300-mile, verdant valley penetrating the "barren grounds" to shelter muskoxen, caribou and tundra grizzlies while offering canoeists wildlife without wild water.

Number seven is the Big Island of Hawaii. Taller than Mt. Everest (from its base in the depths of the ocean to its volcanic peaks), the Big Island represents much of the world in microcosm. An underwater paradise parallels its desert-like Kona coast. On the opposite side, the Hamakua coast begins in a tropical jungle and climbs to the subarctic, often snow-capped peak of Mauna Kea. On its northern coast, its ancient lavas are deeply grooved and weathered, but just 70 miles to the south, molten land pours forth every day from the flanks of Kilauea.

#8: The Swiss Alps.

#9: The Amazon basin, with its myriad life forms, most of them unexamined, yet threatened. Equal in area to the face of the moon, the basin receives almost half of the world's rainwater and is drained by the world's greatest river. Like Lake Baikal, it contains a fifth of the world's fresh water. (The Great Lakes hold another fifth.) Running to 350 feet deep and frequently too wide to see across, the Amazon's silt colors Atlantic waters some two hundred miles out to sea.

For number 10, those who love to travel can visit Australia's Great Barrier Reef. Those who prefer not to cross oceans can visit Canada's Great Slave Lake, while the less adventurous need only head for Lake Superior's northern shore. All three locations bear my last and greatest wonder: the stony remains of STROMATOLITES — the petrified colonies of blue-green algae that, a few billion years ago, began to produce oxygen in the shallows of our ancient seas.

Aided by sunlight and photosynthesis, the algae split water into hydrogen and oxygen, then combined the hydrogen with plentiful carbon dioxide to make simple organic molecules, the forerunners of the carbohydrates we need and love today.

Without competition, the algae became the ascendant life form, producing organic compounds and oxygen for eons, drastically altering the Earth's atmosphere and setting the stage for the rapid evolution of the oxygen-dependent organisms that followed.

Were it not for a curious scientist who decided to slice a stromatolite into ultrathin sections for examination under a microscope, we might still think that these flattened, pillowy, fossilized colonies were just odd-looking rocks, rather than the humble precursors of our lives, the chemical factories that gave us birth.

## Erickson's Twelve Human-produced Wonders of the World

1.  Perhaps the simplest, but most important of all, was the invention of writing, which permitted information to be passed on more accurately than had been possible by word of mouth, followed thousands of years later by movable type, the innovation that allowed the efficient printing of books in large numbers.

2.  The science of the ancient Greeks, as exemplified by Democritus, who proposed the existence of atoms, saw the deceptions of religion as evil, and had no use for gods, and in Eratosthenes, who accurately measured the Earth using simple geometry. Anti-education Christianity swept it all aside, burning libraries and preaching that education was vain and fruitless, leading to the Dark Ages.

3.  The science of Bruno, Bernoulli, Copernicus, Galileo, Darwin, Newton, Priestley and Lavoisier, all of whom, although "religious" in varying degrees, had to tread carefully because of the CHURCH. Bruno was burned to death during the Inquisition for holding the same views as Galileo. Bernoulli fled from Italy to the more tolerant Switzerland. Copernicus delayed

publishing until near death and then had a friend include a mitigating foreword in an attempt to appease the church. Darwin delayed publishing out of fear of the church, going public only when Wallace proposed to publish a similar thesis. Priestley, his laboratory and home set ablaze by religious fanatics, fled England for America, and Lavoisier, the father of modern chemistry, was beheaded during France's Reign of Terror, the presiding judge having dismissed appeals for his life with, "The Republic has no need for scientists."

4. The Magna Carta, the United States Constitution and the Bill of Rights.

5. Immunology and antibiotics, pioneered by Pasteur and Fleming. Many of us are alive because of the work they pioneered.

6. The practical electric generator developed by Michael Faraday. Thomas Edison, the determined genius whose light bulbs illuminated America, remarked that "invention is 1% inspiration and 99% perspiration," (often quoted) and that "religion is all bunk." (never quoted).

7. The internal combustion, reciprocating engine — a blessing and a curse that provides lightweight, reliable, portable power — and pollutes.

8. The harnessing of the atom and its use for peaceful purposes.

9. The jumbo jets, or "heavies" in aviation parlance. Born of the Wright brothers and Otto Lilienthal and propelled by the descendants of Frank Whittle's first jet engine, these technological marvels leap continents and oceans with ease, turning other forms of transport into ox carts.

10. Fiber optics — the new technology that transmits thousands of messages on a single strand and lets us see around corners, benefiting industry, communications and surgery.

11. The multitude of satellites that help keep the peace with their falcon-like eyes as they link nations together with

communications and peer into space (the Hubble telescope) with clarity impossible on the Earth. A "recent" benefit is the global positioning system (GPS) that provides PRECISE navigation (down to a few feet) anywhere on Earth.

12. Computers and the Internet — AMAZING!


Examine this list. Note the void caused largely by the dominance of Christian dogma and tyranny until the 17th and 18th centuries. Note the progress that followed when religion could no longer effectively intrude.

Even though the major religions no longer oppose science, superstition still subverts reason, which damages humankind: In schools, zealots push creationism. In medicine, they oppose abortions, immunizations and even medical care for children. Worldwide, their "go forth and multiply" dogma opposes effective birth control, fuels war and famine, and worsens immigration woes. If these people ever become rational, I will gladly call their conversion the Thirteenth Human Wonder of the Modern World.

# Tradition

The marvelous Broadway musical, Fiddler on the Roof, opens with gravel-voiced Tevye proclaiming the virtues of tradition. Like the fiddler and his family, all of the residents of little Anatevka must strive to keep their balance, and as Tevye says, tradition is their tool. "We have traditions for everything: traditions that tell us how to sleep, how to eat, how to work and how to wear our clothes. ..."

"How did these traditions get started?" asks Tevye, then answers, "Well, I'll tell you, I DON'T KNOW... but it's TRADITION!"

Like Tevye's family, soon to be routed by the pogroms, we also lean on tradition when times are rough. Religious conservatives use tradition to blow back the winds of change. For them, "tradition" is a holy word, now modernized as "family values."

Pat Robertson did just that when he railed against the Equal Rights Amendment, calling it "a socialist, antifamily political movement that encourages women to leave their husbands, kill their children, practice witchcraft, destroy capitalism and become lesbians." Tradition can be mighty handy for keeping women in their place.

In much of the Christian and Muslim world, tradition promotes large, double-digit families in a world of limited resources. A few years ago, a report on Canadian television provided an outrageous example. In the '90s, Canada endorsed a population boosting policy, largely through immigration, but I was nevertheless stunned to see Prime Minister Brian Mulroney, in his home province of Quebec, distributing awards to mothers of FIFTEEN or more children. What an affront to those who limit family size, and eventually, what a crime against our planet. For me, it was a revolting sight, but for those in the cheering throng it was another cherished tradition.

With cries of "tradition," we mask our reluctance to learn new ways. Led by people like George Will, we run from the metric system, preferring to perpetuate an erratic, illogical system based on the dimensions of a British king's anatomy. With inflammatory, Limbaugh-like language, Mr. Will blasted the "Commerce Department Gestapo" that would introduce kilometers and liters. Never mind that the metric system is easily learned and more user-friendly, or that it has been adopted by most of the world. It represents change. It's not our tradition, so it must be bad.

Tradition perpetuates our chaotic spelling system, forcing generations of children to learn it the hard way. We'd rather have them waste time, intellect and material with the complex spelling of "thought" instead of "thot." Why "praise" instead of "praze?" Why "phone" rather than "fone?" Perhaps becuz wr lazy and self-sentrd.

But wayz kan chanje. Fonetik speling izn't so hard, and it's much mor kunsistent. Fonetik speling apeerz to be that uv the unedukated, and sumtimez it iz, but it makes perfekt sens to those who r not indoktrinated into the k-os of old english speling. It iz the rezult of a lojikul aproche.

Howevr, George Will (xsepshunz r aloud for propr namez) kan b xpectd to leed the rezistens with inovaytiv, katchy termz like "speling Gestapo." So, if fonetik speling ever arivez, I do not beleev that George wil akwe-s. Insted, I think George won't. He is very tradishinul.

# The Toolbox — A Hazard for the Home

Let's face it. You've always envied those handy folks who build a fifty-foot deck complete with a gazebo before breakfast, or repair your garage door while you are still looking for the owner's manual — and now you're determined to join their ranks, equipped with a brand new tool box and all the goodies that are usually found therein.

Don't do it! The toolbox, which was invented by a woman named Pandora, has brought grief and injury to do-it-yourselfers since the days of the early Greeks, who until that time had been content to write poetry and run marathons.

However, for those who choose to reject my advice as an expert on self-injury, I offer the following guide:

TOOL BOX: A metal box for hiding tools from men who intend to commit carpentry. A cloth bag or old water pail will do just as well and costs much less, but if you are concerned with appearances, a tool box is essential. Also purchase a LARGE first aid kit, disability insurance and scratch 911 on the cover of the box.

A flat black finish ensures that the box will be easy to lose and hard to find, and installing a combination lock adds a nice safety feature for those with failing memories. Get the biggest, heaviest, most expensive box available, thus reducing its portability and frequency of use, and consuming some of the money you might otherwise waste on tools.

HAMMER: A good hammer tops the list, primarily because people like to hit things. Hammers have heads made of metal or rubber or plastic, plus a handle capable of raising blisters in two minutes. There are claw hammers, tack hammers and ball peen hammers, to name just a few. After years of practice, a skilled professional can hit a tack, nail or a ball peen on at least one attempt in three. All hammers carry a warning that forbids striking one hammer against another, thus frustrating one of our innermost desires.

SCREWDRIVERS: Often called PLIERS by the truly ignorant, screwdrivers can be purchased singly or in kits containing all 83 varieties. Square shaft models can be gripped with pliers, permitting one to ruin the slot of the screw more quickly. In the screwdriver department we find the basic philosophical question of the carpentry world: Who is Phillip, and why does everyone want to use his screwdrivers when they could easily use their own?

LOCKING PLIERS: Also known as Vise-Grips. If you miscalculate, these pliers, unlike ordinary pliers, will continue to crush your finger for however long it takes to locate the release lever. Pass this one up and get a NEEDLE-NOSE pliers instead. These are much less hazardous in that they traumatize a smaller area, release instantly, and are useful for removing fishhooks and (as the name implies) hairs from inside one's nose.

DIAGONAL WIRE CUTTERS: Only necessary if your home has diagonal wiring instead of the tangential wiring, which has been used since 1963.

ADJUSTABLE WRENCH: Use this tool to attempt to turn a nut or a bolt that is often welded in place. Adjustable wrenches are never quite tight enough, causing the shoulders of the nut to round off, which permits one to experiment with a Vise-Grip, (not recommended) which completes the rounding of the nut and the scarring of one's knuckles. This calls for the application of a COLD CHISEL, or a NUT SPLITTER and, frequently, purple prose. Rounded nuts such as these demonstrate the Erickson CERTAINTY PRINCIPLE, a corollary to the Heisenberg UNCERTAINTY PRINCIPLE: No matter how many nuts one removes with ease, the last will be permanently locked in place, proving that there really are immoveable objects.

MEASURING TAPE: Carpenters, when working for themselves always "measure twice and cut once," but those who are paid on a cost plus basis reverse the dictum by measuring once and cutting as many times as they please. However, measuring tapes are intended only for beginners who have no eye for distance. Advanced craftsmen with one or two birdhouses behind them usually remove the tape from the case on their belts to save weight while still looking classy.

CUTTING TOOLS: Cutting tools are extremely dangerous, as they do not discriminate between hands and hemlock. Worse yet, the hazards have been increased by ignorant, self-styled "craftsmen" who claim that dull tools require greater force, and therefore cause more slips and excursions into soft tissue than their sharper counterparts. This is correct only because these tools are still TOO SHARP! A properly dulled tool will cut as nicely as a tennis ball, avoiding any possibility of injury. With this in mind, we now proceed to:

CHISELS: Chisels are not recommended. Save money on this item because no one knows if the bevel should be up or down. Use one of your 83 screwdrivers as an economical substitute.

CROSSCUT SAW: Used to cut long, narrow boards into short, narrow boards.

RIP SAW: Used to cut long, wide boards into long, narrow boards and for sectioning saw horses that one forgets are holding up the board. Save money here by purchasing only short, narrow boards that can be glued together end to end — no sawing needed.

PLANES: These devices are designed to remove thick shavings of wood or nothing at all. A mechanism is attached that is supposed to adjust the depth of the cut. Do not touch this! If you do, the blade will cut lower on one side or fall out. When your plane finally refuses to cut anything, buy a new one, or better yet use your screwdriver chisel.

FILES: The most common file is the bastard file, but in polite company it is called the illegitimate file, and its cutting grooves run in only one direction. Files, including those that are legitimate and have grooves running wherever they please, are used to remove metal. Files can be made into excellent knives and scrapers, but they will turn to rust if someone exhales in the same building, which is why there are so many knives and so few files.

HAND DRILL: This tool is basically an egg beater with a drill bit on one end for producing smaller holes than those made by your hammer. When you crank the handle, the bit enters the wood, making a hole. If you crank it the other way, the bit backs out of the hole, which closes behind it. (Just joking there.)

SANDPAPER: This product, popularized by 3M™ and the lumber companies, converts good wood to dust, which most carpenters inhale because they like the smell and don't want to live forever. Sandpaper comes in a variety of grits, from extra-coarse for cleaning battleships to superfine which hardly cuts at all but is great for exercise.

POWER TOOLS: No one should use power tools. They are the most dangerous of all inventions and are surrounded with magnetic fields that will result in three-eared progeny and a lot of ill will. Furthermore, all of the power tool companies are owned by doctors who work in emergency rooms, profiting not only from your purchases but from repairing you as well. They want you to have tools, which is why some companies will give you a new tool FREE if the old one breaks. Just see, though, if they'll give you a new arm. Not likely, because that's where the real money is. Finally, if you can't resist buying this stuff, go for it, but don't say I didn't warn you!

# Letter to God

A few years ago, I received a group email from a very religious relative who began by asking God about the children who died in a series of school tragedies, one of which is mentioned below. I inserted my responses within his message and sent this reply to him and to everyone who received his email

**Dear God: Why didn't you save the school children shot at Littleton, Colorado?**

**Sincerely, a Concerned Student**

Good question, but why not ask about children killed in accidents on their way to church or church camp, or why a tornado destroys a church and those who seek shelter within it while tearing up a town? How about those who died in Katrina? How about GWB?

**Reply: Dear Concerned Student: Sorry, I am not allowed in schools.**

**Sincerely, God**

God, according to believers, is everywhere, and no restriction against his, her or its presence will have any effect, so to say that God is not allowed in schools is an evasion of the religionists' real gripe.

In public schools, school-sponsored or school-led Christian, Muslim, or Jewish prayers — or the prayers of other sects — are not permitted because they promote one religion over all other views and are, as a consequence, divisive. If children want to pray, no one forbids it — but they must keep it private by keeping it inside their heads. Prayer *is* allowed, but the proselytizing effects created by school-approved, audible prayers are not — and there is a difference. That difference is usually ignored by those who are always pushing prayer.

The email continued,

**"I think this started when Madeline Murray O'Hare (sp) complained about prayer in schools. Then, someone said, you better not read the Bible in school — the Bible that says "Thou shalt not kill, Thou shalt not steal, Love your neighbor as yourself."**

The Bible, one of <u>many</u> "holy" books, says a lot of things, many of them quite horrible and hard to defend as practices of a supposedly loving god.

To blame our troubles on Madalyn Murray O'Hair is simplistic and heavily biased. The problem is rooted in the old practice of Bible reading in public schools — which always used the King James Bible, which upset Catholics because they used a different version. In response, Catholics started parochial schools to prevent their children from being exposed to Protestantism. Those schools and the divisions they represent are still with us. Now we also have "faith-based" schools — all of which damage the best melting pot we ever had — the public school.

You want the Bible in school? Then offer a comparative religion and ethics course taught by an <u>unbiased</u> teacher. Where this has been tried, it has usually been opposed by parents who do not want their children exposed to other beliefs — or worse yet, taught how to employ critical thinking. Instead, most parents want their children to be clones — to hang onto beliefs that were drilled into their once open minds.

I did not always think like this, having once been an elder in a large Presbyterian church, but exposure to other beliefs began to make a difference, and I now look at religion as I do at politics or buying a car. I'm now from Missouri — the "show me" state.

Perhaps the only thing of value in the email was a quote near the end — **"WE REAP WHAT WE SOW,"** which is often true. Unfortunately, many ill-informed people who won't change their minds despite the facts keep sowing these biased half-truths to advance their one and only true theology while ignoring the dozens of competing theologies that also claim to possess the truth.

In response to the email's biased question **"Why can't our children** read a Bible in school, but can in prison?" I'd again note that they can read it in an appropriate, balanced course on religion and philosophy guided by an unbiased teacher.

In addition, if all students were required to take a course in critical thinking and ethics, fewer would end up in jail — like convict Chuck Colson who, while in jail, memorized one book and — voila, took up a new and profitable occupation upon his release.

Most freethinkers know the Bible better than those who push it but refuse to read anything that disputes its validity. The contents of books by Sam Harris or Richard Dawkins, or my *Time Traveling With Science and the Saints* will never enter their minds.

On the other hand, it's more fun (and much easier) to just forward every badly-researched, biased and distorted email, as long as it advances one's programmed-from-childhood bias. No work or study is involved. Just be a faithful cog in the great proselytizing machine fueled by those who preach about love but are the first to pound the drums of war.

Comedian George Carlin, whom I manage to enjoy despite his often "salty" language, is an expert at poking holes in our pretensions and sacred beliefs.

Carlin says that he has "begun worshipping the sun for a number of reasons. First of all, unlike some other gods I could mention, I can see the sun. It's there for me every day. And the things it brings me are quite apparent: heat, light, food, a lovely day. There's no mystery, no one asks for money and I don't have to dress up. Furthermore, I noticed that of all the prayers I used to offer to God — or even Joe Pesci — are being answered at about the same 50% rate. Half the time I get what I want. Half the time I don't. Same as God — 50/50. Same as the four leaf clover, the horse shoe, the rabbit's foot, and the wishing well."

If there is a god that takes an interest in human affairs, he must really like Mr. Carlin, because Carlin has done very well, which must prove what many conservative pastors (who have apparently forgotten Jesus' views on the rich and the accumulation of wealth) have been loudly preaching: God wants you to be rich! Given the choice between some God preferring these guys to Carlin, I'd bet on Carlin — and give odds of fifty to one!

# Always a Bridesmaid

I have never been a juror. During several decades of eligibility, I've not once been summoned to weigh a defendant's guilt or innocence in my even, judicious hands. I'd wondered why I hadn't been called, but dropped it from my mind, so imagine my surprise on receiving my county's version of "Uncle Sam Wants You!"

As I leaf through a stack of letters, JURY SUMMONS leaps out at me from an official looking envelope that directs me to report to the Ramsey County Court House for one week, on Monday, May 9, unless I can show evidence of inability to serve. The county promises to pay $15 per day and 24 cents per mile, and warns that failure to appear could result in a summons of a different sort.

By the time I finish reading the summons and begin to respond to the juror questionnaire, I am polarized: part of me is elated at this potentially rewarding experience, but the other is yelling, "Not the week of MAY 9, not MAY 9!"

The timing is awful. The ice will have just left Lake Vermilion, restoring access to our island cabin, to walleyes, and to my bulldozer with four acres of brush and forest. I scan the questionnaire, hoping for a loophole through which I might escape with honor, but find none.

Nevertheless, for each question, the grinch within suggests ways to evade my duty:

"Occupation" — <u>Hit Man.</u>

"Do you have a physical or mental disability that would affect your ability to serve?" — <u>Tourette's Syndrome and Allergy to Attorneys</u>

"Have you been convicted of a felony?" <u>No — I got off.</u>

In the end, "George the Good" triumphs over "George the Grinch" and on Monday, May 9, I pay $3.50 for civic center parking, stroll along Kellogg Avenue while longingly scanning the greening banks of the Mississippi River, and enter the bowels of the courthouse where, along with 120 other conscripts, I surrender my week to the Ramsey County Courts.

I am deep into the "Juror's Handbook" when a pleasant young man introduces himself and describes the mechanics of the court system and the jury selection process. He then yields to Ms. S., the young man's coworker who will be our overseer, announcing periodically who has been selected for which court, when to leave and when to return.

After watching a redundant, twenty-minute court system video, I return to the handbook, there to discover the two oaths used by the Ramsey County Courts, both ending with "so help me God." I search the handbook for an affirmation, but find nothing that doesn't involve a deity. Seeking out Ms S. in the assembly room office, I ask about affirmation.

"No problem" she says, and prints AFFIRMATION in bold letters after my name on the jury candidate list.

I ask, "Would it be possible to include the affirmation oath in the Handbook along with the two traditional oaths, so that jurors would realize they had the option?" Ms. S promises that an affirmation will be included in the next printing — due later in the year.

Ten of my county's 24 courts are in session. The first call comes at 10 a.m. — a stabbing. As a felony case it requires 12 jurors plus an alternate. Ms. S. reads the names of more than twenty prospects who head for the courtroom, there to be questioned by the judge and attorneys.

Not being called, I open my copy of the "Used Aircraft Buyers Guide." I have progressed to the pros and cons of the Cessna Skylane when Ms. S. returns with another jury call — this one a civil case requiring just six jurors plus an alternate. This time I am called.

A few minutes later, we enter the chambers of Judge C. Drawing names at random, the clerk seats seven of us 12 in the jury box for questioning, leaving the rest to watch.

In an unusual switch, a corporation is suing one of its former managers for return of severance pay. The judge and attorneys question the panel, searching for evidence of bias. A juror who has been involved in a similar dispute is dismissed, replaced by a woman on my right. With the attorneys content, we rejects return to the assembly room just in time to be dismissed for lunch.

Monday afternoon brings five more calls, none involving me, and at 4:15, Ms. S. releases us.

Tuesday begins badly. 3M has reserved the entire civic center ramp for its annual meeting, and downtown parking is nil, requiring a long walk from a distant $5 lot. Even so, May 10 is gorgeous, with Rice Park's flowering crab trees in blossom and birds in song beneath a spotless, cerulean sky.

We jurors are beginning to lighten up. People chat in little groups, play cards and noisily gather around a Donahue program that promises to feature men's underwear, which my flawed hearing presents as "nun's underwear," a translation that I share with my neighbors, bringing roars of laughter.

My group includes a 20-year-old with a faded "Just Do It!" T-shirt stretched balloon-like across his ample belly, a leggy, mini-skirted legal secretary who has just bought her first Harley motorcycle, an amiable, middle-aged man in a three-piece suit, a marginally articulate, 19-year-old male whose life revolves around traffic citations, a scruffy young fellow who, having heard my parking lot complaint, hands me a useful bus schedule, and a plain-looking, 30-something woman who glances incessantly at the leggy blond.

Two juries are called, the "rejects" of one returning shortly along with those called for the second case, which was settled as the selection process began. Once again, I am not included. But on the third call I am not only summoned, but am also chosen to enter the jury box for questioning.

It's a felony case: a young woman charged with attempting to redeem an altered gambling ticket. She has the sort of brainless look that I'd associate with such a scheme, but I ask myself how I would look if I were sitting there, unjustly accused. Guilty as bin Laden, I conclude.

When Judge S. arrives, the clerk of the court proceeds to swear us in, using the conventional God oath. I refrain from joining when the jurors reply, "I do," fully expecting to be asked to remain standing for an oath of affirmation, but nothing happens. I decide that they will swear me again if I pass examination, and that if they don't offer, I will have to request it.

Judge S. is impressive. He instructs the jury calmly, as if measuring each word, urging us to remember the presumption of innocence, and emphasizing that the burden of proof rests not on the defendant, but on the state. Then, with consideration and sensitivity, he questions us, gently probing personal issues, impressing me with his professionalism.

I am stunned that eight of our twenty reply "Yes" when asked if they have ever been a victim of crime against their property or person — with 30% of the women reporting rape.

The defendant's attorney, a conservatively-suited young woman, asks the expected questions: Do you gamble? If so, how often? Have you ever been charged with a crime? Did the case go to court? Were you satisfied with the result? When you make up your mind, do you ever change it after consultation with others?

The state's attorney is a tall, spare, smiling man who tries to appear friendly. He repeats a few of the defense attorney's questions, then moves on to his own, including "Why do you think you would be a good juror?" In an interesting reversal, some of those who had protested being required to serve while in the assembly room are suddenly selling themselves as if competing for a prize. Their questioning complete, the attorneys finally inform the clerk who will stay and who will be dismissed. I am dismissed, as are the other prospective jurors who do not gamble.

Lunch time, and I opt for a nearby restaurant and a hot turkey sandwich served by a genuinely friendly, middle-aged waitress who is the epitome of everyone's Mom.

The "corral" is even noisier when I return, buzzing with rumors of possible trips to the Maplewood courts in northern Ramsey County, but the afternoon jury calls never mention Maplewood — and never mention me.

On Wednesday morning, I park free near Sears and, after a seven-minute bus ride, arrive at the courthouse. When I enter, I am instantly struck by the 36-foot onyx Indian statue, the "God of Peace" standing at the far end of the hall. A plaque at its base reveals that the statue revolves very slowly, but although I watch carefully, I detect no motion, then discover that its control switch is locked at "OFF."

As I head once again for the basement, I reflect on my career as a juror.

Like the onyx Indian, I am undeniably present — but going nowhere.

I strike up a conversation with an amiable, graying computer programmer for the Minnesota income tax department, but we are interrupted by three jury calls, the last one taking him. I am beginning to think there must be blood on my door, for I am once again passed over.

Noon arrives and I realize that I have never eaten at the Radisson's top-floor Carousel Restaurant. To my surprise, I am seated immediately. At several nearby tables, bailiffs sit with jurors to ensure that they do not discuss their cases among themselves or with others, a service that even includes escorting them to the bathroom.

I open "Wrinkles in Time," a book on cosmology, while I wait for my lunch, and although I had been making good progress, by the time my chicken BLT arrives, the wrinkles are getting deep. As the St. Paul panorama drifts slowly by I muse that if I were one of those fundamentalist "the universe was made just for man" types, I might also believe that I am stationary, and the world is centered on me.

When I return, the corral has the appearance of a flophouse minus the beds. People are draped across chairs, feet up, with eyelids drooping. Boredom permeates the air.

Wednesday is a pivotal day. If we are impaneled, the odds are good that our work will conclude before the weekend. If not, Thursday or Friday could ensnare us in a case that will involve the following week. A few say they wouldn't mind, but most of us are anxious to return to our lives.

A jury call arrives in the afternoon. It declines my presence, and we are released at four o' clock.

Thursday morning finds me waiting for bus 12A amid the fragrance of fresh lilacs on another lovely day. Back at the corral, conversations begin to focus on ways to avoid selection — some subtle, some outrageous, but none really serious.

One person says he will tell the judge that he has an appointment with a bucket of minnows; another suggests telling the defense attorney that the justice system is so perfect that indictment is proof of guilt or, conversely, one might inform the prosecution that courts are so biased against defendants that jurors should always vote for acquittal. As an alternative, I propose that during the questioning process, one could exclaim, "Brothers and sisters, have you been saved? Have you been bathed

..." and carry on until led from the chambers.

At 9:30 and again at 10, Ms. S. appears with two jury calls — neither involving me. She also warns us not to worry if we smell smoke; some Indians will be burning a bit of sage during a renaming ceremony of the great onyx "God of Peace," who will become "Vision of Peace." This is fine with me — and what's the difference between gods and visions anyway? We are dismissed at 11:15. Hooray!

By Friday I have my schedule down pat, and as I survey our thinning ranks (those who have already served are not required to return) I note that Ms. mini-skirt, Mr. "Just Do It" and the three-piece-suit are absent.

The morning creeps by, but at 11, Ms. S. announces, "I have good news for you. The remaining cases have been settled or postponed. You may leave; thank you for your patience."

I trudge up the stairs and pause at the foot of the massive "Vision of Peace," then catch its inverted image in the mirrored ceiling above. Disconnected but almost real, it hovers there like a prospective juror who almost made the cut. Content that I tried, I head north on I-35, then stop for groceries and gas — and an extra-large bucket of minnows.

The following week I write to the assembly room staff to thank them for their efforts to keep us informed, for their cooperation in seeing the affirmation option added to the handbook, and to inform them that writing "Affirmation" across my juror's data sheet had proved futile.

I also sent the following letter to Judge S.

Dear Judge S.

Last week I had my first experience as a potential juror. When I read the Juror's Handbook and noticed there was no provision for affirmation, I mentioned it to the assembly room staff, who printed "AFFIRMATION" in bold letters across the front of my form.

On Tuesday, I was one of those called to your courtroom. We were all sworn with the standard oath, to which I did not respond. Frankly, I expected my affirmation to immediately follow, but it did not. Instead we were questioned first by you and then by the attorneys.

I want to add that I was impressed with your short address to the prospective jurors, with your restraint, concern and the clarity of your comments and questions. You made us feel at ease while informing us and asking questions.

While the attorneys questioned us, I decided that if I were selected for the jury I would, unfortunately, have to interrupt things to request affirmation. I assume that I would then have been required to state that my responses already given remained unchanged. I am sure that you see the problem: a juror later found to have been improperly sworn could be a gift to the losing side. However, I was not selected, leaving the question moot.

I assume that judges run their courts in similar, but not identical, ways, and I am concerned that my experience might not be rare. I realize that few panelists request affirmation, partly because affirmation has not been listed as an option in the Juror's Handbook. Even fewer would feel free to stand up in court and request it when it is overlooked.

I hope you will find a standardized way to remedy this issue. Those of us who maintain morality and ethics without reliance on supernatural beliefs do not want to present problems for the courts, but we cannot ethically take god oaths either. Thank you for your consideration.

Sincerely,

George A Erickson, President

The Humanist Association of Minn. and St. Paul

One week later, the judge replied, thanking me for my letter and noting that my point regarding affirmation was well taken. He then continued, "I intend to incorporate an affirmation option in my courtroom procedure so that it will be standard for all future jury trials. I will suggest that all the other judges do so as well.

"I don't know what happened with your affirmation request. We would not have deliberately ignored it and we should not have overlooked it. In any event, my new procedure will ensure that (in this court) this will not be a problem in the future."

Last fall, I phoned Ms. S. and asked her to mail me a copy of the revised Jurors Handbook so that I can send copies to officials in other Minnesota courts, but it has not yet arrived.

If you ever encounter similar discrimination I hope you will politely resist. We can be ignored only if we allow it.

# If I Were a Rich Man

Could you use a few million dollars? Better yet, why not 100 million; or in order to avoid any hint of stinginess, let's just make it 100 BILLION. Consider it done — a little gift from me to you.

Invested at a paltry six percent (tax free, of course) this Georgesend will earn you $6 billion per year, or 17 million dollars per day. Next to you, Ross Perot is a pauper, as are Bill Gates and the Sultan of Brunei. Wrapped in your immense security blanket, you can burn the tent, buy an extra Veg-O-Matic and "direct your feet to the sunny side of the street." But then comes the hard part. What will you do with 17 million dollars a day, and the power it represents?

In "Fiddler on the Roof," Tevye, the loving Jewish patriarch, unaware of the coming pogrom, lustily belts out the song of our dreams: "If I Were a Rich Man." Unfortunately, shortsighted Tevye opts for property and status, including "an extra staircase leading nowhere just for show."

In "The Man Who Would Be King," Rudyard Kipling composed a tragic answer that would provide a couple of actors named Sean Connery and Michael Caine the roles of their lives.

However, most gifts come with strings, and this is no exception, so before I encumber you with such a responsibility, I will need to assess your character in case you are just another Tevye, your vision extending no further than a larger gaggle of geese or a superfluous stairway. As for me, having thought it over for all of several minutes, I know precisely what this freethinking liberal would do if all of that money were mine.

First, guided by Humanist principles, I would dedicate my resources to public education via every means available. I would buy a controlling interest in a major newspaper chain and, along with it, one or two of the major TV networks. Our editors and producers would be chosen from those attuned to programs like "Discovery," "Nova," "60 Minutes," "Nightline" and the fine programming that often runs on PBS, condemning those who focus on American Idols, the Octo-Mom and Brangelina's baby to watch endless repeats of Fox "News."

My channels will offer a mix of comedy, news and entertaining-but-educational programs that critically address all issues, including the sacred cow of religion. And unlike the current practice, my newspapers would give error corrections the same prominence as the original mistake.

Second, I would campaign for approval of RU-486, subsidize its use, and provide free sterilization and abortions for all who want no more children. I would support research into other methods of male and female contraception and campaign to limit immigration to levels that balance emigration. I would advocate free trade with every country that enforces environmental laws equivalent to or better than our own. I'd raise the minimum wage, lower taxes on family incomes below $70,000, and increasingly tax the rich.

Third, I'd fund a campaign to end religion's tax-free status and the diversion of tax revenue to church projects. I would establish a fund to reward whistle blowers who report environmental violations or reveal corruption.

Fourth, I would support a determined, rational media campaign to reduce homophobia and to help homosexuals develop a coordinated public relations campaign to counter the negative attention given their minority.

Fifth, I would support a national health plan similar to Canada's, where care is not tied to one's ability to pay, nor do medical costs rise at three to five times the rate of inflation. In addition, I would support reforms to our legal system that would end the advantage of those who can afford endless litigation, to the disadvantage of those who can barely afford a defense. And I would support adoption of English as the official language of the U.S.

Sixth, I would seek to end commerce with repressive regimes, promising our cooperation when new leaders arise or the abuses end. I would support and fund a United Nations force to indict and punish leaders for the war crimes they commit or allow. In time, presidents and generals would learn that supporting wars that brutalize people has consequences.

Seventh, I would contribute heavily to pro-environment candidates and liberals in general while promoting tax breaks for those who drive economy cars.

Finally, after establishing a website asking for suggestions on what else I might do, I would try to persuade Congress to scrap the electoral college and severely restrict the ability of the executive branch to classify documents and use executive privilege to hide its misdeeds.

If some of you are thinking that my 100 billion won't do — that it can't possibly stretch that far, you might be right, but I have an answer. I'll order up another 100 billion, and maybe several more, because when it comes to dreaming, one might as well dream big!

# Is Anybody Out There?

from *True North: Exploring the Great Wilderness by Bush Plane*

Fed and soon to retire, I sit, elbows on knees, on a gently sloping beach with a fire at my side. Overhead, a blanket of cirrostratus clouds slips across the darkening sky to intercept the light of the thousands of stars that our unaided eyes can see. To circumvent my censored sight, I envision the Andromeda galaxy, which is said to be our twin, and I wonder if, on the beaches of distant worlds, other life forms are looking up and asking, "Is anybody out there?"

More than two thousand years ago, the Greek philosopher, Metrodorus, reasoned that "to consider the world the only populated world in infinite space is as absurd as to assert that in an entire field sown with millet, only one grain will grow." Epicurus agreed, as did Lucretius: "Nature is not unique to the visible world; we must have faith that in other regions of space there exist other earths inhabited by other people and animals."

Were Lucretius to return to us, he'd be pleased to find the scientific community firmly on his side, arguing that amino acids, the simple building blocks of life, are easily formed in the billions of galactic kitchens whose starry cauldrons brim with primordial soup. In contrast, some fundamentalists embrace a doctrine of "just one Earth, just for man." Really? And should pigeons believe that the skyscrapers on which they roost were assembled just for them?

Lucretius and I, being agreed that other life forms almost certainly exist, must respond to the question raised by the American nuclear physicist Enrico Fermi: "If there are others out there, WHERE IS EVERYBODY?" I don't know, of course, and with Lucretius indisposed, I move on to a more easily answered question: Why don't we know?

In the first place, the distances between stars are so vast that even with fantastic speeds, the timetable for interstellar travel is reckoned in thousands of years.

Second, even if we try to communicate with other solar systems by radio, the time/distance problem is still enormous. Assume that the nearest star has planets. Assume that one of those planets shelters a technology equal to ours or better. Assume that their transceiver is aimed at our tiny portion of their sky and is scanning the frequencies we send their way. If all of this works, it would require at least ten years to send a message and receive a reply.

Warming to my subject, I conjure up Dr. Fermi and convince him that the odds of *nearby* celestial civilizations achieving technological parity at the same time as ours are not very good. Most other life forms will either be primitive, compared with our own, or more advanced. The primitive society could not receive our signals, let alone reply.

As for the advanced civilization, Dr. Fermi suggests that we might have already been evaluated, using methods beyond our dreams. On observing that we still fight like children, they'd probably not return for several hundred years.

I offer a different approach: when we ask why others haven't contacted us, we assume that life on other worlds will evolve as it has on Earth, producing beings with similar technologies. In so doing, we ignore the fact that with millions, perhaps billions of suitable planets to work with, the potential life forms are limited only by time and the laws of physics. Perhaps there are non-materialistic intelligent beings out there that communicate among themselves, develop societies, loyalties and show compassion but lack technology.

Consider the whales and dolphins that communicate over great distances, or the societal patterns of the wolf pack, or elephants that not only assist their injured but appear to grieve for their dead companions. Because communicating by radio with these creatures is not possible, does it mean they don't exist? Dr. Fermi, prompted by my whales and elephants, might wryly add that if these great beasts can survive our brutality, they may yet evolve into creatures of brilliance and great sensitivity — and so might we.

Then, like Marley's Ghost of Christmas Past, another voice intrudes, and Lucretius appears. "There is yet another possibility," he says, "And a grim one it is."

"After a few million years of evolution, humans have developed technologies that can bring great comfort or destroy most of life on Earth. Fail to use that energy wisely, and power-hungry primitives and fanatics who proclaim holy wars could snuff out our beacons of light when they've just begun to shine.

"Other worlds may well have evolved parallel technologies, broadcast for a few decades, then reaped the whirlwind and vanished into silence, only to begin again the long climb back from the stone age or beyond, if life survived at all."

Lucretius dims and vanishes. Fermi, too, is gone, leaving me to ponder what message I would send if I were in charge at the SETI Institute (Search for Extra-Terrestrial Intelligence). "Perhaps the safest thing to do at the outset, if technology permits, is to send music," said Lewis Thomas, an American pediatrics professor and the author of "Lives of a Cell."

I'd also use music to send my universal message. Thomas cast his vote for Bach, but I would send the soaring rhythms of Brahms's First Symphony, or Tchaikovsky's disquieting "Pathétique" to probe the distant stars.

# Doctor K. and the Christmas Star

Every year, as the winter solstice draws near, a small pleasant man — a scientist — begins to make the rounds of our Twin Cities schools and churches, offering large, uncritical audiences a much-publicized program called the Star of Bethlehem. And as you might expect, the intent of the doctor's program is to make the story of the nativity star seem plausible.

Doctor K. is an appealing, elderly man, the sort who'd make a nice grandfather. Possessed of warmth and wit, he uses both to suggest that Jupiter and Saturn arose in close proximity just before the sunrise on the day of Jesus ' birth. So close, he believes, that they appeared to be the single bright star that led the Wise Men to Bethlehem. He then proposes that the three men were astrologers who, having seen the conjunctive planets on a night when the "star" was south of Jerusalem — in the direction of Bethlehem — had headed south toward the "star." Naturally, the "star" slowly moved westward during the night, so the three travelers took a fork in the road — and came to Bethlehem. Now isn't that neat — and improbable.

Three of the four synoptic gospels fail to support this myth. Neither John, Luke nor Mark mention such a star, and Mark, the earliest and therefore the least likely of the gospels to have been embellished, makes no mention of a birth at all. No stars, no wise men and no heavenly hosts. Of course, it's quite possible that a conjunction of the planets occurred, but that doesn't prove anything. Unless Dr. K. has a bias, why hasn't he used the tools of science to investigate astronomical events that were said to attend the births of Krishna, Moses, Buddha, Yu, Lao-tse, Abraham, Aesculapius, Alexander and several of the Caesars?

Unfortunately, pseudo science still falls on receptive ears. By supporting a cherished myth with carefully selected schemes, Dr. K. leads good minds astray and undermines the science that has provided his living, at one point even laughingly dumping science aside, saying, "After all, logic is simply an organized was of thinking to help one go wrong!" That's terrible! Does he prefer the opposite? Would he turn instead to tarot cards and casting the bones — to voodoo or leaves of tea?

Most discouraging, however, were his closing remarks. In what was probably intended to be a plug for the spiritual, he ventured that despite all our technology and science, humankind is not much happier. I strongly disagree. Science has been relatively unfettered for only 200 years, yet most of us live in surroundings that no king of old could have hoped to attain. Think of our many choices for travel, our progress in medicine, our cornucopia supermarkets, the real "miracles" that modern medicine has produced, the abundant stores of knowledge in libraries and on the 'net, our marvelous communications systems, and above all, the freedom to inquire, with no church powerful enough to prevent us from reading a book.

Compared to recent years, the preceding centuries overflowed with despair, ignorance, disease and filth, due largely to the relentless opposition of religionists to the efforts of science to better understand the world, and to make it a better place.

Dr. K. is undoubtedly a nice man. He has fun with his program, but if he were living in the days of Bruno, Copernicus and Galileo, he wouldn't dare speak of an Earth that revolved around the sun, for those were the "happier" days when spiritual leaders ruled, and even kings took pains to measure their words.

The Star of Bethlehem is a Christmas fable that deserves no pseudo scientific prop. Let it go, dear Dr. K. Leave the tale for those who think like children. As your Bible says, it's time to think like a man.

# Close Encounters of the Surgical Kind
from MPLS/ST PAUL magazine

"Get that one!" I shout, pointing to a ragged stalactite hanging from the cavern's milk-white dome. As if in response, a stainless-steel tube angles upward, its Pac Man head devouring the triangle of tissue. Lowering its sights, it darts across the cavern's floor, snapping up shreds of raw, bacon-like debris. As it does, my wife and I lean closer to the television set, urging it on like frantic fans at a homecoming game; for the cavern lies inside my knee; the voracious little Pac Man is the star of the show, and the game is called "Arthroscopy."

My role began a year ago when, as the terror of the tennis courts, I attempted an Agassi, twisted my knee and, worse yet, played on, limping my way to the end of the set. I erred.

My doctor prescribed anti-inflammatories and TLC. When they failed, he suggested I contact Dr. C., who injected cortisone, providing a marvelous, short-term recovery, and then a relapse.

Dr C. then recommended surgery, the sort that uses a fiber optic light/lens (an arthroscope) inserted through a small incision to illuminate and video the interior of the joint while the Pac Man and his toothy friends tidy up my knee.

Though content with the advice of Dr. C., I consulted the real experts, my tennis friends, only to discover that most of them had already met the Pac Man and liked his work. Then came the jokes, usually about repairs to the wrong limb, or even the wrong patient.

My buddy, Bill, never one to take chances, claims that prior to surgery he wrote across his good knee, "Not this one, dummy!" Being less confrontational, I considered encasing my good knee in a stovepipe — no access, and no offense.

Two weeks later, I limp into Mercy Hospital, pondering the implications of its name (they showed mercy? — he begged for mercy?) and follow the signs to SHORT STAY SURGERY.

After donning paper slippers, a gorgeous pea-green gown slit from stem to stern, and a blue privacy robe, I am asked for the 43rd time, "And which knee are we working on today?"

"The left one," I reply, though the imp within me urges, "tell her the wrong one and watch her face."

She hands me a copy of "The Patient's Bill of Rights" (free speech while comatose), two patient education forms and a schedule called:

### Welcome to Short Stay Surgery
You will be called to the pre-surgical area at 8:30.
Your surgery is expected to start at 9:00.
You will arrive at Phase I recovery at approx. 10:30.
You will be expected in Phase II recovery at 11:30.
Your estimated discharge time is 12:30.

I'd been warned that the ghost of Henry Ford haunts the halls of short-stay surgeries. One of my tennis friends, Fred the Unrefined, calls them the equivalent of "Wham, Bam, Thank You, Sam." Fred, as usual, had it nailed, for the assembly line spirit prevails.

The beds in pre-surgery are lined up like race cars, four or five on either side of the room, all angled slightly toward the swinging doors. From my horizontal viewpoint, I study the driver to my left, a woman ten to 15 years older than I. She'll be no problem, but her bed looks fast. On my right is a young guy so ensnared by pre-op sedation (and his comely nurse) that he'll never see the starting lights.

The anesthetist strolls in, making small talk, and I wonder if he is embarrassed by the redundancy of his obligatory, "And which knee is it?"

"Still the left."

As he checks it off his chart, I grin foolishly at my sudden recollection of his profession's more descriptive name: gas passer.

He is followed by the affable Dr. C., who seems to have lost his chart.

"So, it's the right knee, is it?"

I stare at him briefly, wondering if he is serious, and conclude that he is.

"NO ... it's the LEFT!"

Suddenly I am moving, leaving the gal in the flashy bed behind as I accelerate through the doors.

The operating room is cool — deliberately chilled, they say, to retard the growth of bacteria. The real reason, however, is more apparent: they have sold tickets and the place is SRO.

Then, just as I am getting comfortable on the operating table and am about to toss a witticism to the crowd, the **GAS PASSER** pulls this dirty trick on me. No explanation, no warning, no counting down by sevens from one hundred and three. Suddenly— nothing.

I awaken in Phase One recovery feeling fully alert, but like a driver who suddenly finds himself 60 miles farther along the Interstate than he expected. "What the hell?" he thinks. "What happened to Hinckley?"

As my copy of the surgery video plainly shows, somewhere near Hinckley the Pac Man withdrew, surrendering his portal to a side-cutting Roto-Rooter, an expert at trimming the mohair cartilage that arthritis creates, and to a tiny lobster claw that snipped away an interfering plica, pronounced "pleeka," which is probably Latin for "something unexpected, but profitable."

Now, three months post Pac Man, I once again prowl the tennis courts and poach from my partner, who claims that Dr. C. did his job too well. I have paid all my bills, including the hospital's minutely detailed masterpiece that somehow missed "envelope — $16.48" and "First Class stamp — $10.89." The statement also contained a surprise — the source of the hospital's name, revealed when I reached the bottom line and heard myself cry for MERCY!

# The Dundee Enquirer: A Success Story

We've all rolled our eyes at those absurd-but-intriguing National Enquirer headlines while we shift from foot to foot in supermarket checkout lines. In fact, just a few months ago, I memorized a few while the customer ahead of me dreamed on until her groceries were totaled, and then began to dig for her checkbook in a handbag large enough to dwarf a Holstein's udder.

One journal proclaimed, "Sinead O'Connor Exposed as Cross-Dressing Priest." Another cried "Texas Woman Impregnated by Aliens Gives Birth to Titanium Baby," while a competing publication revealed, "Scientist Finds Cancer Cure in Toenail Clippings" and "Louisiana Man Loses 640 Pounds to Qualify for Olympics."

As the woman ahead of me probed, armpit deep, in her bag, I contemplated a headline for the next issue: "Frustrated Shopper Stabs Woman With Cold, Crisp Carrot in Supermarket Brawl." However, recalling my Humanist ethics, I switched to "Woman Accidentally Tumbles Into Giant Handbag Containing Black Hole."

As I pulled out of the parking lot, I reflected on the bias of the tabloids for "Alabama Man..." or "Texas Teen..." Granted, the South seems saturated with characters destined to appear in "News of the Weird," but to focus on them to the exclusion of mid-Westerners seemed not only elitist, but downright offensive.

Don't Iowans ever find little statues of St. Joseph holding tiny "Buy Me!" signs when they spade the corner garden of their newly-purchased home? Don't Minnesota men treasure forty-pound cysts that encapsulate the still-living goldfish they swallowed in 1962? And don't Wisconsin residents occasionally gasp in midnight surprise when they discover a fifty foot obelisk where the outhouse once stood? Of course they do!

By the time I turned into my driveway, I'd decided to introduce a competing tabloid to highlight the sparkling personalities of the upper Midwest, something with a name like The St. Paul Expose, The Des Moines Tattler or "Rochester Revelations." I considered, then rejected, The Grand Forks Gossip and The Madison Insider, finally settling on The Dundee Enquirer, what with Dundee, Minnesota — my tiny home town — being the cultural and intellectual center of the Upper Midwest. Besides, I'm fond of titles that are self-explanatory — like the UTNE Reader.

Because of my clever concept and the classy title, financing was a breeze, and the Dundee Enquirer hit the supermarkets before the month was out. (Only Bill Gates turned me down, and is he SORRY now!)

With eye-catching headlines like "Minnesota Timber Wolves Win a Game" and "Man-Eating Carp Sucks Fisherman to Death," every issue quickly sold out. We doubled our print run, then doubled again, and still sold every copy. Confronted with a shortage of the cheap paper that tabloids use, we began to maximize headlines and minimize text. Sales soared.

We cut text further, printing ever more issues with the same amount of stock — and sales continued to increase, with profits keeping pace. Finally, realizing that readers preferred headlines to text, we transformed the Enquirer into the mature publication it is today: All headlines — and not one word of bothersome text.

Printing costs fell, sales rose; profits increased, and along came problems. In setting aside increasingly large areas for stacks of the Enquirer, store managers began cutting into space once reserved for pickles, anchovies and greeting cards.

When narrow-minded shoppers complained, we countered by delivering the Enquirer at 1:00 a.m., assuming that aficionados would snap them up by dawn. We were right, but with extra clerks required for the midnight shift, managers began to howl.

Well, in just three months we'd made such a pile that we decided to drop retail sales and switch to mail order at 10 bucks an issue. Subscriptions went wild, confirming our hunch that folks only bought that boring stuff about Hugh Grant or Brittney Spears when they had nothing better to read.

However, just to be sure, we tried an issue featuring real hotshots like Sean Connery, Julia Roberts, Bernie Madoff and Senator Larry Craig, but it just wasn't us, and it bombed.

What was us was the latest on Evelyn Peeps, the scrappy octogenarian who staked a mining claim on the fifty yard line of the Metrodome, and the whiny, wealthy team owners who cry for public funds, but our record-setting issue was the one that disclosed the clandestine romance between Clay County hog farmer Erling Verdis and (you read it here first) Martha Stewart.

Being a sprinter instead of a marathon man, I eventually lost interest in the Enquirer, and put out the word I was ready to sell. After turning down that Gates guy (he'd had his chance), I made a deal with a bunch that has done very well with snippets and sound bites — a consortium of well-heeled neocons.

I'm happy to say that having plenty of money hasn't changed me. Knowing that the rich are often criticized for being tightfisted, I still send a fiver to the Red Cross at the end of every year. And to stay in touch with my humble past and the folks who brought me wealth, I sometimes stop at the supermarket to check out the competition while I quietly wait in line. In a sudden burst of pride, I nudge the customer ahead of me — who has finally found her checkbook. Smiling broadly, I point to the headlines and exclaim to the mystified woman, "Hey lady, ain't America great?"

**Notice:** Astute readers who would like to invest in original copies of a collector's edition of a facsimile of the Dundee Enquirer may send one hundred dollars per copy (cash only) and a stamped, self-addressed manila envelope to the Dundee Enquirer, Dundee, MN 56126. Hurry. Supplies are limited.

# Turn Your Radio On

Tucked away in a corner beneath a layer of dust, the old radio barely caught my eye, and I looked again more carefully to be sure of what I'd seen. But there it was, its big Z-for-Zenith pointer spanning a circular dial dimmed with grime. I wondered how long the 1930s radio had waited there, silent and unwanted on a paint-splattered chair in the Cobweb Antique Shop of Ely, Minnesota.

Its face proclaimed that it could call in short wave stations from around the globe, from the police, fire and aviation bands as well as the broadcast band, with push buttons for Midwest favorites like WGN, KOA, WCCO, KSTP and WDGY. And though its handsome walnut finish bore the scars and scratches of time, it looked just great to me.

I had been searching for just such a radio; one that could amplify the feeble emanations of Minneapolis' WCCO that barely reach our cabin in the Minnesota North, where modern radios with speedy transistors and ferrite antennas are worthless for 'CCO. But I was sure that the Zenith's seven, slow-to-warm tubes and its directional antennae could still snare the airwaves that once carried Cedric Adams and the news from Zanzibar.

The asking price was $45, so how could I go wrong? I agreed to the price if the radio worked, prepared to offer 30 bucks if it failed.

We plugged it in. The dial lit. The push buttons glowed. The hummer hummed, and I was like a kid — in love again. Soon WELY bathed us in music, but alas, no KSTP or 'CCO. However, having fallen in love, and knowing that Ely lies on the outer reaches of the communications galaxy, and that I could add another antennae, I bought Zelda, wrapped her in a blanket and drove home, humming old-time tunes for mile after mile.

Before the unveiling, I informed my wife that this was her birthday present, having learned that ploy from a milkshake-loving son who gave his mother a blender for Christmas.

That evening, I attached the external antenna, poured a small glass of Chardonnay and, with lights down low, flipped the switch and punched the button for 'CCO.

Wonderful! Good volume, no background noise and great clarity. Same for Denver, Yankton and Chicago. Then, not having heard a short wave station for years, I changed bands and slowly tuned across the dial.

Zzzzzeeeoowww—bbbbbbsttttttiiinnnggggee... announced today that her Royal Majesty will address the House of Lords on Decem... Eeeaaaarrrruupppsttt... must send your money now. Not just twenty dollars, not just fifty dollars, but a hundred or more, for God loves a... ttsssaaanggffffttttt... ahora los Estados Unidos es un... yyyowrowrowrowrowreeeepp... must get right with Jaysus NOW, NOW, N... a release from Reuters News Service quotes Yassi... eeeeeeeeeeeeeeeeeee... Trust me, right here in Revela... zzzzzzsssssssssppp... in dem finanziellen Markt die Mark... yyyeeeooowwwwrrr... en el nombre del Padre y del...

I almost gave up. Across much of the dial, religion rode high. Baited with warnings of dire consequences that would bring charges of extortion in other fields, Christian broadcasters had spread their nets across the airwaves. Like the drift nets of the Japanese, they ensnare those not strong enough to break free — fishing for souls and filleting their wallets.

I shouldn't have been surprised. Religious organizations began purchasing FM stations decades ago, so why should AM or short wave be spared?

Still, I persisted, and finally, amid the warblings of the ether goblins, soothing music broke through, lingering for half an hour before finally fading away.

For two more hours I traversed the dial, finding French, German and Spanish, and languages for which I had no name. But something had changed. Not the radio, and certainly not its yowls and hisses, or the science that makes it work. What had changed was the message. Where once the airwaves primarily entertained, informed and politely advertised, the message had shifted toward pressure to BUY, PLEDGE, JOIN, CONTRIBUTE, PAY, GIVE and TITHE.

Later that night I returned to 'CCO, where I briefly sampled a conservative talk show host called Dark Star, a name he richly deserves, although "black hole" or a "total eclipse" would be better. Disgusted and longing for the long lost, friendly voice of Cedric Adams, or the soothing tones of Franklin Hobbs, I finally drifted off between stations, lulled to sleep by the ether goblins' quiet whistles, squeals and beeps.

# Terracide and Mother Goose

In the youthful days of science fiction, one of its early masters (Heinlein, Bradbury or Asimov?) coined the word "terraforming" to describe the remaking of an asteroid or even a planet by carving and shaping its alien realities into an Earth-like world — a terrestrial twin. Now, centuries after Malthus' "Essay on the Principle of Population" and decades since Paul Ehrlich's "The Population Bomb," perhaps another new term is needed, a word to describe irresponsible acts that threaten the viability of the Earth and its life-sustaining biosphere.

We need a critical word, a word that condemns the continued release of chlorofluorocarbons, our profligate waste of energy, the removal of rainforests and mindless reproduction along with the religions that promote it. We need a word like TERRACIDE.

Unfortunately, too many people lack the good sense to perceive, or the integrity to admit, that limited resources require a limited population. This country is no longer empty, nor are others. The spaces that remain are largely desert, mountain or bog. Many farms are overworked and are losing soil to constant erosion.

We can no more grow apples in the Arctic, corn in the ocean or wheat in a rainforest than we can grow hair on a bowling ball. To fail to act on these realities is to continue down a disastrous path that will eventually change Cincinnati into Calcutta and bring Mexico City to Minneapolis.

Even Mother Goose knows better, telling of the "Old woman who lived in a shoe. She had so many children she didn't know what to do. She fed them some broth without any bread, then whipped them all round and sent them to bed." Compared to many today, her children were wealthy. They had broth AND a bed.

We live on our little island, relatively secure and comfortable, though muttering about any increase in crime, about rising welfare and unemployment costs, about cuts to education and libraries, and we've sat stunned before our TVs as we've watched hundreds of Mexican immigrants sprinting through traffic past helpless border guards.

If there was ever a country where religion had a chance, it was Mexico. There, in spite of its cruel past, Catholicism has become the equivalent of the state religion. And its fruits? Poverty, hunger, overcrowding and a future so bleak that many Mexicans will pay any price to leave it behind. They flee from a country where, for many, the only options are to endure, to reproduce or to run. So they flee to America and reproduce here, where things are not so bad — yet.

Beset by a flood of Russian Pentecostalists with double-digit families, all of them honoring the biblical command to "go forth and multiply," the Sacramento area now bears escalating welfare costs.

The days for this sort of reproduction are long gone. We need to acknowledge that those who continue are saying to us, "I want many children, and YOU are going to foot the bill."

Consider Sayed, an Egyptian from the pages of Tony Horowitz's *Baghdad Without a Map*, which describes the realities of life in Israel and in the Arab States.

In his crowded dwelling, Sayed spoke of his sister, "… still the most beautiful woman in Shubra. At twenty nine, she already has eleven children." Sayed reveals that his father married at age 11 and his mother "… bore her first child at 12, and twenty five years later went into the bathroom and gave birth to number *seventeen*." Thus, like some conservative Christians who breed with biblical zeal, convinced that God will provide, Horowitz's confidants continue to "muddle on as they have for millennia, muttering *'malesh'* (never mind) and gazing towards Mecca in prayer."

So what to do? For a start, get informed. Read. Check out the public television and network news. Use products that are environmentally safe. Minimize energy use. Examine the variety of Earth-sensitive organizations, join one and get involved. Support candidates who advocate choice, early sex education and birth control with contraceptives in the U.S. and abroad. Campaign against all who would continue the

Reagan-Bush policies against family planning, sex-education and birth control abroad. Write letters to your legislators and to newspapers at least once a month. Be critical of those who expect science to work miracles or believe that a few billion dollars can solve every ill.

To do less is to surrender to those who mutter *"malesh"* and rely on a god instead of learning and using new words — words like TERRACIDE.

# Manna From Heaven

I like short stories — perhaps because I'm not an excessively patient person. Consequently, I couldn't resist buying a copy of *Great Short Stories of the World* in a used book store I frequent. In it I found "The McWilliamses and The Burglar Alarm," by Mark Twain, a humorous tale showing that security has never been guaranteed and was a consideration even in the days of Twain. But the second story, "A Letter To God," written by an author unknown to me, impressed me as the epitome of a short story.

The author, one Gregorio Lopez Y Fuentes, began with images of a poor Mexican's parched corn fields thirsting for rain. On the horizon, dark clouds bloomed with promise. The rising wind brought a fine mist, then wonderful rain, then beautiful pearls of sleet and hail.

Within a few minutes, Lencho, the farmer, is transformed from someone who could provide for his family to a destitute man with no crop at all.

Lencho did not sleep at all that night, and in his agitation he eliminated all possibilities of hope except for an appeal to God, the God whose eyes see everything, "even what is deep in one's conscience."

Lencho began to write a letter, "a letter asking for one hundred pesos that he himself would carry to town and place in the mail. It was nothing less than a letter to God."

Lencho's letter amused the postal workers, but they later reflected on the simple faith that it represented. Lest the sender be disappointed, they decided to answer it. But, upon opening it, they found a need for "something more than goodwill, ink and paper."

In an act of charity, the postmaster donated a few pesos, as did other employees and a few of their friends. They sealed their pesos in an envelope and affixed the name, Lencho.

When Lencho returned to the post office to ask if there was a letter for him, he was not the least surprised to learn that there was, nor was he surprised to see that it contained a stack of peso notes. But his mood turned to anger when he counted the money. "God could not have made such a mistake ..." thought Lento.

Lencho went back to the post office window, requested a sheet of paper and an envelope, turned to the public writing table, wrote for a few minutes, slid the letter into the envelope, sealed and stamped it, and across its face he once again wrote "to God."

The moment the letter fell into the mailbox, the postmaster, who had been watching, ran to open it. It said: "God, of the money that I asked for, only seventy pesos reached me. Send me the rest, since I need it very much. But don't send it to me through the mail because the post office employees are a bunch of crooks. Lencho"

Lopez Y Fuentes' story appeals to me because of its three-page precision and its clever ending. But what attracts me most is its vivid portrayal of an old injustice: When charitable, humanistic acts support people in need, as when taxes are used to support Catholic Charities or Lutheran social services, religion gets the credit, but when things go wrong, secular society often gets the blame.

# Plates, Planes, Prayers & Pele

The Earth, the sphere on which we ride, is cracked like a giant eggshell. Between those cracks, the continental plates slowly slip, dip and hump their geologic version of a bump and grind. When examined every million years or so, as with time lapse photography, what was once undetectable becomes the casual dance of the continents.

Western California, beset by irreconcilable differences with the rest of North America, has filed for divorce, and is slipping off to the northwest along the San Andreas Fault. Given another ten to twenty million years, Los Angeles will cozy up to San Francisco and, as Jonathan Weiner predicted in "Planet Earth," that "the Giants and the Dodgers will again be cross-town rivals."

On the other side of the globe, the opposite occurs. India, once an island continent, continues to press against the belly of its lover, Eurasia, producing the earth's largest, longest and most indeterminate pregnancy — the bulging Himalayas.

The continental plates are made of lighter stuff than the semisolid mantle below. In that mantle, near the center of the great Pacific plate, lies one of the few active, longstanding features of the Earth: a tremendous plume of molten rock that is coursing upward to penetrate the slowly-moving crust, spewing fiery jets of lava across a span of thirty million years. Like a candle held beneath a moving sheet of paper, it torches through the drifting plate, building one island after another during times of high activity, and subsurface ridges during lows.

The youngest and southernmost of the island chain, the Big Island of Hawaii, rose above the ocean less than a million years ago. Farther north, and fully three million years its senior, Oahu calls to tourists with the beach at Waikiki and two famous craters called Punch Bowl and Diamond Head.

Beyond Midway Island, some two thousand miles northwest of the even older, dwindling island of Kauai, nature has reduced Hawaii's senior relatives to little more than reefs. Thus, the Hawaiian Islands line up as if for a family portrait, youngest to oldest, although in this family, size runs counter to age.

In January, 1983, following a silence of several years, the great molten plume burst free, sending waves of excitement through the crowds at the Big Island's Volcano National Park. In the Visitor Center, rangers explained that the southern flank of Kilauea had split, fountaining lava hundreds of feet skyward.

Fortunately, a park trail led to the top of an old volcanic ridge within eight miles of the eruption, which had already been named Pu'u O'o. (Pu'u is the Hawaiian word for "volcano," and the eruption began in the letter "O" on the Park Service map, hence "Pu'u O'o.")

That afternoon found me trudging across old, rippled layers of pahoehoe lava, heading toward the distant rise that would permit my first glimpse of an erupting volcano. Midway there, the trail wound between hollow columns of lava, formed when an ohia tree's sap hardened the passing flow as it drained off toward the sea. Some of those columns, contorted in an anthropomorphic way, seemed almost human, imaging the Hawaiian belief that those who offended Pele or violated the Hawaiian code of hospitality would be turned to stone.

Fearing that the eruption would stop before I topped the ridge, I panted up the long, steep slope toward those already above and cheering, then joined the gesturing, chattering crowd of ecstatic magma celebrants. Having regained my breath, I began to carefully photograph the spectacle, convinced that I would never again witness such a sight. Then, remembering the magic carpet that resides in my wallet — my pilot's license — I realized that the best might be yet to come.

That evening, I called the Hilo airport and reserved a plane for the following day, my last in the islands. Luck was with me, for by morning a rare offshore breeze had cleared Hilo's often weepy skies, and on the horizon, the eruption still flared.

In the next hours, I orbited Pu'u O'o as lava jetted from its massive throat seven hundred feet into the air, rocketing past the Cessna's wings as it cooled from rose to purple to grey.

Flying higher, I laid the Cessna on its side and aimed my camera into the giant's mouth. Turbulent air heated by the 2,500 degree, block-wide lava flow jarred the Cessna, blurring more than half of my photographs, even a few of those shot at a thousandth of a second. But what I recall most vividly is the roar and the chaos of glowing, leaping, liquid rock that exploded skyward, then thudded back into the radiant cauldron below.

As I flew over the glowing magma that spilled through a breach in the crater's wall, its heat needled me through the Plexiglas and the plane leaped higher, born aloft by expanding, sulfur-scented air. Finally, out of film and satiated, I rolled out of orbit and returned to Hilo. That evening, the eruption stopped, not to begin again until long after I'd left the islands. Later, a Hawaiian friend would tell me that I had flown with the fire goddess, Pele, and had ridden on her breath.

To the older Hawaiians, Pele was an 'aumakua, a lesser god. But because she has always been associated with Kilauea's persistent lava flows, Pele has survived.

In the 1950s, journalist Bob Krause received several reports of islanders who claimed to have picked up an old woman along the road. After climbing into the back seat, she asked for a cigarette. Receiving one, the smell of sulfur filled the air. Later, when the drivers looked back, they found an empty seat, and believed that Pele had been testing their hospitality. Having passed the test, they escaped the fate of those who failed — bad luck, or even death, like the petrified Hawaiians on the lava plain.

Nevertheless, in the way of all non-flesh, Pele is slipping from goddess to myth, as gods are prone to do. Even so, there was a time when she was strong, requiring offerings of 'ohelo berries, flowers and poi, ruling much of Hawaiian life with her rituals and taboos. Thus, early Hawaiians were impressed when the high priestess Kapi'olani converted to Christianity, traveled to Kilauea's rim and defied Pele. Conversions soared when she survived.

Protestant missionaries soon began to dominate Hawaiian life, even arranging the banning of Catholicism during the early 1800s, a prohibition ended by the French frigate L' Artemise, which blockaded

Honolulu. Undeterred by all the fuss, Pele rumbled on, ignoring wars and insurrections, and the Cessna I steered around her lava fountain as I wondered when, or if, her flows would reach the sea.

Over the next three years, Pele flared through the ohia forests, incinerating hapu ferns, consuming the homes of Royal Gardens and entombing fire hydrants and traffic signs that vainly ordered, "STOP." Nearing the ocean, she torched the asphalt of the Chain of Craters road and descended towards a village known as Kalapana.

Kalapana had been threatened many times, but Pele had never touched the town. Accustomed to such deference, Kalapana residents remained confident that their stunning, black sand beach and two historic churches would again be spared. However, as the lava inched closer, the members of the Congregational church yielded to reality, removed whatever they could and left. The Catholics delayed, praying that their church would be spared, and that this flow, too, would pass them by.

I returned to the Big Island a few years later, having heard that the village of Kalapana was gone, and with it, the Congregational church. I had read that a new lava plain had obliterated the black sand beach, although the flows had spawned new beaches farther up and down the coast. But I was curious about the Catholic church and, as I prefer to portray it, "the prayers vs. Pele affair."

As I drove through Keaau and the ramshackle village of Pahoa, I wondered what I would find — a triumphant church, untouched, or a church in ashes. I found neither, for when I turned at the Y to Kalapana, I discovered the Catholic church a mile or two from its former home, standing beside the road on five-foot stilts.

They were right. The flames had failed to touch it. Sensing danger, the church had sprouted legs and hobbled uphill, where it now rests, having sensibly decided to retain its legs in the event of another flow.

Meanwhile, Pele's lava still explodes into steam and jet black sand where once stood Kalapana — and she's found an alternate route. In a flanking attack, she is bursting through the ocean floor just twenty miles to the south. Loihi, the someday island, is already 13,000 feet above the ocean's floor, with only 3,000 more to go before she breaches the foam and breathes Pacific air.

When Loihi has cooled, I wonder what sort of humans will climb her slopes. Will they be burdened with dogmas that claim to own the ultimate truths, though the fruits of these dogmas are overcrowding, starvation, intolerance and war? Will Hindu, Muslim, Christian and Jewish fanatics still talk of "holy" wars and jihads? Will religious zealots still stroll away from bomb-laden vehicles, firebomb Planned Parenthood clinics, and substitute prayer for medical care for their diseased and dying children?

Perhaps their leaders will mellow, finally embracing the values of love, tolerance and peace that often touch their lips but so rarely touch their hearts.

While we wait, cultures, like islands, will rise and fall. The continental plates will still be dancing, but when people come to orbit Pele's child, as I once circled Pu'u O'o, will some still be asking their god to stay the course of nature? Will some hear still Pele's sighs?

# George Carlin and the Fetus Lovers

Remember George Carlin, the scrawny, talented humorist who made people laugh for forty years? Some of us remember George from his hilarious critiques of the English language on the Ed Sullivan and Johnnie Carson shows. George, however, limited his popularity by his willingness to include words that many found just a little too crude.

Consequently, I was once surprised to see George Carlin performing on the Mister Rogers show in the role of a gentle, mild-mannered train conductor. George, as expected, did an excellent job, leaving me wondering if George might have mellowed. Not two days later, I came upon an HBO program featuring one of George's many comedy club performances — and George had not mellowed.

George, who had no use for religion, first took on the pro-lifers: "When Cardinal O'Connor has had a few periods, labor pains, several kids and is pregnant again, I'll be glad to hear what he has to say about abortion ... These pro-lifers and conservatives enamored with the UNBORN are obsessed with the fetus from conception 'til nine months. But once you're born, you're on your own! No prenatal care. No neonatal care. No pregnancy leave. No preschool. No head start. No school lunch. No food stamps. No welfare. No nothing. If you're preborn, you're wonderful; if you're preschool you're "screwed!" (George chose a different word.) "They'll do anything to save a fetus, but if it grows up to be a doctor, they just might have to kill it."

George then puzzles over the fact that "Catholics and other Christians who are against abortions also oppose homosexuals — and who has fewer abortions than homosexuals?"

Switching to crime, George has a few practical, and typically Carlinesque, suggestions: "For violent criminals, we'll empty out the whole state of Kansas, giving everyone maybe $200 for their inconvenience. Then we'll build a big wall around it and toss in the crooks. No food, no fuel — just lots of guns and ammunition so they can communicate in a meaningful way."

George notes that "If we outlawed religion, most of the sex crimes would disappear in a couple of generations, but we don't have time for rational solutions. So we fence off Wyoming and toss all the perverts and child molesters in there." (George prefers rectangular states as they can be more easily and economically fenced than states like Maryland or Kentucky.)

Carlin died in 2008. I can picture him seated at the right hand of God, regaling him with hilarious, knee-slapping stories while Billy Graham, Robertson, Swaggart, Hinn and Falwell, plus a string of popes and all of the other sour-faced snake oil salesmen are forced to wait in the wings. Quite a philosopher, that Carlin.

# The Performance

AS THE ASSEMBLED MULTITUDES APPLAUD, THE MAESTRO STRIDES ACROSS THE STAGE, ADJUSTS THE ELEVATION OF HIS LUSHLY-PADDED CHAIR, SEATS HIMSELF AND FLEXES HIS FINGERS IN A GRACEFUL GESTURE OF AGILITY AND POWER. HIS RIGHT HAND RISES, THEN FLASHES DOWNWARD TO ACTIVATE THE "ON" SWITCH OF THE MASSIVE AND POWERFUL IBM PC JR, FOLLOWED BY A NEARLY INVISIBLE FLICK OF THE LEFT POINTER FINGER, CAUSING THE MONITOR TO SPRING TO LIFE.

THE CROWD TENSES, EMOTIONS BUILDING AS THE ACs RIPPLE THROUGH THE GIANT MAINFRAME, THE RECTIFIER RECTIFIES AND THE NEWLY TRANSMORGIFIED DCs BURST FORTH.

THE MAESTRO, EVER THE CUNNING AND SKILLFUL SHOWMAN, ALLOWS ONE HAND TO DRIFT SUGGESTIVELY IN THE DIRECTION OF THE PRINTER. THE CROWD GASPS — WOULD HE? COULD HE? NOT SO SOON! BUT HE WITHDRAWS HIS HAND. HE IS TOYING WITH THEM, KNOWING THAT HE WILL RESERVE HIS PRINTER VIRTUOSITY FOR THE FINAL MOVEMENT, THE FAMOUS PRESTISSIMO CON BRIO.

HE LEANS OVER THE KEYBOARD, CONCENTRATING AND GATHERING ENERGY. THE LEFT HAND RISES, THEN GENTLY FLOATS DOWN TO THE KEYS — AND THE PERFORMANCE BEGINS:

Dear All,

As you know, the Chinese have the "Year of the Dragon," or the monkey or the lizard. Pretty soon they will work their way down to the year of Jimmy Swaggart, Benny Hinn or Glen Beck, but that is sinking pretty low.

At any rate, we Americans, with our short attention spans, cannot devote a whole year to anything, our longest possible period of dedication being one week. And recently out here in a rural corner of the great Midwest, we endured THE WEEK OF THE SEWER.

It began with a slight congestion of the basement floor drain, causing minor, though alarming regurgitations from the floor trap. Armed with a primitive device that is aptly called a snake, I advanced upon the floor drain, having become a basement [not closet] proctologist, and proceeded to give her the old "reameroo."

Preferring to use the clockwise twist, I advanced el snako steadily, first 10 feet, then past the sewer vent stack, then 20 feet. At 30 feet I calculated that said snake was now screwing around in the septic tank, but my drain was still plugged. Therefore the "estoppage" — a touch of elegance there — must lie somewhere in the 70 feet of overflow tile that led from the septic tank to its outlet on a nearby slope.

When the snake and I rappelled down the embankment, we found the end of the six-inch tile wide open, but no evidence of fluids. The snake, however, found an interesting blockage about 18 feet in. A woodchuck had apparently explored the drain, and, finding a break in the tile, had made a nice hacienda beside the fracture. Being a discriminating ground hog he decided to block off the odors emanating from the septic tank, so he plugged it up, using paper torn from bundles of shingles I had stored on our back porch, plus lots of dirt and scraps of black plastic which he probably made in his lab. This I could not breach, so I call the pros, who brought beefy equipment.

Mightily, and briefly, did they ream, and the waters came forth, and they flowed for 40 seconds and 40 more. Then they ceased and I was happy, for once again mine flusher flushed and mine effluent flowed. (And compared to me, my wife was ecstatic!) I then jammed chicken wire into the drain to circumvent further home building within it. We slept well that night.

Twenty four hours later the estoppage did return, but the lakeside chicken wire remained undisturbed. This time the problem was apparently between the basement and the tank, so I returned to the floor drain with Sam the snake. Unfortunately poor Sam, while going down the tube, both literally and figuratively, had accumulated several displaced vertebrae, which made him cranky and less effective. At any rate we didst persevere and after an hour of delightful diversion didst clear el plugo. We slept well that night.

Twenty four hours later the wind did shift and the house began to stink as it had done on other occasions and we concluded that the sewer stack that travels from basement to roof must have a defect where it passed through the wall between the bathroom and our bedroom closet. This being the Week of the Sewer, I purchased twenty feet of plastic sewer vent pipe, intending to use it as a liner inside the larger cast iron stack.

From atop the roof, a very steep roof, I might add, I fed the plastic pipe downward inside the old pipe. I had planned to stop it just above the entry of the "water closet" effluent into the stack so that it wouldn't obstruct the flow that issues therefrom. However, the old cast iron stack was far from straight, and the plastic pipe would not flex enough to navigate the slightly angled joints. In addition, the pipe was filled with corrosion and scale, so that, even if it were straight, the new pipe could not have passed through.

The vent pipe was too heavy to lift out through its hole in the roof, so I decided to break it about a foot above the basement floor. Fortunately, cast iron is brittle, so I detached the first floor toilet (our unfinished basement ceiling granted easy access) and out came the sledgehammer. Working from the bottom, I smashed the cast iron piece by piece as it descended from the heights into the basement.

When done, I fed the plastic pipe through the hole in the roof, reconnected the toilet and inserted the bottom end into the cast iron fitting that protruded from the basement floor, then sealed the two together in an everlasting embrace with silicone sealer and a sense of relief, and told my wife she could "let 'er rip."

Our home no longer had B.O. We both slept well that night.

On Sunday, a cold rainy day, we decided to celebrate the end of the Week of the Sewer with a trip to the big city of Sioux Falls, but as we passed the scenic penitentiary, the Reliant began to falter and didst finally expire, coasting to a stop within fifty feet of the Eternal Rest Monument

Center — General Motors Only. We had entered the Week of the Automobile.

We didst crank so hard as to turn the key four times around in the socket to no avail. We didst wait for 15 minutes and tried again and lo and behold, the Reliant did finally rely. We proceeded another 10 blocks, where the Reliant did expire for good at the stoplight on 10th and Main — in the rain. My dear wife didst steer the auto as I pushed it through the intersection to a service station, where I determined that the defiant Reliant had an abundance of vital fluids, but there was no spark to be found, and darkness prevailed upon the interior of the cylinders. Being Sunday, there were no mechanics about, so we pushed the Reliant to the Dodge dealer with an Avis rental car and drove the rental home.

The Reliant is now repaired — bad coil. Sally took back the Avis and returned with the Reliant — probably disappointed that it wasn't the camshaft. (She always says, "It's the camshaft.") Love, Pop

THE MAESTRO RISES FROM HIS SEAT, BOWING AGAIN AND AGAIN AS THE WAVES OF APPLAUSE ROAR THROUGH HIS EARS, MAKING LITTLE FLAKES OF WAX DROP TO THE BOTTOM OF HIS EAR CANALS, TICKLING AS THEY FALL.

"YES, APPLAUD ME, YOU PEASANTS," HE THINKS, "BUT IT'S MONEY I WANT."

"I'LL FIX THEM! I'LL SEND THE WHOLE PERFORMACE SINGLE SPACED." AND WITH A SWEEP OF HIS IRIDESCENT CAPE, HE LIGHTLY TOUCHES "SEND," THEN TURNS AND STRIDES FROM THE STAGE.

# Off With Their Heads?

Lewis Carroll's Queen of Hearts would have objected to the question mark at the end of my title, preferring instead a series of exclamation points. But despite the fact that the Queen sought capital punishment, and I occasionally agree with her, the question mark must remain.

Society has long argued that punishments should fit the crime. Even the illustrious team of Gilbert and Sullivan echoed that sentiment in the "Mikado," a spoof set in early 20th century Japan. In one of its famous passages, the Emperor sings "My object all sublime I shall achieve in time, to let the punishment fit the crime, the punishment fit the crime!" And so, in the Mikado, a billiards hustler is condemned to play "On a cloth untrue with a twisted cue and elliptical billiard balls."

It would seem, therefore, that in cases of murder, Gilbert and Sullivan might sing along with "an eye for an eye" or "a life for a life." But if you know your "Mikado," you'll recall the Emperor's earlier, catch 22 decree that a person "Cannot cut off another's head until he's cut his own off."

The Queen of Hearts and Gilbert and Sullivan represent the capital punishment dilemma within the United States, where proponents and opponents each claim the majority, each citing polls that use different methods and timing. Taken during the height of a crime wave, it's often "thumbs up" for a lethal injection, but a few months later, sentiments swing toward, "Aw, what the hell."

In the United States, the death penalty is reserved primarily for premeditated murders, such as murder for profit, multiple murders, or murder to silence witnesses. Some view the decline in executions (in early Virginia the death penalty even applied to those who stole grapes or disbelieved in God) as a tacit admission that the death penalty is immoral. Others counter that past overuse of the penalty argues not for its elimination, but only for a reduction.

Death penalty arguments usually focus on six areas:

1. Incapacitation: An executed murderer will never commit another crime. Society has a right to rid itself of deadly individuals, just as we seek out and destroy our own cells when they turn malignant. In that light, failing to eliminate murderers would seem irrational. However, if the convict is innocent, another crime will occur.

2. Deterrence: Proponents argue that murderers should not be allowed to outlive their victims, and that in the absence of the death penalty we are telling prospective murderers, "Don't worry, no matter how many you torture or kill, YOUR life will be spared." Opponents claim that death penalties deter no one; that those intent on murder are either too driven or too deranged to consider the consequences, while others are convinced they will never be caught. Nevertheless, there are occasional admissions that the existence of a death penalty prevented an assault or robbery from escalating into a murder, which leads many to ask: If the death penalty deters even a few cases, why not keep it on the books?

3. Retribution or revenge: Although retribution is of limited importance to society as a whole, in many cases, it can play a large part in allowing a victim's friends and relatives to make peace with their loss. Whether retribution should provide such a release is debatable, but the fact remains that, for many, it does.

4. Constitutional: Some assert that the death penalty constitutes a cruel and unusual punishment that is unconstitutional and inhumane. Others ask, "Is it not equally cruel to cage a person for the rest of their life?" In fact, a few prisoners, faced with that question, have demanded execution rather than face a life behind bars. Some commit suicide. Proponents will argue that murderers have shed their humanity, becoming beasts, and that

in regretfully killing a killer, society reaffirms the value of the victim. Nevertheless, most of those who have attended an execution or have read detailed accounts of executions by gas, hanging or electrocution will confirm that the process is often revolting — a fact now rendered moot by the introduction of painless, rapid-acting lethal injections.

5. Equality before the law: Opponents claim that the death penalty is used far more frequently against nonwhites, yet a study by L.W. Johnson, using Department of Justice statistics, reveals that although whites commit less than 40% of homicides, they represent more than half of the inmates on death row. What seems beyond dispute, however, is that capital punishment has often come to mean that those without the capital get the punishment. With the advantage of wealth, the sky is the limit, while others quickly exhaust their funds, and are forced to manage with court-appointed attorneys who operate on a limited budget and whose experience and interest in capital cases may be close to nil.

6. Cost factors: Execution advocates claim enormous savings compared to the expense of housing convicts for the rest of their lives. That may be, but it has little to do with the ethics of whether execution is appropriate punishment. An offsetting factor is that death penalties tend to generate more appeals and legal costs than life sentences. For example, one capital case underwent twenty court reviews, reached the Supreme Court four times, and involved 118 state and federal judges over a period of ten years.

Having reviewed the arguments, we now need to drill down to the "nitty gritty," a favorite phrase of Ross Perot. We need to decide how our philosophy informs our opinion. Assuming that we agree that the death penalty should be severely restricted, let's look at a few cases where I think it still should apply.

Consider Dan White, who murdered San Francisco Mayor George Moscone and then sought out and killed town supervisor Harvey Milk. Dan White, an overtly Christian, Caucasian male, escaped with a manslaughter conviction and was paroled after five and one-half years, despite convincing evidence of premeditation. His sentence is an example of unequal, inappropriate justice and an insult to society and the survivors. Mr. White later passed the appropriate sentence on himself and committed suicide.

Consider the physician who tortured his wife with unspeakable brutality, using acids and other atrocious means. She was left crippled, blind and deaf, barely able to speak or swallow, pleading to be helped to die. Modern medicine couldn't help her, and society allowed her murderer to continue his life on Earth. Should he have received a death sentence? Yes! Am I wrong? Maybe.

Consider the Chicago man who hired two thugs to rape and murder his wife so that he could use her insurance money to buy a motorcycle. He plea bargained down to a lesser charge, receiving life in prison, but many life sentences are later reduced. Should he have been executed? Why not?

Finally, I bring you two North Carolina men who went hunting. When they were unable to find anything to shoot, "not even a dog or a cow," they decided to kill a black person, which they did. Should they have been executed? Yes! Were they? No.

The sentencing of criminals deserves our close attention, but by focusing on the weeds, we often neglect the lawn. In my view, those who favor broad use of the death penalty are like doctors who prefer the certainty of amputation, claiming that corrective surgery, antibiotics, immunization and good nutrition are not 100% effective.

Instead, we need to prevent crime by reducing poverty and ignorance. We need family planning agencies that are not crippled with gag rules and restrictions engineered by the extremists of the religious right. We need economic opportunity to eliminate despair and to provide the hope of success. We need rich Americans to financially support the country and the people who made them wealthy, to turn from amassing greater fortunes in offshore bank accounts to helping others build better lives. We need Americans who love their country more than they love their things.

As for enforcement, we need an ample, well-trained, <u>responsible</u> police forces. We need more public and private support of civil liberties unions. We need prosecutors who seek the maximum <u>provable</u>

indictment and who turn to plea bargaining only as a last resort. We need to (gasp) "socialize" law so that all defendants receive equal representation, sentencing and accommodations — no country club jails for the rich. We need court records to be available to those who determine verdicts and sentencing. We need mandatory sentences for specified crimes when prior convictions for violent crimes exist. We need to be less lenient on those who claim mitigation due to drug or alcohol use.

When education and social equity improve, perhaps there will be no need for capital punishment. But in the meantime, as we send soldiers off to murder and die in undeclared wars that are waged for economic gain or political advantage, many will continue to wonder why their deaths are lauded, while the execution of a tried and convicted murderer is not. As a consequence, in our less than perfect world, I reluctantly support <u>tightly restricted, and racially unbiased</u> use of the death penalty. Yet, because of my high regard for the many civil libertarians who dispute me, and my distaste at being in the company of the Queen of Hearts and "leaders" like G. W. Bush, I hope someone proves me wrong.

# Gods Made to Order

First came designer jeans — fashion products aimed at the super-svelte and at those who believe that wearing a fancy label lifts them up the ladder of style and appeal.

Not long after came designer genes — products of science that not only can prevent certain birth defects, but have the potential to fulfill the Army's promise to help us "be all that we can be." If genetic engineering were allowed to proceed rationally, unencumbered by religious reactionaries who fear to intrude on what they perceive as their God's turf, humanity could make great strides. Within a century humans could finally become "healthy, wealthy and wise," having genetically remodeled the genes that had endangered health, undermined intelligence and promoted aggression.

Perhaps to achieve that goal we need a new version of an old story: designer gods, for we humans have always invented gods — usually in our own image: Women invent goddesses — men invent gods. Furthermore, all gods mirror those who made them, women's gods being more benign and men's gods more aggressive. With male gods having been dominant for the last two millennia, it is not surprising that times have been brutal, Christianity having provided the bloody Crusades and the Inquisition, both of which enriched the Roman Catholic Church. Catholics and Protestants then dreamed up the witch hunts, while in later years Christian dogma provided the motivation for the Holocaust, Apartheid, Slavery, the Klu Klux Klan, James Jones' Jonestown massacre, David Koresh's Waco wackos and paramilitary zealots who operate Bible-based militias.

In making our new god we must first acknowledge that WE are creating IT, thereby intercepting those who would assert that the reverse is true. Our second step would grant the god certain attributes, and though our preferences would undoubtedly differ, my god would promote intellectual inquiry, education, personal responsibility, tolerance, good humor and situation ethics. (In order to avoid lying, would you reveal Salman Rushdie's whereabouts to the ayatollahs if you knew where he lived and were asked?)

In churches led by religious moderates and humanistic liberals, the Christian god, with its traditionally violent, aggressive and acquisitive nature, is being slowly moderated by the gene therapy of applied humanism. Given enough time, there is hope that even the Roman Catholic and fundamentalist churches will shed their dragon skins, abandon their quest for power and evolve toward higher, less self-centered ethics.

What humanity could become without the hindrance of primitive religion was once well illustrated in a cartoon from the now defunct English humor magazine, *Punch*. The cartoon depicted a corpulent English gentleman peering over a fence at a fine healthy bull. The Englishman, bursting with admiration, says to the bull, "My, what a magnificent creature you are!" The bull replies, "And you would you be too, had your ancestors been as carefully selected as mine."

In short, it's all in the genes. Will the "gods" we create lead us to use genetic engineering to rid ourselves of disease and disabilities or should our futures be guided by reactionary religionists who would leave it all to chance?

# Georgia On My Mind

from *True North: Exploring the Great Wilderness by Bush Plane*

Canada, like most countries, has many towns that are named for individuals: Churchill, Gillam, Thompson, and so on. My favorite place names, however, are those that spring from optimism. Some, like Fort Enterprise, Fort Reliance, Fort Confidence and Resolute, ring of determination. When optimism waned, Fort Good Hope and the Bay of God's Mercy showed up on the map, while those beset with troubles left behind Dismal Lake, Repulse Bay and the Funeral Range. Today, however, a more prosaic name confronts me, for Fort Smith, which lies dead ahead, will be my first stop.

As I taxi up to Fort Smith's Loon Air docks, a Beaver pulls away from the pumps. I'm still long on fuel, but I need to add oil, and I want to call my wife. Having passed up the radio telephone at Reliance in my rush to depart, I have not spoken to her since I called from Baker Lake.

Peace River, my next stop, is only four hours away, so I empty my gas bags into the mains while Scott adds a liter of oil. Knowing I'm American by the Cub's registration numbers (Canadian aircraft use letters), he asks where I've come from. When I explain he erupts: "My God, man, that's fantastic."

He slides a hand along the Cub's cowling. "I tell you," he says, "Someday I'm going to buy one of these little beauties. I'll take off for two weeks straight — no, I'll take three — and see the country. God! I'd give anything to go along with you."

Laughing, I say, "I don't want to hurt your feelings, but a nice-looking gal back at Red Lake said those exact words, and I passed her up, so you know what the odds are for you."

As Scott fills out the charge slip, I ask if I can make a credit card call. "Sure," he replies. "Just go through that door and down the hall. The phone's in the first room on your left — under Georgia."

"Come again?"

"On your left under Georgia."

Figuring that they have a wall map of the United States over the pay phone, I head for the office, where I discover that Georgia is a gorgeous Playboy centerfold. "Wow!" I exclaim to the grinning clerk who's watching me, for I can't be the first to be stopped in his tracks by this eye-popping Georgia peach.

I stare at her. A bath towel V's suggestively upward from between two perfect legs to end conveniently an inch below her breasts. Her hazel-eyed gaze is direct and slightly inviting. She's stunning — a modern Rubens or Venus without the fat.

"Think you're man enough for her?" asks the grinning clerk as he eyes my graying hair.

"Sure am," I reply, and as my eyes sweep Georgia's curves, I tell him about the elderly gent whose friends expressed concern that bedding his bride of twenty-eight might become too much of a strain. "What the hell," he replied, "If she dies, she dies!"

While Georgia watches and the clerk listens, I try to call my wife. But the operator claims ignorance of my long distance phone company, and I'm forced to call collect.

"Hi, it's me," I say, forgetting that the operator has already told her. "I'm in Fort Smith."

"Where's that?"

"Northern Alberta," I respond, deliberately turning my back to Georgia, for I'm uncomfortable talking with my wife while my eyes cruise Georgia's curves.

"I thought you were going to Yellowknife," she says.

"Well, the weather forced a change of plans, so I'll probably stop there on the way back. I should reach Peace River today and Fort St. John — that's in British Columbia — tomorrow. You getting along OK?"

"Oh sure. You too?"

"I'm fine. Beautiful country north of here, you know."

"I suppose."

I pause, trying to think of something that might interest her, but she's heard it all before. Though our worlds intersect in many rewarding ways, flying isn't one of them, and as our conversation dwindles, I decide that the clerk and Georgia must think that I'm terribly dull.

"Well, I'd better be going. I'll call from Fort St. John."

"OK. Take care. Goodbye."

"Miss you," I quickly add, telling myself that I am sincere and not just responding to Georgia's scenery. I wait for a response, but my wife is gone.

When I return to the Cub, a smiling Scott asks, "Did you find the phone?"

"Sure did," I reply. "I bet you have guys flying a hundred miles out of their way just to use that phone."

"Wouldn't be surprised," he says.

As I wipe a smudge from the Cub's yellow cowling, I think of Jim Kimball, my friend who fished for grayling in the fog at Baker Lake. After watching Wes and me fuss over our Pipers day after day, he claimed that pilots' wives have a right to be jealous of the attention we heap on our planes.

"Think about it. You treat them like lovers, touching them, adjusting and loooobricating them," he said, drawing out the word with a leer. "You fuel them, polish them and fly off together, then do it again and again."

At the time I thought that Jim was either a little nuts or that he'd been away from home too long. But as I slide a hand along the Cub's rounded cowl and strap her idling, vibrating frame to my body, I wonder if maybe Jim wasn't right, and I'm the one who's been gone too long.

# Stayin' Alive!

Every February, when winter is half over and a dozen or more pilots have converted their airplanes to scrap, aviation magazines begin to feature articles with "catchy" titles like "Winter Flying," or titles that reveal the obvious, like "It's Cold Out There." The truth is that these articles are written by self-styled experts who drone on about the hazards of snow-covered wings, frosty runways and water in your fuel while they slurp pina coladas in the balmy Bahamas.

Those of us who fly the northern Minnesota bush know these writers for what they are — tender souls who avoid flying on frigid 50 degree days because it's so difficult to enter waypoints while wearing electrically heated gloves. And so, to counter the unbelievably bad advice that these dilettantes dispense, my friend Hugo and I now offer a few of the useful techniques that we've learned in these northern climes.

First of all, the ice-on-the-wing experts only confuse the issue with their incessant chatter about lift and drag and blah, blah, blah. Sure, ice isn't good, but it really isn't a worry unless it gets pretty thick, which is why the guys who flew the Gooney Birds over the Hump during the Big One waited a while to inflate their wings' leading edge boots. Thick ice cracked and fell away, but thin ice just hung in there. So if you find your plane covered with light ice, don't sweat it unless you're at least 20% over gross. After all, it might be warmer aloft, where nature can melt it way. If the ice gets too thick after takeoff, just land (which is easy with all of that ice) and remove it — which leads to the next topic.

Here in northern Minnesota, the bush flying center of the universe, (Alaska doesn't count because it's just a U.S. colony populated mostly by demented former Minnesotans) we can't afford to flood our wings with expensive deicing stuff like the airlines do, so we use the next best thing — a hammer — the heft of the hammer being determined by the thickness of the ice.

For light ice, a tack hammer works quite well, but for serious ice, a ball peen's just the thing. As for the dents you create, consider the fact that foolish aircraft owners are paying thousands to have vortex generators installed on their wings despite the fact that dents do just as well. A good row of properly placed dents can suck that boundary layer down so tight that your bird won't want to quit flying. Be warned, however, that unless you enjoy flying with a heap of aileron and rudder or want to fly in circles, you should keep your wings equally dented because a well-dented wing creates heaps of lift.

Hugo, the optimist, always parks his airplane facing east in the hope that the sun will melt a handy little window in the windshield ice. But up here, the January sun is too feeble to melt snow, let alone ice, which means that you have to look for the hammer again.

The Bahama boys also make a big deal about covering up the pitot tube, which is a word I hate because when people ask "What's that thing?" I always have to tell them three times, and even then they don't believe me. The way I look at it, if you really need some tubey thing to tell you how fast you are going, you shouldn't be flying, so park it and take a bus!

As for snow on the wings, we say leave it there and give it a try. Every year guys die of heart attacks while clearing their roofs of snow, and a wing is just a smaller roof — so why risk it? Runways these days are plenty long, and most of the snow will blow off anyway. Just remember that if it blows clear off one wing and not the other, you just might go inverted, but what's life without a thrill now and then. Besides, decent pilots should be able to fly their birds with a little snow — even when over gross. That Max Conrad guy flew all over the world while way over gross, so what's a little snow? And if it's just you and your sweetie in the old Cherokee, you're light, so you don't need all that wing anyway.

I hate to admit it, but I agree with the guys who say we should remove the wheel pants — but for a different reason. They worry that they'll fill up with slush and freeze. Well, so what? It sure improves the braking! I look at it this way: Without the wheel pants a 180 is a proud, nose-in-the-air workhorse, but in panties she's a gussied up debutante waiting for the ball. So I say take the pants off and leave 'em home.

For those who fly with skis, one humorist suggested placing garbage bags under the skis to prevent them freezing down. The Hefty bag people will love that one! Tell me — how do you taxi onto a garbage bag without blowing it away, or how do you push a floppy bag beneath the ski? Better to carry a kid's plastic roll-up toboggan that's been cut in half lengthways. Just lift the front of the ski and slide it underneath. You'll stop most of the ski from freezing down and the rest won't matter. On ice, do the same thing but shove in a stick, which you can leave behind. There's no shortage of sticks and they're biodegradable.

One genius said we should loosen our control cables because the cold weather makes them shorter. Well, I tried that one year, but although the airplane shrinks, so do the cables. (On a really cold night up here, a 4-seat 172 can turn into a 2-seat 150.)

Then there's this silly talk about batteries. In the good old days, real aviators knew how to swing a prop, and airplanes didn't need batteries. The battery people won't admit this, but even the "cheapest" (ha!) are meant to last twenty years, so that battery stuff is a lot of hooey. Besides, since someone invented external power plugs, we can jump-start our birds, which adds years of battery life.

They say it's a good practice to check braking action during the run up, the idea being that if the plane moves despite heavy braking, guess what — it's slippery. However, according to my mechanic, engines that can't drag their planes across bare cement need to be overhauled, which explains why he gets to write articles about pre-heating from Palm Beach, and I stay in Minnesota.

So what about tying your aircraft down on one of our deeply frozen lakes? When you land on the ice at Walker to wet a line at the Leech Lake Eelpout Festival, you can secure your plane by freezing short lengths of chain in the ice. Just be sure to leave your tie downs a little slack unless you want to share the fate of my buddy Hugo, who ties his plane nice and tight. During the night, a warm front began to expand the lake's ten mile-wide lens of ice. The expanding ice had nowhere to go but up or down, which it did by creating a two-foot pressure ridge directly beneath Hugo's tightly secured Champ. The wings bowed and the struts collapsed as Hugo's pride and joy gave sad new meaning to "negative dihedral."

According to the palm tree crowd, the two most serious winter concerns are water in the gas and weather. This makes no sense. If it gets cold enough, water in your tanks will turn to ice, which can't go anywhere. Furthermore, as long as your engine is running there's plenty of heat to melt any ice inside the cowling, and even a sick engine can suck water through in a flash. Besides, an engine that coughs now and then keeps your passengers entertained.

My advice on weather is simple. If your winter weather gets anything like ours in Minnesota, there will be times when you'll look out the window and think: This weather really sucks! Well, that's the time to get going, because if you wait too long, it'll surely get worse.

It's hard to believe, but up here we lose more pilots to a dangerous condition called CAVU (a no-weather condition that happens maybe two days a year) than we do to running scud. On CAVU days, wise pilots hug their dear ones, have a beverage or two and polish their planes while neophytes take to the air. Unlimited by the usual stratus, they climb higher and higher, enthralled by the endless view.

Some might think that pilots like us who live in the center of the continent would be acclimated to height, but except for a few wrinkles near the Canadian border, we're as flat as Florida, and not much higher. As a consequence, these high flying beginners quickly become anoxic. Their thinking gets fuzzy. Illusions arrive. "By God," they say, "I can see the Hawaiian Islands! Perhaps I should fly to Japan!" Ensnared by the rapture of the heights, they fall asleep; they spiral down. The lucky ones, guys like Hugo and me, awaken just in time to survive, duty bound to tell young pilots to avoid the dangerous, deadly blue skies.

There's a lot more we could tell you, but by now you've figured that out, which is why it's unnecessary for that Keillor fellow to keep reminding the world that up here the women are strong, the men are handsome, and all of the pilots are above average — except for Hugo, who went flying this morning, and is, for some reason (again) overdue.

See you at the Eelpout Festival!

# Blind to a World of Wonder

When I was the educational vice president of a Toastmasters Club, an organization designed to enhance public speaking skills and reduce stage fright, our members' most common complaint was that they couldn't think of anything to talk about. This amazed me, and because I always had a surplus of subjects, I offered to give each member a list of three topics every week from which to select. It worked for a while, then faltered when it became obvious that they disliked the necessary reading and preparation, preferring to speak only on what they already knew. That can work for the world's Shaws and Asimovs, but it's a dead end for those whose scope is narrow — and often shallow as well.

Most of them, though "hail fellows, well met," hadn't darkened a library door in years. So I told them, "Just look around! The water glass at your hand holds at least three subjects: a history of glass making, a talk about water, without which we are dust, and a discussion of optics, which would be prompted by the refraction of light produced by water and glass.

"The tableware in front of you could inspire a lecture on basic metallurgy, including alloying, annealing and tempering, and the notebooks that you carry cry out for talks on paper making and a history of writing tools." Unfortunately, most of my listeners were victims of inertia, intellectual tunnel vision or eyes that could not see — and few responded.

What a shame it is that so many people plod through life with a muted sense of wonder, never asking why ice always floats, why biscuits rise, and how an east wind brings rain with a storm from the west. Some ask the questions, but never root out the answers, living in a world in which things makes sense, but never learning why.

# Wish List

As children we wished upon stars, repeating the magic words: "Star light, Star bright, First star I see tonight, I wish I may, I wish I might, Have the wish I make tonight."

Later, with the help of lovable characters like Pinocchio and Snow White, the Disney folks taught us that "When you wish upon a star, makes no difference who you are, When you wish upon a star, your dreams come true."

More recently, Aladdin's genie sprang from the magic lamp to flash across our movie screens as he made his master rich. Experience, however, tells another tale: that wishing alone will not make it so; that it never caught a fish, built a home, or ladled up a lover.

Nevertheless, since the thought is often father to the deed, and if there are enough sympathetic souls who agree with me, a little wishing might someday bear fruit. So here is my wish list, arbitrarily limited to ten admittedly unlikely prospects.

1. I wish people would realize that failing to limit our population is already degrading our lives and will severely limit the lives of our descendants. In this wish, I am opposed, as usual, by the pro-birth conservative religionists who seek more bodies to vote their way, and by an economic system that prefers growth to stability.

2. I wish that access to education, health care and legal representation was EQUALLY available to all, without regard to income. Were that so, the great disparities between the curricula and facilities of the wealthy school districts and the poorer school districts would

disappear; an abandoned child would have the same access to a potentially lifesaving MRI as a wealthy septuagenarian, and the rich and poor would finally stand equally before the law.

3. I wish that churches would practice the love that they preach and abandon their pursuit of wealth, power and property.

4. I wish for true separation of church and state, without preferential treatment that exempts churches from real estate and gift taxes, and allows their more primitive sects to deprive their children of medical care.

5. I wish that churches were subject to truth-in-advertising laws.

6. I wish that our Congress (and all our legislatures) were unicameral — like Nebraska's —, having but one legislative body, thus economizing while cutting confusion, buck passing and the old fraud of supporting legislation in one body that you have arranged to have killed in the other.

7. I wish that interracial marriages would be seen as desirable, gradually eliminating the visual evidence of race that makes it so easy to know whom to hate.

8. 1 wish that our news media had the guts and integrity to print more freethought letters and articles, rather than the usual pap about "Bikers for Jesus," and to air rational responses to the nonsense portrayed as fact in pseudo documentaries like the "Discovery of Noah's Ark." I am angered that Public TV aired a three-hour special called "Mine Eyes Have Seen The Glory," without any opportunity for critical review. And I am reminded that it was the Republicans who scuttled the fairness doctrine regarding equal time.

9. I wish that we would stay out of other nations' idiocies, becoming involved only in concert with other countries at the request of the U.N.

10. I wish that wealth bred concern and generosity, rather than greed and indifference. Unfortunately, the children of the rich

frequently inherit their parents' indifference along with their assets, or at least that portion not willed to an equally grasping church. Occasionally, in a play at generosity, the wealthy make foolish, vanity gifts, as one mogul did in donating a freakish, metal-sheathed art museum to the University of Minnesota, an organization then in far greater need of double-glazed windows and a modern heating system. By ignoring sensible needs while providing a splashy bauble, the regents and their "benefactor" revived the 18th century dictum of "Let them eat cake."

10 a. I wish I were as rich as Bill Gates so I could better work to implement this list.

10 b. I wish I had the wit and wisdom to go with it.

10 c. I wish I had a better backhand.

# Parochaid — Sounds like Kool-Aid Tastes like Bile

According to *Time* magazine, the day the communist government of Poland fell, the priests arrived at the schools to begin religious "education." In the United States, as elsewhere, a similar result is sought as Catholics and fundamentalists push for "parochaid " and "tax credits" that will be the ruination of the public school system if they are passed.

This is nothing new. Religious leaders have long known that the young are the most easily indoctrinated, and that beliefs inculcated during childhood are strongly held and not easily abandoned.

Leo Tolstoy, author of "War and Peace," knew this and lamented the indoctrination of children by the Russian Orthodox Church. Like many others, then and now, Tolstoy viewed the indoctrination of children in the Christian fantasies as a grave offense against them, an offense for which they have no defense, likening the indoctrination of a child's mind to "driving a wedge into the floor of a granary," rendering it unable to retain useful material, no matter how much is added.

The efforts of the churches to ensnare the immature demonstrates their moral bankruptcy and their fear of intelligent questions. They are no different from those who sell multiple insurance policies to our often-confused and fearful elderly — policies that they don't need and can't afford.

Fortunately, many resist the attempts of the conservative religious factions, speaking out at every opportunity, as did our former AHA president, Edd Doerr. In his excellent article, "Bush-Whacking Education and the First Amendment," he revealed what will happen under Bush's plan to include religious schools in the choices available under open enrollment.

As Doerr pointed out, "logic" is the buzzword, but the bottom line reveals that including parochial/private schools in open enrollment will cost far more than the one billion tax dollars they already consume each year. In the vast majority of these schools, sectarian indoctrination is mandatory, and the plan is for us to foot the bill.

J. B. Haldane, English geneticist, is more specific. After asserting the incompatibility of science education with religion, he provides examples, "... This means that children will have to learn about Adam and Eve instead of evolution; about David killing Goliath instead of Koch killing cholera; about Christ's ascent instead of Montgolfier's and Wright's. Worse than that, they are taught that it is a virtue to accept statements without adequate evidence, which leaves them prey to quacks of every kind ... and makes it difficult for them to accept the methods of thought which are successful in science."

Indeed, the parochialists already teach the propriety of setting aside one's common sense, of acceptance on "faith," which Mark Twain defined as "believing what you know ain't true."

Worse yet, the support of schools that are based on religious or ethnic divisions is counterproductive, if not un-American.

These schools work against the ethic of the melting pot — a pot in which children of a variety of beliefs and cultures can learn to set aside the differences and prejudices of their ancestors as they are taught by instructors chosen for their ability instead of their religious affiliation. As Doerr put it, "The great virtue of the comprehensive American school is that it tends to bring all sorts of students and teachers together in a democracy-enhancing enterprise."

Furthermore, many thoughtful people feel that choice for some will result in an increase in segregated private schools; not schools with a formal color standard, but schools that use economic and other ploys to ensure the exclusion of minorities.

Edd Doerr is joined by many in his support of public schools, among them Joseph Fernandez, former New York City Public Schools Chancellor. As a former parochial school student, Fernandez has seen both sides. In a letter to *Time* magazine, he argued that advocates of religious schools fail to acknowledge that much of the costs of parochial schools are already borne by the public schools system. Included are "costs for food, transportation, testing, remedial reading and math instruction, and substance abuse education, costs that artificially inflate the public schools' budgets. Public schools serve all children, regardless of race, gender, physical or mental handicap. Catholic schools educate only those students they choose to accept."

In conclusion, Fernandez says, "I wish Catholic schools the best but I urge them not to proclaim their success at the expense of the public schools, one of this country's greatest institutions."

Mr. Fernandez, you are a dreamer. They will proclaim whatever they wish because, in this country, you can get away with almost anything in the name of religion. The fundamentalist and Catholic supporters of parochaid who teach children that fables are fact will continue to aim wrecking balls at the public schools, for as long as the public schools are up and running, the superstitions of the past are in peril.

If, in our United States, we do not want the divisions of Ireland, Iraq and India, we will need the unifying effects of the public school system. If we are to continue our progress in science and education, we need Thomas Huxley's ethic that "the deepest sin against the human mind is to believe things without evidence." If we are to have better schools and a better nation, we need to heed the words of Thomas Edison, who had the brains and the guts to assert that "Religion is all bunk."

# Confidential Report

We had assumed that the U.S. would never suffer another power outage as severe as the one that totaled the Eastern seaboard on November 9, 1965. As you will recall, the outage was triggered when an undersized relay tripped out when power demands rose above the design limits of the relay. The shutdown increased loads on adjacent generating stations, which also tripped out to protect the generators. By the time the outages had cascaded to the limit, millions were without power, approximately 300,000 were trapped in subways, and the affected area reached from New York to Toronto to Boston and beyond.

Unfortunately, our confidence in the new equipment that was recently installed was unfounded, as demonstrated by the catastrophic power loss sustained on the eve of October 3, 2006.

With the use of power station logs, it has been possible to trace the series of events that led to the collapse. That chronology is now well understood, although its cause is difficult to accept, despite the proof available and the testimony obtained from the perpetrator.

At the risk of sounding anticlimactic, I will tell you that it all began at the interstate power substation at Dundee, MN when a resident named George Erickson turned on his antique PC!

**10:02 p.m.**

Hi Everyone,

Greetings to one and all out there in Bushland. Since you are probably awhirl over which country our self-declared war president will invade next, I will divert your mind with news from the swamp.

**10:05 p.m.** — Relays at the Dundee substation trip out.

We survived the Week of the Automobile and headed north on

Friday to the cabin. Arrived just in time to meet Chris and the kids. We kept them busy 'til Sunday afternoon, taking multiple walks and boat rides and eating rutabaga pasties. Later in the week, a bear visited us several times, once tearing down the birdfeeder during the night and consuming all the sunflower seeds. During another night, the local otter lifted the top off our minnow pail and ate about two dozen minnows, leaving the pail upright and half full of water.

**10:09 p.m.** — All southwestern Minnesota counties lose power, but the PCJr continues to operate due to a north-south, two-way power feed unique to the Dundee area.

Later in the week we drove around the Echo trail. Lovely day, but red leaves all gone. On Thursday night, I caught a nice northern pike from the dock, about five pounds. The next night, I left the line out overnight and when Sally went to move it so I could pick her up at the front dock for a plane ride, she discovered there was a bigger northern on the line and had to drag it ashore. On Friday, also caught a very nice walleye, about three pounds. Decided to take the line in to avoid the risk of catching more fish.

**10:14 p.m.** — Relays at the Missouri River's Gavins Point dam and the Oahe dam fail to trip out, fusing all generators. Nuclear plants in Minnesota and the upper Midwest drop offline for self-protection.

Headed home on Monday, towing the big boat with the Suburban, which was slowly enlarging several small holes in the headers as we roared along. Near Minneapolis, the Sub began to miss, so new plugs and a tune-up are probably in order. Got home and changed oil. Discovered a leaking power steering hose. I'd better get the Suburban some attention, including a new set of headers. I will buy a set of cheapos since they will outlast the car.

**10:22 p.m.** — NORAD base at Omaha now operating on emergency power and on red alert, suspecting that spreading destruction of the power grid is a dirty commie plot. Power now out from New Orleans to Winnipeg, and Denver to Chicago. (Pat Robertson, on the air when told of the spreading power loss, commands it to stop. Later explains his failure by saying he thought electricity was AD and BC, not AC and DC.)

I've hired some roofers to shingle the north slope of the roof. In preparation for their arrival I have replaced the three-tiered trim all the way around the roof with new wood, painted it, removed the peak flashing, taken down the antennas and removed the eve trough. The roofers are now three days late getting here. They had better get here soon or I will finish the job myself.

**10:28 p.m.** — Grand Coulee facility down, as is Boulder dam. Bush goes on TV. Says that the power is on everywhere and those who report otherwise are "terrists."

Got a call from the bank today. Seems they hold the opinion that they wrongly credited my account with 10,000 shekels. I have yet to check their story. If they are right, I've had the use of their 10,000 little ones for three months, so that's OK. If they are not right, I will enlighten them. Have to work Saturday. It's a cruel world. Love, Pop

**10:34 p.m.** — Total U.S. power failure. A "black hole" in southwest Minnesota consumed all power. (Robertson operating by candlelight. Says he is better at diverting hurricanes.) Source of the outage is finally traced to a PCJr in Dundee, MN. Perpetrator admits to using the equipment and bargains with the authorities. Agrees to destroy the PC in exchange for a lifetime supply of Ju Ju gummies and a new minivan. End of report.

# Birds of Prey

Australia confines the koala;
    the Arctic... the polar bear.
      But, as you'll agree,
        birds are quite free:
          and there are vultures everywhere

They had to pay bribes to leave Shanghai — under-the-table money to those who could "get things done." He came to get his masters degree and then a doctorate; his wife came to study English. They both work part time, living the frugal life that is so common to married students.

We met them through the MIC, the Minnesota International Center, an organization that encourages Minnesotans to befriend foreign students and visitors. They learn about ordinary Americans, instead of John Wayne, Britney Spears or Donald Trump, and we get to meet some very bright, energetic, serious young people who are striving to gain that which we take for granted. We asked them to supper and an evening of conversation at our home — an evening that passed well, with only a few awkward moments as we groped for common ground. They brought a small hand fan and a lovely scarf, gifts that they probably could not afford. And we all talked too loudly, as if volume would somehow increase the clarity of our speech and improve our comprehension.

A month later we were invited to their home, an apartment that took us back 40 years to the days of one-bedroom student housing, complete with bare walls and noisy neighbors. We dined on several delicious dishes, with mushrooms, egg rolls, napa cabbage and squid. Our four chairs were well used and of different colors and design. The table rocked a little; the silverware was a riot of mismatches, the plates assorted styles, but the soup bowls matched ... complete with a portrait of Big Bird in their bottoms.

We talked about our cultures, of events in Russia, and about the rush to a better China that was derailed in Tiananmen Square.

Our friends had joined a demonstration at the University of Minnesota to protest their government's actions, so they fear returning to China. They need different visas that will allow an extended stay, and for her, a green card for full-time work. They need a car to replace their disintegrating Honda that he repairs, and they need to see a movie once or twice a year. They both need dental work. I've taught him tennis — and he's getting too good!

A law firm contacted them (and other Chinese students) offering to TRY to get the visa changed for $1,500 per person, and to TRY to get a green card for $5,000. Easy payments of $250 per month, and they had already made two payments, taken from savings.

We were stunned. We told them that they could file the same forms at no cost by working directly with the Immigration and Naturalization Service, that the MIC might be able to help them, that our bureaucracies may sometimes be slow and confusing to deal with, but that they are basically honest and are not to be feared. We told them that in America we are free to seek alternatives to exorbitant charges, free to get a second opinion, and free to demand a refund of the unused balance of our "easy monthly payments."

We are working on it, gathering data and seeking advice. As with the attorneys, we'll TRY to change the visa and TRY to get a green card, but win or lose, our friends will save close to $6,000.

The vultures will survive. They'll find others who fear the system, who do not understand how it works, and they'll prey on those who think they must pay and pay and pay.

# It's a Crime and Shame

Like most children, I occasionally misheard some of the adult phrases that drifted past my ears, one of them being "a crying shame," which I heard and repeated as "a crime and shame" until someone straightened me out. Nevertheless, it really is a crime and shame that, until George Seldes came along, the major books of quotations were "sanitized" by men like Bartlett, whose religious and establishment bias disallowed dissent. When embarrassed by the remarks of their leaders or stung by the perceptive observations of the nonreligious minorities, editors like Bartlett simply left them out.

Seeing the need for open-minded, uncensored books, George Seldes, then in his sixties, began to compile *The Great Thoughts* and *The Great Quotations*, completing them when well into his eighties. Thanks to Seldes we know that Thomas Edison, the famous inventor who said, "Genius is 1% inspiration and 99% perspiration," also said "Religion is all bunk." Bartlett includes the genius quote, which is fine, because it supports the work ethic, but he predictably omits "Religion is all bunk."

Mark Twain, a favorite target of fundamentalists, wrote, "Faith is believing what you know ain't true." Bartlett not only excludes that statement, he also shuns the anti-Semitic teachings of Martin Luther that led to centuries of German Lutheran hatred of Jews. Combined with the anti-Semitic bigotry of the Roman Catholic Church, these two dogmas prepared German soil for the seeds of Hitler's Holocaust.

Seldes' books contain an unbiased selection of the words of tyrants, patriots, persons of honor and famous frauds: Words that inspire and words that repel from those who influenced public opinion, advancing or retarding the progress of humanity. *The Great Thoughts* and *The Great*

*Quotations* can be ordered in soft cover from any bookstore, but here's a sampling of Seldes' 20-plus years of research.

**President John Adams** — "The question is whether the god of nature will govern the world by his own laws or whether priests and kings shall rule it by fictitious miracles."

**Aristotle** — "A tyrant must put on the appearance of uncommon devotion to religion. Subjects will less easily move against him, believing that he has the gods on his side."

**St. Augustine** — "All diseases of Christians are to be ascribed to demons."

**Alan Barth**, American writer — "Character assassination is easier and surer than physical assault and involves less risk for the assassin. It leaves him free to commit the same deed over again and again, and may win him honors even in the country of his victims." (Joe McCarthy and Jerry Falwell come to mind.)

**Ambrose Bierce**, author — "Religion is a daughter of hope and fear, explaining to ignorance the nature of the unknowable."

**Susan B. Anthony** — The religious persecution of the ages has been done under what was claimed to be the command of God. I distrust those people who know so well what God wants them to do to their fellows, because it always coincides with their own desires."

**Justice Hugo Black** — "The framers of the constitution knew that free speech is the friend of change and revolution; but they also knew that it is the deadliest enemy of tyranny. The first amendment has erected a wall between church and state. That wall must be kept high and impregnable."

**Martin Buber**, theologian — "I don't like religion much and I'm glad that in the Bible the word is not to be found."

**Pearl S. Buck**, Nobel laureate — "I feel no need for any other faith than my faith in human beings. Like Confucius of old, I am so absorbed in the wonder of Earth and the life upon it that I cannot think of heaven or angels."

**Canon law** — "The church abhors bloodshed." (1163) (In obedience to this decree, the Inquisition burned the accused alive so as to avoid shedding blood.)

**Mark Twain** (Samuel Clemens) — "Man is a religious animal. He is the only religious animal. He is the only animal that has the TRUE RELIGION — several of them. He is the only animal that loves his neighbor as himself but cuts his throat if his theology isn't straight ... It (the Bible) has some noble poetry in it; and some clever fables; and some blood-drenched history; and some good morals; and a wealth of obscenity; and upwards of a thousand lies."

**Confucius** (One of many sources of humanist ethics.) "What you do not want done unto yourself, do not unto others. We don't know yet about life. How can we know about death?" (500 BCE)

**Clarence Darrow**, attorney — "I don't believe in God because I don't believe in Mother Goose."

**Charles Darwin**, biologist and agnostic — "For my part I would as soon be descended from a baboon as from a savage who tortures his enemies, treats his wives like slaves and is haunted by the grossest superstitions."

**Justice William Douglas** — "Restriction of free thought and free speech is the most dangerous of all subversions. It is the one un-American act that could most easily defeat us."

**Thomas Edison** — "I have never seen the slightest proof of the religious theories of heaven and hell, of future life for individuals, or of a personal god. Religion is all bunk. Religion ... is all a damn fake. I do not believe that any type of religion should ever be ... introduced into the public schools of the United States."

**Albert Einstein** — "Do you think that religion will help promote peace? It has not done so up 'til now. I cannot imagine a god who rewards and punishes the objects of his creation, whose purposes are molded after our own — a god who is but a reflection of human frailty. Neither do I believe that the individual survives the death of his body. I am convinced that some activities of the Catholic organizations are dangerous. I mention here the fight against birth control at a time when overpopulation has become a serious threat to health and to any attempt to organize peace on the planet." (1954)

**Benjamin Franklin** — "When religion is good, it will support itself. And when it does not, and God does not care to support it, and its professors call for the help of a civil power, 'tis a sign of its being a bad one." (School prayer, parochaid, church tax exemptions?) ...

Lighthouses are more helpful than churches. I have found Christian dogma unintelligible. "

**Sigmund Freud** — "Religion is comparable to a childhood neurosis."

**Mohandas Gandhi**, in praise of women — "Is she not more self-sacrificing, has she not greater courage. Without her, man would not be. If nonviolence is to be the law of our being, the future is with women."

**William Gladstone**, English statesman —"Liberalism is trust of the people tempered by prudence. Conservatism is distrust of the people tempered by fear."

**President Ulysses S. Grant** — "I suggest the taxation of all property equally, whether church or corporation."

**J.B. Haldane**, scientist and geneticist — "Scientific education and religious education are incompatible. The clergy have ceased to interfere with education at the advanced state, but they still control that of the children. This means that children will have to learn about Adam and Noah instead of about evolution; about David killing Goliath instead of Koch killing cholera; about Christ's ascent into heaven instead of Montgolfier's and Wright's. Worse than that, they are taught that it is a virtue to accept statement without adequate evidence, which leaves them prey to quacks of every kind and makes it difficult for them to accept the methods of thought that are successful in science."

**Adolph Hitler** — "As a Christian ... I have the duty to be a fighter for truth and justice. ... the government ... regards Christianity as the unshakable foundation of morals and the moral conduct of the nation. I believe today that I am acting in the sense of the almighty creator. By warding off the Jews, I am fighting for the Lord's work. Women's world is her husband, her family and her home. We do not find it right when she presses into the world of men. Secular schools can never be tolerated because such a school has no religious instruction. Consequently all character training and religion must be derived from faith. We need believing people."

**Victor Hugo**, author of *"Les Miserables"* and humanist — "Hell is an outrage on humanity. When you tell me that your deity made you in his image, I reply that he must have been very ugly."

**Robert Ingersoll**, attorney, orator, humanist — "Blasphemy is what an old dogma screams at a new truth. There will never be a generation of great men until there has been a generation of free women."

**Thomas Jefferson** — "Fix reason firmly in her seat, and call on her tribunal for every fact, every opinion. Question with boldness even the existence of a god, because, if there be one, he must more approve of the homage of reason than that of blind faith. In every country and every age the priest has been hostile to liberty. He is always in alliance with the despot ... The day will come when the mystical generation of Jesus in the womb of a virgin will be classed with the fable of the generation of Minerva in the brain of Jupiter. Question with boldness even the existence of a god because if there be one he must approve more of the homage of reason than that of blind fear. Christianity is the most perverted system that ever shone on man. I do not find in our particular superstition [Christianity] one redeeming feature."

**Immanuel Kant** — "The death of dogma is the birth of reason."

**President John F. Kennedy** — "I believe in an America where the separation of church and state is absolute."

**President Abraham Lincoln** — "I belong to no church." "The Bible is not my book and Christianity is not my religion. I could never give assent to the long, complicated statements of Christian dogma. My earlier views on the unsoundness of the Christian scheme of salvation ... have become clearer and stronger ... and I see no reason for thinking I shall ever change them."

**St. Ignatius of Loyola** — "We should always be disposed to believe that which appears to us to be white is really black, if the hierarchy of the church so decides." (1500 CE)

**Martin Luther** — "Reason is the greatest enemy that faith has. Whoever wants to be Christian should tear the eyes out of his reason ... Concerning the Jews: set fire to their synagogues ... destroy their houses ... drive them from the country." (He also advised killing them.) "No one need think that the world can be ruled without blood. The civil sword must be red and bloody."

**President James Madison** — "Who does not see that the same authority that can establish Christianity in exclusion of all other religions may establish any particular sect of Christians in exclusion of all other sects. What has been its [Christianity's] fruits? ... pride and indolence in the clergy; ignorance and servility in the laity; in both, superstition, bigotry and persecution."

**Ferdinand Magellan**, circum-global navigator —"The church says the Earth is flat, but I know that it is round, for I have seen its shadow on the moon and I have more faith in a shadow than in the church."

**Massachusetts Bay Colony** — (The encyclopedia merely says that the Puritans were "unfriendly" to other religions. In fact, other religions were outlawed.) Capital laws: 1. If a man be convicted of worshiping any other god but the Lord God, he shall be put to death. 2. A witch shall be put to death. 3. Blasphemers shall be punishable with death. (1641)

**Herman Melville**, author of *"Moby Dick"* — "Of all the preposterous criticisms of humanity, nothing exceeds those made on the habits of the poor by the well-housed, well-warmed and well-fed."

**H. L. Mencken**, author and editor — "A Galileo could no more be elected president than he could be elected pope. Both posts are reserved for men favored by God with an extraordinary genius for swathing the bitter facts of life with bandages of self-illusion. I believe that religion, generally speaking, has been a curse to mankind. I believe that it is better to tell the truth than to lie; I believe it is better to be free than to be a slave; I believe it is better to know than to be ignorant. Sunday school — a prison in which children do penance for the evil consciences of their parents."

**A. A. Milne**, author — "The Old Testament is responsible for more atheism, agnosticism, disbelief — call it what you will — than any book ever written; it has emptied more churches than all the counter-attractions of cinema, motor bicycle and golf course."

**Michael Montaigne**, philosopher — "Man is certainly stark mad. He cannot make a flea and yet he will be making gods by the dozen."

**Napoleon Bonaparte** — "If I had to choose a religion, the sun as the universal giver of life would be my god. Religion is excellent stuff for keeping common people quiet." (It worked beautifully on slaves, and it still helps to keep blacks and other minorities pacified.)

**Friedrich Nietzsche** — "All religions bear traces of the fact that they arose during the intellectual immaturity of the human race, before it had learned the obligation to speak the truth. Not one of them makes it the duty of its god to be truthful and understandable in his communications.

It is all up with priests and gods when man becomes scientific."

**R. M. Nixon**, resigned president — "When a president does it, it is not illegal."

**Thomas Paine**, American patriot, deist, source of inspiration for the Declaration of Independence and the "father" of the American revolution — "One good schoolmaster is of more use than 100 priests. My mind is my church. Of all the systems of religion that were ever invented, there is no more derogatory to the almighty, more unedifying to man, more repugnant to reason and more contradictory to itself than this thing called Christianity."

**Blaise Pascal** — "Men never do evil so completely and cheerfully as when they do it from religious conviction."

**Pope Pius XI** — "Mussolini: a gift from providence."

**Red Jacket**, a Seneca Indian Chief — "You have got our country; you want to force your religion on us. You say there is but one way to worship and serve the great spirit. If there is but one religion, why do you white people differ so much about it?"

**Bertrand Russell** — "God and Satan are essentially human figures: the one a projection of ourselves, the other of our enemies."

**United States Senate**, June 10, 1797 — "The government of the United States is not in any sense founded on the Christian religion." (A UNANIMOUS declaration of the U.S. Senate on the Treaty of Tripoli, signed by President John Adams.)

**Carl Sagan**, astronomer and cosmologist —"Skeptical scrutiny is the means, in both science and religion, by which deep thoughts can be winnowed from deep nonsense."

**Arthur Schlesinger**, historian — "Those who are convinced they have a monopoly on the truth always feel they are only saving the world when they slaughter the heretics."

**Albert Schweitzer**, Nobel physician and philosopher — "Humanism, in all its simplicity, is the only genuine spirituality."

**Seneca**, Greek philosopher — "Religion is regarded by the common people as true, by the wise as false and by the rulers as useful."

**Socrates** — "My plainness of speech makes them hate me. And what is their hatred but a proof that I am speaking the truth."

**Elizabeth Cady Stanton**, social activist and abolitionist — "The bible and the church have been the greatest stumbling blocks in the way of women's emancipation."

**Billy Sunday**, evangelist — "When scholarship says one thing and the word of God another, scholarship can go to hell. America is not a country for a dissenter to live in."

**Henry Thoreau**, author and philosopher — "I do not see why the schoolmaster should be taxed to support the priest, but not the priest to support the schoolmaster."

**Voltaire**, 1720 — "If you have two religions in the land they will cut each other's throats. But if you have thirty religions, they will dwell in peace." (As in Ireland and Bosnia-Croatia-Serbia.) "As long as people continue to believe absurdities they will continue to commit atrocities."

**Walt Whitman**, poet — "The churches are one vast lie; the people don't believe them; the priests are continually telling what they know is not so and keeping back what they know is so. The spectacle is a pitiful one."

**Kaiser Wilhelm II** — "The German people are the chosen of God. On me the spirit of God has descended. I am his sword, his weapon, his vice-regent." (Like David Koresh of Waco, Adolph Hitler and James Jones of Jonestown.)

**Thomas Wolsey**, English cardinal — "We must destroy the press or the press will destroy us."

# Salvation for All

Dear sinners,

Salvation from your sins and earthly cares is finally available.

I, George Erickson, the Flying Spaghetti Monster Incarnate (the only begotten son of the Great Flying Spaghetti Monster) hereby offer you membership in the Fellowship of my Father, the GFSM.

For your *Salvation Certificate* (see sample below) mail your $10.00 membership offering or item of comparable worth to George Erickson, FSMI, 4678 Cedar Island Drive, Eveleth, MN 55734. Your certificate will arrive within thirty days. This is a limited time offer. Only one certificate per supplicant. No exceptions.

---

Sample certificate of membership in the congregation
of the Great Flying Spaghetti Monster.

Be it known that on (date here) in the year 1 of our GFSM, (your name here) did remit to the George Erickson, the Spaghetti Monster Incarnate who is the only begotten son of the Great Flying Spaghetti Monster, the sum of $10.00 by personal check in full payment for membership in the congregation of the GFSM universal. (Stamps, cash, free lube jobs, etc. also accepted.)

Be it also known that dear _____, who has our complete confidence, shall henceforth be known to fellow servers of the GFSM as Apostle __ ____ I.

Apostle _____ I is now authorized to bring others to our saving grace so that they will not be "left behind" and to spread our spicy gospel to all the lands, telling potential converts that salvation can be achieved only through the S M Incarnate, who will give each and every supplicant his loving attention.

This, I promise. I have therefore affixed my signature below with noodle # 69.

George Erickson, the human iteration of the GFSM.

**May the sauce be with you and bring you cheese.**

# Fireworks of Sky and Mind

On Independence Day, thousands watched the darkened sky erupt with colored light and thrilled to crashing sounds. I was one of those thousands, and as rockets streaked across the sky, I thought of a simple lab demonstration that introduced a bit of sodium into a Bunsen burner flame, producing a yellow fire. Copper created turquoise blue; barium, green; rubidium, lavender, and strontium delivered a crimson red flame.

One pure white starburst jogged my memory further, filling my mind with the small brass tube in which I first saw sparks created not by ten-pound rockets, but by the tiny explosions of a very special element that burst on the scene more than one hundred years ago. That element was radium.

Shaped and sized like a Kodak film container, my brass tube differs in what it contains. Like the light-sensitive film that Kodak produces, the inside of the far end of my tube is coated with zinc sulfide, a chemical that reacts not just to visible light, but to other radiation as well. Inside the tube, a needle tipped with a tiny amount of radium chloride hovers in front the zinc sulfide screen, and to help us see the show, the front of the tube contains a magnifying lens.

Our tube needs a name. Galileo called his first telescope a "looker," and then an "optical tube." The word "telescope" came later. These terms make sense to our modern minds, but Sir William Crookes, who invented the tube that we use to spy on atoms, chose the name "spinthariscope," which comes from the Greek word for "spark."

Our spinthariscope needs no batteries, and it will work for close to forever, for the tiny pin's coating contains millions of radium atoms, and similar tubes made a century ago still produce the flickering lights *with an undiminished flow.*

One further thing is needed — a very dark room. Be patient. The eyes needs time to adjust, for the tiny flashes that speckle the screen lie just within the limits of dark-adapted eyes. One caution: Do not uncap the tube except in a darkened room, for light will render it useless by setting the screen aglow.

Look now, and marvel. The tiny sparks that you see provided the first visual evidence that Democritus was right when he argued (about 400 BCE) that matter consisted of tiny particles that he called atoms. See how the flares dance upon the screen, flashing randomly like short-lived shooting stars as the radium atoms decay, rocketing out alpha particles, a few of which brighten our zinc sulfide screen.

Many scientists had noticed that radium glowed, but not until Sir William Crookes devised his ingenious tube, were they able to dilute the process, "slowing" it enough to be able to witness the breakdown of *individual atoms* by using a tiny sample, a darkened, sensitive screen and a magnifying lens. (In 1960 radium cost $500,000 per ounce, but our diluted, miniscule sample costs just a few pennies.)

It's almost a hundred years since Sir William devised his tube, and science is marching on. It claims no miracles. No chants or incense needed.

But because our country is swayed by the faith-based crowd, when we oooh and aaah at the rocketing reds, purples and yellows that brighten our 4th of July skies, we need to remember this: It was *science* that raised the colors aloft and created the thundering sounds. And it's *science* that will carry you back to your home and a life that few could have dreamed of on that first Fourth of July evening more than 200 years ago.

# If you're feeling sad and blue,
## stop at Tillie's and hoist a few.

For fifty years, this bit of poetic advice on the wall of Tillie's Bar beckoned to travelers who passed through Cloquet, Minnesota on highway 33. And although I reject Tillie's advice as ill-advised, I'm sure that Tillie's spirits were lifted whenever money crossed her bar.

During Tillie's years of service, many undoubtedly accepted her invitation. Perhaps most of them departed only mildly impaired, but it's just as probable that the feet of a few went strolling down the path to addiction.

Any physician or honest addict knows that addiction involves not only dependency on the drug, but requires increased amounts to provide the same result. Physical dependence reveals itself not only in a powerful urge to seek the drug, but in the onset of severe withdrawal symptoms when usage is stopped. In fact, quitting cold-turkey refers to the chills and gooseflesh that heroin addicts endure when the drug is withheld. So powerful are addictions that former addicts often find themselves fighting relapse years after breaking free.

Oddly enough, some of the most addictive drugs chemically resemble substances that our brains manufacture: endorphins. Like morphine, endorphins alter nerve transmission, which affects how information passes through the brain. Our brains however, have the good sense not to make endorphins unless needed, as in handling a crisis, or in the brains of those all a-swoon with love.

Nevertheless, endorphins have not undermined our culture and created our futile and expensive war on drugs. Those we owe largely to a simple poppy plant from which come opium, morphine and heroin.

When the German chemist Frederick Serturner isolated morphine in 1806, the hypodermic syringe had not yet been invented. Fortunately, it arrived soon after, allowing injectable morphine to ease the pain of our Civil War wounded. However, it also led to an addiction that, by the end of the century, came to be called "the soldier's disease." About that time, the Bayer Company, which would soon synthesize aspirin, introduced heroin. Derived from morphine, heroin was promoted as "a non-addictive opiate." They were wrong.

If Western nations have a drug problem today, it began in large part with the policies of their predecessors. By the early 1800s, Great Britain, France, The Netherlands, Portugal and Spain dominated almost a third of Asia, profiting hugely by trade with China, a trade that included selling opium from Turkey and Greece. But the Manchu government resisted by closing every port but Canton and making opium illegal. Britain declared war (the Opium Wars) which eventually led to a role in "The Sand Pebbles" for actor Steve McQueen. Naturally, we Caucasians were portrayed as the good guys and Britain's attempt to promote opium traffic in China went unmentioned. Unfortunately, Britain won.

Karl Marx likened opium to religion, calling religion "the opiate of the masses" because he knew that opium could temporarily sweep aside their tragedies and numb their pain. But since Marx, the poppy and its derivatives have found less essential uses. While some of our soldiers returned from Vietnam with Asian brides, others brought addictions acquired not from treating wounds, but from their first experiences with mind-altering, "recreational" drugs.

Like the opiates, the nicotine-tinged smoke that blued the lights in Tillie's bar — not to mention the alcohol that Tillie served — first found use as medicine. Over the millennia it has been prescribed for everything imaginable, and red wine is currently said to help ward off heart disease. In the 16th century, on the advice of Jean Nicot, tobacco cured the headaches of Catherine De Medici, the wife of France's King Henry II. Three centuries later, when tobacco's active ingredient was isolated, it received the name of "nicotine" in honor of Jean Nicot.

Today, nicotine and alcohol are "starter drugs," training wheels for those who might someday move on to bigger and better things, while enriching the CEOs of Philip Morris and the owners of Budweiser and Coors. Fortunately, most of us who use these drugs use them sensibly. But having seen where addictions can lead, and knowing that "feeling sad and blue" is more safely remedied with support and counseling, I wish that Tillie's sign had read:

> If you're feeling really great,
> Let's moderately celebrate.
> But if you're feeling sad and blue,
> A counselor's the thing for you.

# The Happiness Machine

Everything has a price — even happiness, they say. Ray Bradbury, who with Isaac Asimov, a past president of the American Humanist Association, led several generations of science fiction lovers to a world of new ideas, certainly must have agreed. In Bradbury's story, "The Happiness Machine," he told of a tireless inventor who builds a machine in which all can enter the world of their dreams.

In the tale, the inventor's son sneaks into the machine before the inventor can test it, and emerges sad and disheartened. His distraught wife, who is determined to root out the cause, quickly climbs into the machine, shuts the door and turns it on.

From inside the machine come peals of laughter, shrieks of joy, beautiful music, sighs of pleasure and a hint of perfume. "I'm dancing," she cries. But a few minutes later, the sound of weeping begins. She emerges, her face awash in tears, for she has seen what she knows she never will see, and has briefly lived as she knows she never will. "It's the saddest thing in the world," she says — and then goes on to explain.

"Leo," she says to her husband, "You had me dancing. We haven't danced in twenty years."

When he tells her "I'll take you dancing tomorrow," she argues, "No, no. It's not important. It shouldn't be important, but your machine makes it important.

"What you forgot," she says, "is that we just can't stay there — that the dream must end, that we have to come back to a life on a budget, to dirty laundry, to difficult people and unmade beds."

Bradbury's happiness machine was, of course, a fiction, the product of his inventive mind, but I can't help wondering if the escape his machine provided, and the crash that followed, is akin to being hooked on drugs. Those who try to escape with mind-altering drugs like heroin, speed, cocaine, alcohol or Ecstasy often suffer the same fate as Leo's wife, who couldn't stay there forever, and found that returning was ever so hard to bear.

To solve the problem, Leo set his marvelous machine ablaze. End of story. No machine, no way to get addicted. But those who are addicted to chemical highs have a harder row to hoe, for the drugs are always calling, and for those who have tripped with drugs fantastic, reality can be very hard to bear.

So why have I told you this story? Because you, too, might have a son, a daughter — perhaps a grandchild who pleases you, whom you treasure very much. You know that time and chance will someday tempt them, and if it is hard for you to find the right words, or the words sound too harsh, you can offer this story — a story that says that happiness comes not from needles, bottles or pills but in hands that are held, in hearts that are cherished — and from hugs. Tell them about Janis Joplin, Elvis Presley, Judy Garland, Michael Jackson and the hundreds of others whose lives were cut short by drugs. It's the Humanist thing to do.

# Life Ain't Fair

Every night and every morn,
Some to misery are born.
Every morn and every night,
Some are born to sweet delight.
William Blake

Those well born to sweet delight
Will fight to keep it day and night.
With devious words and slippery phonics,
They sold us Voodoo economics.
"Patience," cried those who wear the crown,
In time, our wealth will trickle down.
George Erickson

# Hot Stuff

"My first hot flash showed up when I was twelve," said ol' Charlie Fletcher. Me and Charlie'd been settin' on the shore of Cross Cut Lake for close to three hours fishin' for bullheads and chewin' over whatever came to mind.

We'd been popin' bullheads out of the lake so fast that it weren't fun no more, and then Charlie starts talkin' about hot flashes. Claims he's always been hot one way or another. His wife says he's got a metabolic rate like two hummin' birds makin' love. I'm not sure about that metabolic thing, but I get her drift.

Well, anyway, Charlie said, "Jess, the only thing that keeps me cool these days is moving. I swear I'll cremate myself when I die if they don't get a fan on me quick."

"I know what you mean, Charlie," I said. "Sometimes I get those hot spells too, only with me the flu comes next."

"That's not the same," said Charlie. "I'm hot *all* the time! When the missus and I go to bed, she's wrapped in six blankets and a snowmobile suit, and there I am — on top of the covers, naked and steamin'."

"How about that air conditioner you got last spring? Don't tell me that it's caved in already."

"Nope, it hasn't, but I don't like it — plugs up my nose. It's like breathin' through a brick. You ever hear those TV fellas talkin' about them football guys that got hot hands? Well, they can't hold a candle to me! That's a joke, Jess!

"One time I got the whole Omaha Fire Department out with just one of my flamin' fingers," he said as he wiped the sweat from his forehead.

"Okay, Charlie," I said, "tell me about it, but let's try to keep within sight of the truth."

"It's all true," said Charlie, "200 proof, and ain't nothin' better than that. You can even ask the missus.

"We'd decided to run off to Omaha to get away from the kids. Picked up I-29 at Sioux City, gettin' into Omaha 'bout noon. We cruised around for a spell, checkin' out the movies and lookin' for a good hotel. Finally, on one of them big, five-lane, one-way streets we spotted a pretty good one — the Downtowner Motor Hotel. Never did decide which it was, hotel or motel. Maybe they couldn't either.

"Anyway, we got us a sixth floor room that looked towards the Missouri River. Real pretty view. I was lyin' there on the bed in my shorts tryin' to get cool while the missus unpacked, when I noticed the ceilin' was one of those new suspended jobs with panels settin' in a frame that hangs from the ceilin'. You can put all the plumbin' and air coolin' and wires above them panels and they won't show, but they're easy to get at when the time comes.

"Now you know I'm just nuts about how things work, so it wasn't ten seconds 'til I had a couple of them panels out and was checkin' on all that gear up there. Pretty dark though. Really didn't see much. Just got it put back together when I spotted this shiny thing stickin' out of one of them panels."

"Bet it was one of them sprinkler deals," I stuck in quick. (That Charlie hardly stops once he gets his tongue revved up.)

"That's what I thought too, Jess, but it weren't. I looked it over real close. It was about the size of a golf ball cut in half with a flat part glued to the ceilin'. And there weren't no holes in it or any way for holes to open up to let water out. All brass, too — really had me stumped!

"So there I am, standin' on the bed, lookin' this thing over, and I says to the missus, 'I wonder if I should touch this thing.' Unfortunately, at the same time that I'm wonderin', I'm also touchin' — and suddenly all hell breaks loose. There was bells ringin' like crazy, Jess. I'd set off some sort of alarm with just one hot little finger.

"I jumped off the bed, grabbed the phone and dialed the front desk. BUSY! So I headed out the door, gettin' half way through when I remember I'm only wearin' shorts.

"I jammed on my pants, tore down the hall to the elevator and guess what! BUSY!

"So now I go tearing down 65 stairs bare foot and no top — and every floor I go past has bells hammerin' like mad. When I finally hit the main floor, all is peace and quiet, and the desk clerk doesn't have the foggiest idea why this half-dressed nut is runnin' toward him.

"I touched that brass thing in the ceiling," I yelled, "and there's alarms goin' off everywhere but here. That clerk's eyes got real big and his mouth popped open like he'd been shot."

"Oh, my God," he said as he grabbed the phone. "Them alarms are hooked to the fire station."

"That's when I heard the sirens, real faint at first, then louder — and, suddenly I remember I'm only half dressed so I head back up to our room. My missus, who is already upset, isn't helped any when I tell her that we will probably get a visit from the fire department,

"Now, you know me, Jess, and you know my sense of humor never quits. While I'm dressin' — and my wife is lecturin' me about leavin' things alone — I'm thinkin' wouldn't it be great to be checkin' my watch when that marshal walks in, and then say, 'Hmm, not bad. Three minutes and twenty-four seconds! With practice, you could probably get that down to three minutes flat!'

"When he showed up, I explained about touching the thing, and that I didn't know what it was, and that I sure was sorry to have caused such a fuss. Well, he was pretty good about it. Didn't chew me out, and even held back from sayin' I shouldn't do it again."

"Charlie," I said, you're lucky you didn't land in the clink or get a big fine laid on you."

"You're right," he said, "but I'm not done yet. After that marshall left, I waited a couple of minutes and walked down the hall to a window in the front of the building. I could hardly believe my eyes. There was pumpers. There was hook-and-ladders and there was squad cars and rescue wagons, and everything the city had that could wear a red light. That five-lane, one-way street was cut off for two blocks on either side.

"Well, after that we sat around in the room for a while, trying to get up nerve to walk out through the lobby to go for supper. On the way down in the elevator, I asked this guy riding with us if he was there when the alarms went off.

"I sure as hell was," he said. "I was in the bath tub when them bells cut in. Nearly killed myself gettin' outta the tub and into my pants. When I finally got to the elevator, it was gone, so I ducked out the fire exit, ran down the stairs and found the door to the outside locked! When I turned to go back in, the door I had come through had locked behind me. I was wet, mad, scared and trapped! It took fifteen minutes of pounding to get someone to let me in. I sure hope they find that idiot who set off that alarm. I'd like to wring his neck."

And that's when the missus pipes up and says with a grin, "So would I mister, so would I."

# Joe Selvaggio

When the Minnesota Monthly named Joe Selvaggio their Minnesotan of the Year and called him an "Urban Saint," I couldn't wait to read the article. Was he really qualified for such an honor, and was his obvious humanism secular or religious? To the first question, the answer is a solid "yes," to the second, an honest "I don't know." Let me explain.

Joe grew up lower-middle class on Chicago's West Side. After being ordained in the Roman Catholic Church, he was sent to the Deep South, where he angered segregationists for being too supportive of blacks. Transferred to the rundown Phillips neighborhood of Minneapolis, he endeared himself to his parishioners, but irritated the church hierarchy with his views on "silly rules like celibacy, and blacks and whites in different churches, and Cardinal Spellman blessing the warships going to Vietnam."

Joe left the priesthood in 1966, married and began to protest the Vietnam War while supporting Cesar Chavez. Finding little fulfillment in ordinary work, Joe adopted a friend's suggestion that he "sell stock in himself." For $5 a month Joe offered to serve as an advocate for "race, peace and poverty," thus beginning a long career that he still pursues today. He sent out 200 letters to people that he felt cared about these issues. One hundred responded, and Joe began his personal war on poverty via his Project for Pride in Living, Inc., which lends the poor a hand in learning a skill in preference to giving handouts.

Realizing that he was terribly underfunded, Joe turned to corporate benefactors like Gabberts, Fingerhut and the Mall of America for cash and for donations of overstock. Today, Joe's projects brighten an area once described as a "municipal toilet." His general store trains workers in sales and merchandising, just as his nearby tool lending library offers classes and space so that people can learn to use them. His latest project is a car-detailing operation called UltraMax.

Although Joe is a friend of "corporate heavyweights" he has not sought their incomes or their lifestyles. Even his second "marriage" was initially an act of charity to rescue Rose Escanan, a Filipino woman who was being hunted by the Marcos regime for helping to expose military atrocities. Once out of the Philippines on a fiancé visa, Rose lived platonically with Joe for some six months. Love followed and a real wedding soon took place.

Like other genuine humanists, Joe is very concerned about the increasing gap between the poor and the wealthy. Having resisted any increase in his salary for most of his life, Joe declined a retirement package when the time came, noting that his house was paid for, his kids are grown and his wife makes $20,000 per year.

So, is Joe Selvaggio a religious humanist, a secular humanist who has outgrown the church, or just a caring guy who doesn't like labels and the divisions that they bring? Frankly, Scarlett, I don't give a damn.

Joe Selvaggio sets an example for every one of us, and in my book, one Joe Selvaggio is worth a hundred discussers and pontificators who freely give advice and always know what ails the world, but cannot bring themselves to become part of it.

# My God/Your God
from the Twin Cities Reader

"Exit the Shaman," your fair-minded article that defended the Hmong religion, reminded me that, in their arrogant belief that *only they* have the answers and *all* other beliefs are inferior, proselytizing Christians have *always* sought to destroy the religions of different cultures.

In England, Christians swallowed the shrines of other religions by building churches directly on top of them. In Canada, Catholic and Anglican missionaries (while telling lies about each other) first went after the Inuit shamans to destroy their influence. Shamans who refused to convert were beaten and warned that if they failed to "yield to reason," more beatings would follow.

As for the fundamentalist Christians who call Hmong religion "primitive, superstitious and irrational," isn't the pot calling the kettle black? Where is the proof of the trinity, the resurrection, of heaven and hell? Are they not equally suspect?

Where is the "test in reality" of any religion?

When Lee Pao Xiong protests that certain Hmong religious practices can be "very draining on the budget," he touches on an elemental truth: most religions are big businesses. In spite of their wealth, the Vatican and Pat Robertson all keep asking for more as they practice the oldest scam of all: cash NOW for promises they won't have to keep. Always take advantage of guilt. Promise heaven and threaten hell. In secular society it's called extortion, but in conservative religion it's normal practice.

If Tou Ger Xiong knew history better, he'd realize that religion not only is "breaking families apart," its intolerance has caused most of the wars that the world has ever seen. In the former Yugoslavia, Roman

Catholic Croats intermittently warred against Orthodox Catholic Serbs, then united to kill Muslims in a religious war that our press calls "ethnic cleansing."

In the Middle East, Iraqi and Iranian Shiites fight Iraqi Sunnis. In Ireland, Roman Catholics have been fighting Protestants for decades. As George Carlin put it, "Do you believe in god? No. Pow! You're dead. Do you believe in god? Yes. Do you believe in MY god? No. Pow! You're dead too."

Thanks to the power of organized religion, a docile media and timid school boards, no one hears criticism of religion from Magellan and Galileo, from Madison, Paine and Jefferson, and from Asimov and Sagan. If we keep withholding Edison's "Religion is all bunk," and Mark Twain's "Faith is believing what you know ain't true," people will continue to be unable to assess religion intelligently, and religion will continue to deserve Walt Whitman's condemnation: "The churches are one vast lie ... the priests are continually telling what they know well enough is not so, and keeping back what they know is so. The spectacle is a pitiful one."

# Ode to Stromatolites

*from* True North: Exploring the Great Wilderness by Bush Plane

In the Wildcat restaurant, a log-walled relic of old Yellowknife beside the seaplane base, breakfast conversations focus on two issues: forest fires and the weather.

"Dry enough for you?"

"Hell, yes. Last time I remember a spell like this was in the eighties, maybe '88 or '89. Fires all over the place."

"Great year for business, eh?"

"You can say that again." (Charter operators do well during dry years, flying men and equipment to and from remote blazes.)

"Sid get back?"

"Yup, last night about ten. Says the Duncan Lake fire's still cookin' and there's a new one near Desperation Lake. Oh, yaa, there's a big one south of McDonald. He's flying two crews from Snowdrift to the McDonald burn this morning."

"That Sid — if we didn't have enough work to keep us busy, he'd probably be tossing flares out the window right now." Laughter circles the table.

"Naw, Sid wouldn't do that," someone says, then pauses and adds, "not this year." More laughter.

Back Bay is calm. Cleared by the Yellowknife tower, the Tundra Cub skates across glassy water and climbs away from its mirrored image. Turning east, I glance back over my shoulder. A taxiing Norseman makes me wish I'd waited, for I love the throaty rumble of big radial engines. Unlike my quiet Cub, the Norseman will shatter the Bay's serenity, setting the pattern for yet another day.

Forty minutes pass. On the northern horizon, a nuclear bomb-like cloud billows upward from the Duncan Lake burn, lofted by fires hot enough to consume even the shallow tundra soil.

My destination is Utsingi Point, a long sliver of land at the southwest tip of the Pethei Peninsula. There I hope to find the stony remains of the organisms that made life possible for fish and fowl, and for all insects, reptiles and mammals. Called stromatolites, they're petrified colonies of blue-green algae, an early life form that, about two billion years ago, began to produce oxygen in the shallows of our ancient seas.

An hour out of Yellowknife, I descend over Hearne Channel, turn north and fly low along Utsingi Point, searching its weathered limestone for stromatolite remains. Seeing nothing but gnarled, elephant-skin rock, I descend lower, skimming along its wide and barren shore.

Discouraged and unwilling to fly farther north, I turn back, land on Great Slave's wonderfully clear water and idle toward shore. (Unlike the main body of Great Slave Lake, which is opaqued with silt by the Slave and Hay Rivers, the lake's north and east arms are lead-crystal clear.)

As I scan the rocks for something to tie to, the scene snaps into focus. The entire shoreline is an exposed reef of stromatolites. Expecting to see isolated examples of the washtub-sized colonies, I hadn't recognized the mottled mass of thousands that had passed beneath my wings. Now, surrounded by the petrified remains of the cells that breathed us into life, I'm filled with a sense of awe.

For eons, the Earth was a carbon dioxide-rich, oxygen-starved planet. When early life forms appeared, one of them, a blue-green, algae organism called cyanobacteria used photosynthesis to split water into hydrogen and oxygen, then combined hydrogen with the abundant carbon dioxide to make simple organic molecules. These were the forerunners of the carbohydrates that we dine upon today. In so doing, the cyanobacteria changed the parameters of life on Earth. As time passed, they formed colonial structures called stromatolites. Accumulating, they created the oceans' first biological reefs.

With an abundant supply of carbon dioxide and no competition, the algae became the ascendant life form. Oxygen, the "waste product" that accumulated for ages, not only fueled an explosive evolution of oxyphilic organisms, it protected them from ultraviolet radiation with an isotope called ozone, which we have been depleting. As the millennia passed, a few of the stromatolites' descendants developed a taste for their ancestors — the worst being snails, which almost grazed the defenseless stromatolites into extinction.

Scientists are fairly certain that many of the Earth's great iron ore bodies are the byproducts of stromatolite activity. As the organisms released oxygen, it combined with dissolved iron, forming iron oxides that settled in the shallows. Thus, when prospectors discovered Minnesota's Mesabi Range, they often found the ore hidden beneath tough masses of quartz-like rock. Though they cursed the unyielding overlay, they had no way of knowing it contained the stromatolites that had lain down the ore that they prized.

When the same Luis Alvarez who investigated the iridium clay layer that marks the end of the dinosaurs thought to examine stromatolite sections under a microscope, we finally learned that these pillowy, odd-looking rocks contained the humble precursors of our lives.

Fortunately, a few stromatolite reefs have not only survived, but are actually thriving, the largest being located at Shark Bay in Western Australia. North Americans who are content with fossilized reefs can visit Wyoming's Medicine Bow Mountains or Lake Superior's northern shore. Minnesota even hosts a few *living* stromatolite colonies in the depths of its freshwater lakes, all of them spring fed — their locations kept secret to protect them from humans.

As the Cub taxis away from Utsingi's rumpled shore, I'm immensely pleased that, although more than 99% of the earth's life forms have gone extinct, one of the survivors is the simple, two billion-year-old algae that breathed us into life.

# It's a Mad, Mad, Mad, Mad World!

I never read "Alice in Wonderland" because the bits and pieces that I came across convinced me that "Alice" was intended for kids. Looking back, I might have been wrong. Perhaps traveling with Alice to visit the Queen of Hearts, the March Hare and the Mad Hatter would have prepared me for the shifty semantics that allowed David Duke, a former Nazi and Klu Klux Kingpin to win the Republican primary in Louisiana, and perhaps I'd understand why Henry Hyde and Newt Gingrich resent being out-sinned by William Jefferson Clinton. Indeed, if politics is an example of the old saw that "cream rises to the top," one can easily understand the popularity of low-fat milk.

Into this cast of characters we now introduce the charismatics, the Pentecostals and the faith healers, represented by folks like Bakker, Copeland, Roberts, Hinn and Robertson — all of them consummate actors who can easily cry on cue. Consider the "right reverend" Jimmy Swaggart. Caught with prostitute #1, he weeps, wails and confesses — and promises to reform. Caught with #2, he emotes and resigns, then has a conversation with God, who instructs him to tell his flock "it is flat out none of their business." His flock will remain, as will Swaggart and son, for of what use are flocks, if not for fleecing?

Perhaps the Mad Hatter could also explain the actions of Charles Keating, Jr., who describes himself as a "devout Catholic" who has learned a lot from the Church. So much, in fact, that he relieved thousands of depositors of their savings — an outrage that cost taxpayers more than $2 BILLION, half of which was lost by Senator John McCain and his friends — the Keating Five — who saw to it that investigation of the fraud was repeatedly delayed. And where did the money go? It's hard to say, because when you're really RICH one doesn't have to say. It is known, however, that some of the money went to a film designed to lay the attempted assassination of Pope John Paul II on the Kremlin's doorstep. Fortunately, Keating was caught before he had a chance to embezzle another $20 million in order to finish the film.

Why is it that when a VICTIM is religious, the press often includes their religion within its report. How many times have we seen, "Danny J., a choir member of St. Genericus church, was assaulted by a street gang at ...?" But when the CRIMINAL is religious, the headline never reads, "Choir member from St. Genericus assaults youth at ..."

In ancient Greece, it was proposed that no one should earn more than five times the pay of the common worker. Yet today's CEOs have annual incomes that are more than 100 times that of U. S. assembly line workers. In Germany, the CEO-to-worker wage ratio is 25 to 1, in Japan, only 17 to 1. Is any CEO worth $20 million per year while schools, libraries, the unemployed and small businesses struggle? Income ratios now prevalent in the United States fully demonstrate the success of the motivator that fueled Jimmy Bakker, Ivan Boesky and Charles Keating — GREED. If enough of us fail to speak out, fail to call and write legislators in support of a rational graduated income tax, and fail to rise with outrage at stockholder's meetings, these disparities will climb while the money is skimmed from the top, leaving problems to trickle down.

# Boosterism and Unpopular Ideas

During the arms race with the USSR, I was invited to give a Memorial Day speech in the little town of Rushmore, Minnesota. The small crowd that gathered in the small, white-sided Lutheran Church was not very impressive, and they probably thought the same of me. In those days, and perhaps still, Memorial Day speeches consisted of patriotic themes and tributes to the fallen who had defended our liberties with their lives. And though I agree that these sentiments are often justified, I tried to take a broader view, presenting a view of history that was hard to dispute, but far from popular.

I mentioned the fact that arms races had almost always resulted in either war or the economic collapse of one or both nations. And with the Soviet "Union" fracturing and the United States burdened with debt, I wondered if we had finally learned our lesson.

A few years later, I suggested to the board of our Kiwanis Club that we:

1. Stop singing ego-inflating, back-patting songs about how wonderful we were, and devote more time to substantive issues.

2. Send some of our money outside of the community to where it was really needed.

3. Give scholarships based only on need, a change that would have excluded the children of most of our members.

4. Seek and admit women.

My proposals were NOT well received, and we finally parted company after they made a small concession on #2, but failed to yield on the rest.

The story was the same at the Chamber of Commerce. I had been a member of the chamber for years before I realized that the unspoken theme was "bigger is always better," regardless of taxpayer and environmental costs. When I began to question a few of their projects, my questions were shunted aside, so I now generalize these "team player" attitudes as the "chamber of commerce mentality," which is represented by the famous assertion that "What's good for General Motors is good for the country."

Years later, I came upon Aldo Leopold's 1923 speech titled A Criticism of the Booster Spirit. Here was someone who had not only reached the same conclusions, but had presented them to an Albuquerque Civic Society. His speech was a zinger, beginning with the assertion that boosterism had its roots in the mindless misquote from Stephen Decatur that we know as, "My country! May she always be right! But, right or wrong, my country!" Insert the words " city, school or church," and you get my drift. Loyalty first, whether deserved or not! (Leopold, one of the first true conservationists, wrote the marvelous "Sand County Almanac," during his Wisconsin years.)

In his presentation, Leopold listed ten traits at the root of boosterism and then went on to criticize them. Let me mention but four:

1. To be big and grow bigger is the aim of cities ... To stay small is failure.

2. To grow big you must advertise advantages and ignore defects. ... Self criticism is akin to treason.

3. Unanimity is the only defensible attitude towards public questions.

4. Bribing conventioneers or corporations are signs of friendly rivalry.

Imagine! In 1923, there was Leopold, claiming that communities had hidden their warts, stifled dissent and used tax revenue to compete for industry. Unfortunately, it's worse than that. Now we even use tax revenue to help finance church projects!

Ah, churches — ORGANIZED religion — now there's a subject for the skeptical mind. Whatever happened to the separation of church and state?

As the years passed and I eased away from religion, I discovered that my criticisms of religion, like my dislike for mindless boosterism, were far from original. They had been made by hundreds — and even by the famous — but for some reason those thoughts had never appeared in the books of I'd encountered. I had even concluded that religion would someday be treated as an addiction, but as I eventually learned, others had beaten me to it. Story of my life!

# Get a Half-Life

*from* True North: Exploring the Great Wilderness by Bush Plane

When the Cub rises from Owl Lake, the fog is still thick to the north, so I fly west to the Little Churchill River. Thirty minutes later, I'm standing at the front of a float, flipping a jig ahead of the slowly drifting Cub. I let it settle for a second, then add a few twitches. Ziiinggg — it's time to start cranking.

It's a big walleye, quickly followed by several more, but I'd rather have a smaller fish, a two-pounder just for lunch. Finally, after releasing three of its large kin, I catch my next meal just as the current carries the Cub to a sunlit island with a sloping, granite shelf that will serve the Cub quite well.

After roping the Cub to a toppled pine, I return to my still-thrashing pike. As I drag him ashore, my eye catches a lens-shaped fragment of stone — a chip of my bedrock beach. I'm no expert on rocks, but I'm sure that my sharp-edged chip of the Canadian Shield is at least three billion years old. If so, it's just a youngster, for much of the Shield is older still. And as I finger my slender piece of our continent's backbone, which we can now date with ease, I remember that such precision wasn't always possible.

In the fourth century, St. Augustine, the venerated Church father who ordered non-Catholics to "convert or die," proclaimed creation to have occurred in 5500 BCE. About 1,300 years after Augustine, a 17th-century Irish bishop named James Ussher again took up the task. But with nothing more than the biblical "begats" to work with, the archbishop did even worse than Augustine, declaring with laughable precision that time began on "the beginning of the night that preceded the twenty-third day of October (my birthday, how nice!) in the year 4004 BC."

When humans were finally free to employ the tools of science without the hindrance of religious dogma, it soon became obvious that the Earth was incredibly old. In pursuit of determining its precise age, some scientists estimated the time needed for erosion to bring the oceans to their present salinity, while others worked with the probable cooling rate of an originally molten Earth.

By the end of the 19th century, Lord Kelvin, who was the first to allow for the heat generated by gravitational contraction, had extended the age of the earth to fifty million years. Still, something was missing. That something turned up in the work of Antoine Henri Becquerel, who first described radioactivity in 1896, and in the laboratory of Marie Curie, who isolated radium a few years later, which, being 100,000 times more radioactive than uranium, eventually took her life. Her notebooks are still too "hot" to handle.

Upon learning that radium produced enough heat to melt an equivalent weight of ice every hour as it slowly "decayed" into lighter elements, scientists had to acknowledge that even Lord Kelvin's results had fallen far short of the mark. A few years later, when it was discovered that all of the unstable elements decay at predictable, uniform rates, scientists realized that the clock they'd sought had been hiding in the rocks themselves, and the door to the age of the Earth sprang open.

Imagine, for the moment, that we have been given a pail filled with red marbles that we must count at noon every day. On the first day, all 512 marbles are red. The following noon, however, we're surprised to find that 256 (half) have turned blue, leaving 256 still red. On day three there are only 128 red marbles, the rest having turned blue. Day four yields 64 reds and day five only 32, as half of the remaining red marbles turn blue every day. Scientists, observing this transformation, would say that red marbles have a half-life of one day.

Now imagine that we've been given a pail with a mixture of red and blue marbles, then asked how long ago the pail was filled with red marbles. Knowing that the half-life of red marbles is one day, a quick count of each color would provide the answer. Half red, one day old; one-fourth red, two days old; an eighth red, three days old and so on. With such a clock, geologists have determined the age of the Earth.

Geologists, however, work with elements that have immensely long half-lives. The half-life of carbon 14, for example, which all living matter contains, is 5,570 years. Near the far end of the scale is uranium 238, with a half-life of four billion years.

Equipped with half-life dating methods, scientists quickly verified what a few had long suspected, that the rocks of the Canadian Shield are among the oldest of all, ranging back some four billion years. In comparison, the half-billion-year-old rocks of the continental fringes are mere children, and at the mid-Atlantic ridge (or at any erupting volcano), new "land" is pouring forth.

# With a Hey Nonny, Nonny and a Ho, Ho, Ho

In Minnesota, we don't have "chestnuts roasting on an open fire," but we've all had "Jack Frost nipping at our nose," and plenty of "Yuletide carols being sung by a choir," so, since it's that time again, let's examine a few of the customs of Christmases past.

With born again G.W. Bush, Newt Gingrich and Pat Robertson urging us to return to the "religion of our forefathers," we need to remember that the "good old days" were mighty intolerant. For example, in 1659, the Puritans outlawed Christmas and fined anyone who had the nerve to celebrate the "wanton pagan festival."

In 1821, a Divinity professor named Clement Moore published "Twas the Night Before Christmas," but fearing repercussions, he hid his authorship for almost twenty years.

Twenty years later Charles Dickens dashed off "A Christmas Carol" in order to raise some cash. It was overpriced at five shillings, but his book was an instant hit.

Candy canes arrived about 1850, the creation of a Swedish woman named Amalia Ericson.

In 1882, the first electrically lit Christmas tree brightened the home of a New York friend of Thomas Edison.

Congress outlawed child laborers called "Santa's elves" in 1895, liberating children from long hours at low pay during the Christmas season.

By 1898, Christmas and commercialism had become one, with department stores wedding religion to retail via angels and stained glass panels set amid the merchandise, along with paintings of the Madonna and the baby Jesus.

In 1903, Denmark introduced Christmas Seals as a fundraiser. Later, World War I put an end to penny Christmas cards from Germany, which prompted Kansas City's Joyce Hall to begin a business that became Hallmark Cards.

During the depths of the 1933 depression, Sears published its first Wish Book, and a Pennsylvania court held in contempt an honest person who doubted the existence of Santa Claus.

Irving Berlin's "White Christmas" started its record-setting career in 1942 with a recording by Bing Crosby and Marjorie Reynolds.

In 1949, a Bah Humbug banker in Muskegon, Michigan erected a billboard saying "There is No Santa Claus. Work — Earn — Save!" The public howled and the ad came down.

Land O'Lakes moved into the eggnog market in 1955. Five years later, Neiman Marcus offered the first His and Hers Christmas airplanes. His cost $149,000 — hers a mere $27,000.

In 1968, the Catholic Church cut Saint Nicholas Day (December 6) from its calendar. A few years later, even worse awaited Santa. When Mr. Claus arrived at a Fort Lauderdale supermarket, delinquents knocked him flat, and children of all ages ran off with his gifts.

Taking a cue from George Washington, who attacked Hessian mercenaries on Christmas Day, the U.S. in 1972 began the Christmas bombings of Hanoi, dropping 36,000 tons of explosives that killed 2,000 civilians in a pointless war. From an economic point of view, that's 18 tons of explosives per fatality. Now we fight in Iraq.

In response to the popularity of violence-inducing toys like G.I. Joe and He-Man, the Wee Win Toys Co. enlivened the '80s by introducing action figures of David, Goliath, Sampson, and, of course, a muscular Jesus Christ.

As for the religious side of Christmas, December 25 was probably chosen because it fell on (and helped to obliterate) a major pagan festival. In fact, early Christians paid little attention to birthdays, considering them a pagan affair. Moreover, many Mediterranean cultures believed that sometime between December 25 and January 6, the Earth Mother gave birth to a male god, who was destined to die and be reborn.

In usurping beliefs like this, Christianity began a voracious history of gobbling up the mythologies of those it wished to convert.

For example, Christianity claimed that St. Boniface struck down a huge "Thunder Oak" beneath which pagans honored the god Odin. The oak fell, revealing a small fir tree behind it, and a new symbol was born.

These celebrations gradually evolved into Christ-Mass, which maintained many of the pagan traditions until Martin Luther and the Reformation came to town. Out went fun and in came Bible study, a process aided by Oliver Cromwell, who tried to outlaw Christmas by ordering churches closed and shops to stay open. The people rioted, and their holiday was eventually restored.

Some might argue that Christmas has evolved — yes, evolved — into a beautiful, inclusive holiday, but I wonder about that. Do Jews, Muslims, freethinkers, etc. feel included? Should we be celebrating the transformation of the thoughtful Jesus (who warned about laying up treasures on Earth) to the Jesus that is reputed to want you to be rich?

Personally, I like the gift giving, but I need no religious excuse. And I really don't like the fact that some countries' celebrations have even included tanks and rockets.

Give me Santa instead. In the Arctic, Santa travels by snowmobile, but along the Gold Coast of Australia, he leaps ashore from a lifeboat. Skipping the usual Hey Nonny Nonnies and the Ho, Ho, Hos, he pops open a Foster's lager and bellows "Merry Christmas, mates!"

# What's It All About?

There is a small cabin on a Lake Vermilion island in the Arrowhead region of northern Minnesota. I grew up there. My parents sold it in '60 and I bought it back in '69. And as long as I pay my taxes, the government allows me to call the cabin and the two acres that surround it mine.

Until I left for college, nearly every weekend found me tramping the woods and snooping through the bays and shallow inlets. Slowly and subtly, but unaware of the process, I came to appreciate nature — from the ochre lichens scratching a living from shelves of barren rock to the bear and her cubs that wander by, scenting the air for food, not twenty feet from my lawn chair.

I wondered at the horsehair worms in the summer waters, at the delicate, finely curved wavelets stretched across calm waters by the bow of our slowly moving boat, and at the camouflaged caddis fly larva, adorned with bits of aquatic debris, safe from winter's chill (but not my prying eyes) beneath a glassy sheet of ice. Somewhere in it all, I discovered what Albert Schweitzer came to call "reverence for life." And though I have no quarrel with hunters who eat what they kill, replacing beef with venison etc., I now hunt with a camera, joining the thousands who prefer to let a creature live for another day or another decade.

Every season taught me something: which ice could be safely crossed and which winds would drive an underpowered boat ashore. I learned that many questions have several answers, some of them wrong; that today's truth may be tomorrow's myth; that those who show us our errors lift a load from our backs, deserving our thanks instead of resentment, and that even the best educated are often the wisest when they say, "I don't know!"

I learned that there are different people in the world — with different ways. In July, during the "moon of the falling feathers" (the moulting season) some of them would paddle from cabin to cabin quietly offering blueberries for sale.

It is early November when I write these words. The lake will be freezing soon and we must leave the island, not to return until December. As the air nears thirty degrees, a few fine flakes begin to fall. They thicken and grow, settling more slowly as they broaden from flakes to crystalline flowers, the blossoms of the sky. As John Rowlands wrote in *Cache Lake Country*, "Somewhere above, the old lady in the clouds" has begun to pluck her geese. As their frosted feathers float gently down, settling on the cedar boughs that will help sustain the hungry deer, the chickadees pause from their flipping flights and perch quietly, as if in wonder as the sky descends.

A Canada Jay, all dressed in grey and white and black, swoops to the feeder, announcing his arrival with a gentle coo. With one calm eye on me, he stuffs his mouth with seeds, then hurries off to hide them away, preparing for winter's worst. Under the snow, the glacier-scarred granite chills as it slowly surrenders its summer's hoard of heat. The great biological processes of earth begin to slow, but will not cease.

The lake, now stilled and nearly hidden beneath a thickening eyelid of ice, will slowly draw a drifting, downy comforter about its shoulders and slip quietly toward five months of silence, with neither wind nor wave to trouble its rest.

In its depths, and in the long quiet of the nights, will it sense the deepening cold, or remember the promise of spring? Will it ask, as humans sometimes ask, "What's it all about?" Sometimes, though rarely, I've asked that question, and as the years have passed, my answers have changed, becoming less rigid or certain and more open to challenge or change.

I think it's about loving and caring, and keeping an open mind. It's about asking questions, any questions, without fear of where they might lead.

And if you have a different answer, or maybe more than one, I hope that your answers leave room for mine because I've left room for yours.

# From Ibsen and Grieg to Tammy Wynette and From Norway to Tennessee

Long before Grieg wrote the music to Ibsen's Peer Gynt, the story of the wandering, philandering male had been a staple of bards from Nome to Nairobi and from Cape Town to Katmandu. With much justification and a surfeit of examples to draw upon, Ibsen portrayed Peer Gynt as an indifferent son who leaves his ailing mother to attend the wedding of Ingrid, whom he abducts and then abandons in favor of Solveig, who truly loves him, and whom he also loves.

But Peer is afraid of the big C (commitment), so he runs off, only to meet three seductive herd girls who engage Peer in close encounters of the horizontal kind. Moving on, Peer meets and mingles with the Woman in Green, who turns out to be the daughter of the Mountain King of Trolls. The trolls, named Beck, Limbaugh and Coulter, are vicious, single-minded little creatures who are determined to force Peer to marry the Woman in Green. However, Peer seizes a chance to flee and returns to his dying mother, promising that, in death, she will inhabit a great castle.

Peer then travels the globe, loving, laughing and avoiding responsibility while earning and losing fortunes. Shipwrecked, old, broken and full of regrets, he finally returns to Norway where he hears Solveig's beautiful voice in song, but cannot bring himself to face her. In a heart-rending scene, Peer dies, his body scooped up by an immense ladle as he thinks of love lost, songs unsung and tears unshed. To all of this, his mother adds her reproach. Finally, seeing a falling star (these death scenes run on) Peer compares his life to the briefly glimmering star which flashes for just a moment before its light is quenched.

The faithful Solveig, now old and nearly blind, appears and refuses to renounce Peer, claiming that he has made her life a song as she cradles his head in her lap.

With his final breath, Peer sings a lament that we all should heed:

> 0 beautiful earth, do not be angry with me
> that I trod your sweet grass to no avail.
> 0 beautiful sun, you have squandered
> your golden light upon an empty hut.
> There was no one within to warm and comfort
> The owner, I know, was never home.

Peer's irresponsible but adventurous life missed another great adventure — that of living with someone you love in a place that you both call home. Like so many of us, Peer gained wisdom too late, and there the lesson lies.

Peer's story still haunts the airwaves in songs and soaps — all variations on an ancient theme. It's my hope that the Peers of our age will change, and that singers like Tammy Wynette won't amass a fortune by advising women to "Stand by Your Man" no matter how many times he's "done you wrong," for as long as women heed her wailing advice, men will laugh and turn their backs, and continue to run with their Peers.

# Waiting for Perot in '96

I am not a fan of plays. I take pains to avoid them, and I have repeatedly claimed terminal cancer or total paralysis to escape a performance. The actors shout. The crowds are noisy. And apparently, it is written somewhere that a nearby woman will have bathed in perfume that smells like RAID, and her husband, a man of girth who reeks of cigars, will occupy the adjacent seat as well as part of mine.

As a result, I never attended "Godot." Instead, having taken note of its brevity, I read the play.

"Waiting for Godot" is a philosopher's dream, a theologian's all-year sucker. It brings to mind Stanley Kubrick's "Space Odyssey: 2001," the spectacle that left each viewer with a different opinion as to what Kubrick really meant. Unfortunately, like "Space Odyssey," "Godot" (at only 54 pages) was also a little too long.

In Beckett's play we find two men called Vladimir and Estragon, who are waiting for someone called Godot. Apparently Godot (Christ, Buddha, Colonel Sanders), holds the answer to their problems, for they have waited interminably, as if caught in a time warp that endlessly recycles their days. They are to wait many more — never escaping — never finding Godot or a clue as to what Becket had in mind.

I admit it's a stretch, but in the bickering, indecisive and desperate Estragon and Vladimir I see the dilemma of Americans, represented largely by the Democratic and Republican parties. The former, operating with '50s style and '60s technology, have repeatedly fronted presidential candidates of conscience who lack verve and charisma. Worse yet, their leaders have seemed unable to detect a red-hot issue even when it drops into their drawers.

The Republicans, the wonderful flag-and-cross combo that delivered Nixon, Agnew, the Watergate gang, Ronald (Don't Worry, Be Happy) Reagan, James Watt, Robertson and the Bushes, still promote the candidates of the rich while hoping that the Democrats don't realize that cutting taxes for the rich is an issue that could end the Republican reign.

So here are our choices for '96: inept Democrats who couldn't sell water to a man dying of thirst, and the conservative Republicans, so greedy that they'd hold out for more money. Caught between the incompetent and the unprincipled, Americans wait, and some are wanting Perot.

Imagine that! Another Texan, and a billionaire to boot. After LBJ, Tower (of the Iran-Contra Tower Commission) and Bush, perhaps we need our heads examined for even listening to the man. Nevertheless, it was Perot who said that failing to teach evolution made Texas the "laughingstock." It was Perot who had the insight and candor to tell his fellow Texans that the trouble with their schools was TOO MUCH FOOTBALL! And it is Perot who asserts that governments should be servants of the people.

Perhaps Perot will even notice that the thousands of workers soon to be available (we hope) from reductions in our "defense" industry could be employed at road, bridge and building repair, as well as endless other projects that have been taking second place to military hardware. Still, he is a billionaire Republican, but let's admit that, given several decades and a few shots of lightning, even a conscientious conservative could eventually evolve.

Perot is openly pro-choice. He says that Bush's fingerprints are all over the money that empowered Saddam Hussein. He argues against multimillion dollar salaries for CEOs. And he plainly lays the multibillion dollar increases in the national debt at the feet of Reagan and G H W Bush. Still, his past needs scrutiny, as does the record of the military man that he selected for vice president while ignoring many fine women.

What are his views on church/state separation, on the Equal Rights Amendment, on the minimum wage, on assisting needy nations with birth control, and on the conservative tilt of the Supreme Court?

The Republicans will do their best to derail Perot, assisted by people drawn from the mold of Lee Atwater. The Democrats will dither and minimize Perot, forgetting that Truman and Wellstone, despite predictions that they could never win, did just that — and they weren't even *millionaires*.

# Olbers' Paradox and Edgar Allen Poe

from *True North: Exploring the Great Wilderness by Bush Plane*

Far to the north of Yellowknife, it's a cloudy night on the Barrens. The lingering winds of a cold front are sweeping across the tundra, keeping the mosquitoes at bay. Prompted by a star glimmering through a tiny break in the clouds, my idle mind settles on a subject that surely must tantalize every lonely, red-blooded male — Olbers' Paradox: If space is infinite and there really are an infinite number of stars, as many propose, why is the night sky dark?

In 1823, Heinrich Olbers, a German physician and astronomer, reasoned that if space and the number of stars are indeed infinite — as many had said — the sky should blaze both day and night. But the fact that the sky is dark at night, contrary to what reason would seem to suggest, became known as Olbers' Paradox.

Scientists, philosophers and laymen offered solutions — most of them inferior to a theory that a gloomy, American author proposed. In his *Eureka*, that writer suggested that the universe is still so young and the void so great that the light from the most distant stars has yet to reach us. Though we know him only as America's premier author of horror stories, Mr. Poe's explanation ranked with the best.

Later, William Thompson (Lord Kelvin) expanded on Poe and others, arguing that the unlimited but still-empty universe surrounding the expanding, star-filled universe accounts for the paucity of starlight. Some postulated that in a 15 billion year old universe, many stars would have perished, leaving a void where they once gleamed. Later, others suggested that interstellar gas absorbs vast amounts of star light, as do black holes. Still others proposed that, though the universe might be infinite, perhaps there *aren't* an infinite number of stars.

What will happen, I ask myself, if a few billion years hence, our expanding universe slows to a halt, or, worse yet, begins to contract? As our skies brighten, what will we do with street lights, with headlights? What will become of the last drive-in movie? When the earth becomes a sauna, will our M&M's melt in our hands before they get to our mouths?

# In the Beginning
from *Time Traveling With Science and the Saints*

"It is convenient that there be gods, and, as it is convenient,
let us believe there are."
Ovid

When early humans gathered around their campfires, it was only natural that they'd invent gods as they searched for their origins and sought to explain events beyond their control. Around those fires, tribal leaders slowly refined stories of how the earth and the skies were formed, each according to the circumstances that had shaped their primitive lives.

Some North American natives believed that a muskrat dove to the depths of the ocean and returned with a clump of mud; for others, a deep-diving loon surfaced with its beak full of clay. Tahitians also created an aquatic myth, claiming that their islands had been lifted up from the ocean by powerful gods.

A hemisphere away, Sumerians imagined that the earth was formed from a clod of mud thrown by wrestling giants. Farther south, Africans invented a charming tale of a lovely young girl who dipped her hands into a smoldering fire and threw its ashes high to form the Milky Way. The hot sparks flew even higher, and live on as our brighter stars. And on the continent of Australia, aborigines tell of an agile lizard that decided to walk upright — and became the first human.

Today, although many religious conservatives still cling to the mythology of a six day spurt of creation by an omnipotent, omniscient God, most educated people have set creation myths aside and now tend to favor the non-anthropomorphic god of the Big Bang.

When early worshippers envisioned their gods, they quite predictably conceived supernatural creatures that looked and acted like men. Xenophanes, a pre-Christian Greek, plainly stated the facts: "Ethiopians imagine their gods as black and snub-nosed; Thracians blue-eyed and red-haired. But if horses or lions had hands, or could draw and fashion works as men do, horses would draw gods shaped like horses and lions like lions, making the gods resemble themselves."

It's also understandable that as tribes coalesced into cultures, each believed their language to be the first, received directly from a god who was, of course, superior to all others. After all, who would willingly worship an inferior god?

Later, when confronted by the obvious diversity of language, these early cultures once again turned to theological explanations, and perhaps because their brains shared a common ancestry, even widely separated groups often arrived at similar answers: In Hindu legend a great tree that reached for the heavens offended Brahma, who cut off and scattered its branches. The limbs took root as wata trees, and beneath the canopy of every new tree a different segment of the human population found shelter, each with its own language and beliefs.

Across the oceans, Mexican legends tell of a giant named Xelhua, who built a great pyramid in order to reach heaven. The gods, angered at his audacity, destroyed the building, dispersed the people, and forced upon every group a language of its own.

In Jewish/Christian mythology, the Hindu tree and the Mexican pyramid are replaced by the Tower of Babel, which their god saw fit to destroy. Alarmed at the capability of the tower builders, he confounded their language and scattered them across the earth. The facts, however, tell a different tale.

Today, historians agree that structures like the Tower of Babel, which means the *Gate of God*, were primarily used for observing the stars. Believing that the heavens lay not far overhead, observers reasoned that the towers would loft them closer to the nightly mysteries that traveled across the sky. As for the fall of the Tower of Babel, a recently unearthed ceramic cylinder was found to bear inscriptions implying that the tower collapsed due to inept design in a region prone to earthquakes.

Most early humans undoubtedly relied upon mysticism and ordered their lives according to superstition. But, but as early as 4000 BCE a few pre-Christian Egyptians, Greeks and Chaldeans had begun to search for rational explanations, particularly in astronomy, the oldest of the sciences, by mapping the stars and charting their motions.

By the 7th century BCE, the wheel had been in use for 2500 years, and the Egyptians (and others) had been profiting from the virtues of the copper-tin alloy called bronze for more than a thousand years. India had been producing not just iron, but *steel*, which it exported to Syria, where the flat, round billets became exceptionally hard — but tough — sword blades, bringing fame to Damascus steel.

Then, in the 6th century BCE, the seeds of two new sciences — mathematics and geometry — were sown by Thales, a resident of Miletus, the wealthy center of commerce situated close to the Western coast of present-day Turkey. Thales, an inquisitive, perceptive (and rich) olive oil merchant not only amazed his contemporaries by accurately predicting a solar eclipse, but also speculated that life had begun in water, then adjusted to living on land.

Subsequently, a pupil of Thales, the atheist Anaximander, constructed a primitive globe and wrote a treatise, *On Nature*, that promoted the concept of maps as visual displays to replace the custom of relying on literary descriptions of places and distances. (A little more than a century later, the Greeks began to place maps on a few of their coins.) Moving on, Anaximander brought the sundial to Greece, and with it Egyptian astronomy, the science that Plato later claimed "compels the soul to look upwards and leads us from this world to another."

Plato, unlike his teacher, Socrates, who was put to death for offending the status quo with insightful questions and for declining to honor the gods, refused to accumulate knowledge through experiment. And although Plato was an accomplished mathematician, and his Academy at Athens bore the inscription "let none who has not studied geometry enter here," he preferred (like our New Agers) to rely on intuition, and to search for truth with the "eye of the soul." Centuries later, the Neoplatonists, who also held experimental science in contempt, would help St. Augustine conclude that "the only type of knowledge to be desired was the knowledge of God and the soul, and that no profit was to be had from investigating the realms of nature."

Anaximander could well have been the first Westerner to envision a liberated universe — infinite in both time and space. Not content to restrict his mind to the skies, he enlarged upon Thales' theory that the existence of fossils proved that life had begun in an ancient ocean, and speculated that as humans developed, they had passed through a fish-like phase.

A few generations later, Anaxagoras reasoned out the cause of lunar and solar eclipses, contemplated a theory of evolution, and argued that the sun was not a god, for which he was imprisoned. He also advanced the apparently outrageous heresy that the sun was larger than Greece, which by then encompassed most of the land surrounding the Mediterranean Sea, and claimed that the sun "enlightened" the moon — a fact that the Catholic Church would steadfastly oppose for more than 1,200 years.

Shortly thereafter, Pythagoras, of the Greek island of Samos, became one of the first to support the emancipation of women, proposed that the Earth revolves around the sun and investigated the properties of a right triangle, a tool that others would use to determine the distance between the moon and the Earth. Unfortunately, the public found the concept of an orbiting earth preposterous. His liberal policies caused him to be banished. His followers were slain, their meeting places destroyed by religious zealots.

Pythagoras, along with several other pre-Christian Greeks, was also one of the first thinkers in the Western Hemisphere to present the notion of a spherical Earth. "The sphericity of the Earth," he wrote, "is proved by the evidence of our senses, for otherwise lunar eclipses would not take such forms; for whereas in the monthly phases of the moon... the dividing line is always rounded. Consequently if the eclipse is due to the interposition of the Earth, the rounded line results from its spherical shape."

The notion of a spherical earth apparently first occurred (in the Western Hemisphere) to several pre-Christian Greeks, including Pythagoras, who wrote, "The sphericity of the earth is proved by the evidence of our senses, for otherwise lunar eclipses would not take such forms; for whereas in the monthly phases of the moon... the dividing line is always rounded. Consequently if the eclipse is due to the interposition of the Earth, the rounded line results from its spherical shape."

Approximately a century after Pythagoras — around 400 BCE —

another deep thinker named Democritus suggested that all matter consisted of tiny, indivisible particles that he called atoms. Though his atomic theory cast new light on primitive physics and chemistry, the concept was thousands of years ahead of its time. And then, in the middle of the 4th century BCE, came a naturalist named Aristotle.

Aristotle, who knew what had happened to Socrates and Pythagoras, continued to worship the gods, though he candidly wrote of their usefulness to politicians: "A tyrant must put on the appearance of uncommon devotion to religion. Subjects ... do less easily move against him, believing that he has the gods on his side." Aristotle accepted the concept of a spherical Earth, and is said to be the first to propose a system of classification for animals. One could also argue that he became the first embryologist when he systematically began to open fertilized chicken eggs of increasing stages of maturity to better understand embryonic development. Because he believed that nature could be understood through analysis, he came to conclude that natural events had causes unrelated to myths and deities, and argued that humans could control their destinies more effectively through education and reason than with appeals to the gods.

Unfortunately, Aristotle's wide-ranging mind occasionally reached unsound conclusions that would hinder the progress of science. Chief among them was his dogged support of an Earth-centered solar system. As Arthur Koestler wrote in *The Sleepwalkers*, "The Ionians had prised the world-oyster open, the Pythagoreans had set the Earth ball adrift in it, the atomists dissolved its boundaries in the infinite, [but] Aristotle closed the lid again with a bang, shoved the earth into the world's center, and deprived it of motion."

Perhaps no one exemplified Aristotle's philosophy better than Epicurus, the Greek scientist and philosopher who not only rejected religion, but argued that reason must confine itself to the experience of the senses. As a man of ethics, Epicurus urged virtue, not as an end in itself, but as the essential means to a happy life. Thus, in the Mediterranean soils of ancient Greece, the seeds of a philosophy that relied on reason to search for knowledge and a more enriching life took root. With its emphasis on the critical use of the human mind instead of superstition, that philosophy came to be called Humanism. Unfortunately, like Epicurus, who was outlawed for refusing to worship the gods, today's secular humanists still find themselves vilified by fundamentalist Christians.

The tools and methods of the early sciences were, by today's standards, extremely unrefined, so it's not surprising that Aristotle supported a belief first enunciated by Empedocles in the 5th century BCE — that the universe was composed of four elements: earth, air, fire and water — another simplistic conclusion that the church would cling to for at least a thousand years.

About 330 BCE, Heraclites reasoned that the apparent motion of the stars was caused by the rotation of the Earth. Just a few decades later Aristarchus of Samos (like Pythagoras) estimated the distance of the moon at 250,000 miles — with an astounding error of only five percent — and then placed the sun, not the Earth, at the center of the solar system. Archimedes, a young contemporary of Aristarchus, and the first to systematically apply mathematics to the physical world, would later write, "For he [Aristarchus] supposed that the fixed stars and the sun are immovable, but that the earth is carried around the sun in a circle."

Unfortunately, the heliocentric theory that Aristarchus proposed required an elliptical orbit for the earth, and that was one leap of logic that even Aristarchus was unable to make. Not surprisingly, his religious contemporaries charged him with impiety for "moving the hearth of the universe."

Then Euclid, a contemporary of Aristarchus and admirer of the work of Archimedes, devised a system of plane and solid geometry that we still find useful today. Euclid's factual *Elements of Geometry* has been translated and copied more than any other book, with but one very different exception, the Bible. Algebra and trigonometry followed, only to languish a few centuries later when Rome, which had become more interested in obedience and conquest, found an ally in Christianity, which first preached obedience, then conquest in the name of the cross. (In *Euclid's Window*, Leonard Mlindow notes that during its 1,100 years of recorded existence, beginning at 750 BCE, history records not even one Roman mathematician — not a single theorem proven.)

About 250 BCE, the Greek scholar Eratosthenes, who headed the famous library at Alexandria, decided to explore all of the sciences, including mathematics and geography — studies that led him to propose that if the extent of the ocean were not an obstacle, we might easily sail round the world. This was not idle speculation, for Eratosthenes not only *knew* that the earth was round, he had calculated its circumference to within a few percentage points of the figure accepted today.

Knowing that on the equinox the noon-day sun cast no shadow at Syene, while at the same instant casting a shadow of approximately 7.5 degrees at 500-mile-distant Alexandria (which lay directly north of Syene) Eratosthenes asked himself - if a five hundred-mile span causes a 7.5 degree curvature, how many miles would be needed for a full circle of 360 degrees? Since forty-eight 7.5 degree arcs equal 360 degrees, then 48 X 500, or 24,000 miles should approximate our planet's circumference, which it does.

Yet even that achievement pales beside his astoundingly accurate calculation that the sun is 92,000,000 miles distant from the earth! (Unfortunately, about 250 years later, the Greek geographer Strabo somehow — we are not sure by what logic — re-calculated the circumference of the earth at 18,000 miles, a figure that Ptolemy accepted and that Columbus would later rely on when he sought funding for a westerly voyage from the King and Queen of Spain.)

Archimedes, a Sicilian contemporary of Eratosthenes, was the first to use the logic of fluid displacement as a means to assay gold. Moving from geometry and physics to arithmetic, Archimedes suggested in "*The Sand Reckoner*" that very large numbers could be represented by multiples or "orders" of 10,000. Turning to the field of mechanics, he worked out the principles of the pulley and the lever so accurately that no advance was made upon his work until late in the 16th century. As most high school students know, it was Archimedes who uttered the now-famous statement, "Give me but one firm place on which to stand, and I will move the earth."

Around 300 BCE, Alexander the Great, inspired by what he had learned at Aristotle's Lyceum, set out to establish a great museum and two libraries at Alexandria, one of which would become the famous Serapeum. There, prominent thinkers like Euclid, Appolonius, Aristarchus, Eratosthenes and Archimedes would gather to pry open nature's secrets.

Aided by Alexander's protégé (Ptolemy I), the libraries eventually became the Western world's preeminent center of science, mathematics and literary studies, housing some 700,000 scrolls, all written by hand, and many secured at great price. Every ship that sailed into Alexandria was boarded, not just to ferret out contraband, but to search for new works of literature that could be copied and added to the library. In fact, rather than return the original manuscripts of the tragedies of Sophocles, Aeschylus and Euripides to the Athenians from whom they had been borrowed, the Ptolemys chose to forfeit a huge cash deposit — and returned only copies.

In these surroundings, science prospered, unopposed by religion, for the gods of Homer and the pre-Christian Greeks made no claim to omniscience, and were believed to be both capricious and fallible. As a consequence, the early Greeks freely searched for nature's truths — a situation that would begin to change when Egypt and its intellectual center, Alexandria, became part of Rome in 50 BCE, then drastically change with the arrival of Catholic dogmas and the self-proclaimed perfection of Christianity.

During the first century CE, Heron of Alexandria began to experiment with primitive steam engines. But shortly thereafter, science encountered an influential, second-century Alexandrian named Claudius Ptolemaeus who, like Aristotle, favored an Earth-centered solar system. He did, however, propose the use of meridians that converge toward the pole as an aid for mapping the Earth, a concept that would be ignored by Rome, but generally accepted by Arabs and Byzantines. (Claudius Ptolemy was not related to the royal Ptolemys.)

By the time of Claudius, progress in science had begun to slow, partly due to the lack of technology, but also because science held little of interest to the common people or to the dominant culture of Rome. Plato, by calling geometry the highest exercise to which leisure can be devoted, confirmed that only the upper class had the time to devote to science. Furthermore, because the masses, many of whom were slaves, had no access to education, only the elite could understand it. And as science historian Benjamin Farrington noted, societies like Rome, which had an abundance of slave labor, had little incentive to develop the technologies that science can provide.

As interest in science waned, Christianity began to gain strength. Conceived in ignorance and prospering through zeal and deceit, the early

Christian church, which had combined the carrot and stick of heaven and hell with missionary passion, astrological signs, virgin births and assorted miracles co-opted from other religions, slowly began to overcome its competitors.

Growing ever more powerful and unprincipled over the centuries, the churches eventually received the condemnation of Thomas Paine, an early American patriot, deist and defender of the downtrodden, who argued that churches are nothing but human inventions, their purpose being to enslave mankind and monopolize power and profit. When pressed to defend his churchless deism, Paine wrote, "My mind is my church ... to do good is my religion." A century later, Walt Whitman, the American poet laureate, would cast his vote with Paine: "The churches are one vast lie ... the priests are continually telling what they know is not so and keeping back what they know is so."

# On Oakum, Leaks and the Search for Truth

The Viking ships, the caravels of Columbus and the dhows of Dubai had one thing in common — they leaked. Mariners everywhere, preferring a dry hull to incessant bailing, turned to a rope-like substance known as oakum. Soaked with tar, and hammered into the seams of the ship, the oakum restrained the ocean's incessant efforts to reside inside the hull. Thus protected, wooden ships carried fisherman and explorers across the oceans and around the world, troubled only by seepage, and not by floods.

But I have a different ship in mind, a ship whose wake has washed many shores, though it sails upon no sea. It's a ship hard aground where no other ship lives — in Washington D.C.

We call this vessel the Ship of State. Periodically, we elect officers to pilot this metaphor and keep it whole. But, like the hulls of long ago, it also leaks, and in a rather unusual way: It leaks from the inside out.

The officers of Ship of State do not like leaks, preferring to keep the landlubbers informed with speeches and photo ops, and by partially cooperating with an often docile press. The part of their business that they deem too upsetting for ordinary mortals becomes CLASSIFIED or RESTRICTED and is hidden in the deepest hollows of the hull beneath layers of protective procedures. Thus burdened, the seams of the hull of the Ship of State eventually separate and out leaks TRUTH.

Leaks brought us the Pentagon Papers; they informed us of Watergate. A few decades ago, Iran-Contragate oozed forth, and the oakum squads, led by Oliver North, hastened to plug the gaps with shredded documents.

A few years later, President George H. W. Bush nominated Clarence Thomas to help the Supreme Court guide the Ship of State. Presented as being only one step lower than the angels, he was loudly supported by officials of the Roman Catholic Church. Somewhere in the Ship of State, the Senate Judiciary Committee met to consider the nominee. In one FBI report, a former employee, Professor Anita Hill, claimed that Judge Thomas subjected her to sexual harassment as head of the Equal Employment Opportunity Commission. In a statement given under the promise of anonymity, she stated that there was more to St. Thomas than met the press. However, someone found a crack and slipped that item through.

And then, near the end of the reign of King George the Warrior, the hull, weakened from inside by corruption and faith-based maintenance, really began to leak. Out poured: 1. No linkage between Saddam Hussein and al Qaeda, 2. No weapons of mass destruction, 3. No truth to allegations of Iraq acquiring uranium, 4. Secret domestic wire tapping and spying, and 5. The use of torture.

The Ship of State, two battered centuries old, has survived. Not because of the oakum squads, but because of the wonderful leaks that periodically purify its cargo. May that Ship sail on forever, assisted by a hull that seems to know when to pop a seam — and out flows TRUTH.

# Just the Facts, Ma'am, Just the Facts

Like Sgt. Friday of Dragnet fame, I want politicians, retailers, chambers of commerce and writers to stick to the facts. However, somewhere along the road to "success" we were persuaded that bigger is always better, and boosterism was born. Boosterism, like religion, relies on zeal, although there can be an occasional fact or two hiding somewhere in the mix.

In the late Paleozoic era (when I was in grade school) I noticed that adults exaggerated, and even lied on occasion. Nevertheless, I was surprised to discover that they even made ridiculous claims in print when the Lake Vermilion Resort Association distributed a map (still available) claiming that Lake Vermilion had a "thousand miles of shoreline and 365 islands." The figure, 365, seemed too convenient, so I counted the islands, which came to less than a hundred. And although the lake is almost thirty miles long and has a highly convoluted shoreline, an opisometer and a good map soon sliced its "thousand miles" by more than half.

Newspapers and broadcasters often use whatever writers submit, but many writers don't share Sgt. Friday's dedication to the facts. For example, a recent article in the Minneapolis Star Tribune claimed that Jackie Chan, an Asian movie star, had broken "almost every bone in his body." Let's think about that.

If it is fair to assume that a person described as "almost 100 years old" would be at least 85, it seems reasonable that someone who has broken "almost every bone in his body" would have fractured 85% of his bones. And that's "broken," not "cracked, bruised or dislocated."

Given that we humans have a tad over 200 bones, does anyone believe that Mr. Chan fractured at least 170, which would be 85%? How about 150? 100? Would anyone bet that he's broken 50? I think not.

Carl Sagan, one of the few public figures willing to challenge superstitious beliefs, addressed these issues in his excellent book, *A Demon-Haunted World*, noting that science always subjects its conclusions to critical review and continuously tests them against new knowledge. He then says that the failure of religions to do the same "is one of the reasons that organized religions do not inspire me with confidence."

"Which leaders of the major faiths acknowledge that their beliefs might be incomplete or erroneous and establish institutes to uncover possible deficiencies? ... Who is systematically testing the circumstances in which traditional religious teachings may no longer apply? What sermons examine the God hypothesis in a balanced way? What rewards are religious skeptics given by established religions or, for that matter, social and economic skeptics by the society in which they swim?

"Science ... is forever whispering in our ears, 'remember, you're new at this. You might be mistaken. You've been wrong before.' Despite all the talk of humility, show me something comparable in religion.

"People fall prey to pseudo science because they don't have the education and thinking skills to sort out fact from false. They want whatever they can imagine to be true, which is magical, childish thinking. Science carries us to an understanding of how the world is, rather than how we wish it to be. If we shy away from science because it's too difficult or it has been poorly taught, we surrender the ability to take charge of our future ... Our self-confidence erodes."

Sagan noted that people react poorly to science's demands for proof, saying "Where does science come off telling me that a thing I find interesting can't be true? What arrogance!" But Sagan argues to the contrary, saying that "Science is humble. It doesn't impose its own views on the universe." Not so, religion.

A tempest in a teapot? Well, it's not. Every day, thousands are mislead or conned by absurdities in private conversations, in the media, in the work place and in many churches. When critical reading, critical listening and critical thinking become mandatory courses in our schools, gullibility will decline and respect for truth will soar.

Sagan (and I) especially liked this quote from Jefferson — "If a nation expects to be both ignorant and free in a state of civilization, it expects what never was and never will be."

# Sins of the Fathers

from *Back to the Barrens: On the Wing With da Vinci & Friends*

Were I flying higher, the community of Chesterfield Inlet, where native children suffered abuse in church-run schools, would be visible beyond my right wing. Fortunately, those abuses, which were prolonged by government blindness or indifference across much of Canada, are now less likely to occur because many of the church schools that fussed about souls while neglecting health and education have been replaced by secular schools in which health and education come first.

When I wrote of these problems in *True North*, I left out stories of missionaries who ordered the converted to shun the unconverted, causing fractured families, despair and even death when those who needed assistance were deliberately ignored, but I made plain my disgust for the churches that tried to avoid prosecution by hiding behind the statute of limitations.

That evasion brought a letter from an Edmonton attorney whose firm represented hundreds of the victims of church schools, including the school at Chesterfield Inlet. Yes, he said, many of the churches had tried to hide behind the statute of limitations, but, fortunately, Canadian law prevented that clock from starting until the victims understood that the treatment they'd suffered had been discriminatory, inappropriate or sometimes even malicious.

More recently, I've seen notices posted in public areas that advise abused natives to call **866-879-4913** or visit **www.residentialschoolsettlement. ca** to learn if they qualify for any of the $1.9 billion set aside for settling claims of abuse.

All across Canada, children as young as five were taken from their families, their hair was cut short and they were forbidden to speak their native language. Parents were rarely allowed to visit. Some schools became havens for pedophiles. In 1997, outraged Newfoundlanders scrapped the old system and adopted a resoundingly successful system of public schooling. In a report titled "Sins of the Fathers," an Anglican publication revealed that eight Indian men committed suicide rather than answer a subpoena that would have required them to describe the sexual abuse they'd endured as helpless children. A few years later, newspapers reported that claims against the Roman Catholics, Anglicans, United Church of Canada and others numbered in the thousands. The churches argued that if the judgments ran into the millions, which they eventually did, they'd go bankrupt, but despite the fines and their protestations, the churches are still in business.

Like Henry Voisey, the Hudson's Bay Company manager at Padlei, Rankin Inlet mine manager Andy Easton also derided missionaries, describing the community's Catholic, Anglican and evangelical missionaries as "A bloody pain in the ass. They feud like a bunch of castrated hillbillies and don't do a damn thing to help with the real problems of the Eskimos, which are physical — not spiritual."

# Communing With Unok

from *True North: Exploring the Great Wilderness by Bush Plane*

Under gorgeous but darkening skies, the Tundra Cub wings across the Yukon border. Far below its wings, the Pelly River tumbles out of the Mackenzie Mountains and slowly winds out of sight. Dawson lies far to the west — too far to reach before dark, so I angle toward a sunset-bronzed lake where an esker ends at a west-facing beach, then climbs from the depths on the opposite shore to continue its sinuous trek.

Reducing power, I skim the tops of the stunted, black spruce trees that rim the oval lake. The Cub responds to my gentle pull on the stick, raising her cowling to the afterglow of a rosy Yukon sky. She flares out over the water, her engine a quiet rumble, her slipstream receding to a gentle hiss. The Cub and I commune, hardwired by hands, arms, body and brain, sensing the subtleties of lift and drag that flow across our wings. Aided by peripheral vision, diminishing sound and control feedback, we descend as I plan the approaching stall. Three feet, two feet -- one. I raise the nose slightly as we skim across the nameless lake, our floats slicing through its serenity, then settling toward repose.

My campsite will be a strip of level ground beyond a narrow beach. At its rim, moss campion bask in the sunset glow while yellow avens quiver nervously in a gentle breeze.

While a grayling simmers on the Coleman, I slather two slices of sourdough bread with marmalade and decide how to end my day: Do dishes. Read. Build a fire. Take a hike. But with the dishes done, I'm too antsy to read, so I begin to assemble a fire.

Making a fire should be one of our most satisfying acts, but for many, it's become as routine as breathing. For me, fire building is a hands and heart-warming art. Without fail, a fire's first wisps of smoke liberate visions of our prehistoric ancestors worshipfully urging flames from flint-struck sparks. And in the first tiny flames, I see images from Jack London's masterful *To Build a Fire*, in which a freezing trapper struggles to fend off death.

Scraping aside the earth's mossy coverlet, I begin with a few paper scraps, then add a mesh of tinder-dry twigs capped with porcelain driftwood. Were I farther south, I'd begin with nature's pungent, waterproof paper — birch bark.

When the flames are well established, I wet the surrounding ground and stand a slab of rock at its windward edge to thwart the spark-lifting breeze, anoint myself with bug dope and head for the crest of the long, winding esker that forms my narrow beach.

The esker's slopes are dappled with bearberry bushes, but its well-worn crest has been denuded by the migrations of hungry caribou. As I stroll above a sea of scattered spruce, black flies dance in my wind shadow while the bug dope keeps them at bay. I jog briefly, then settle for wide strides until the esker finally ends as it began — at a crescent-shaped beach that cups in its arms another Yukon lake.

Dropping to the still-warm sand, I let my thoughts skip back through the decades to an eight-year-old boy eagerly peddling sled loads of homemade Christmas wreaths. I recall a family friend who offered his science fiction books to a bedridden teenager to help him pass the time. And I think of my wife and our marriage, once green but now mature. Moved by a sense of loneliness, I select a pristine stretch of wind-rippled sand and, with a slender wand of driftwood, inscribe my wife's name in sweeping script.

As I stroll back to camp in failing primrose light, I spot a skull-like dome protruding from beneath the esker's sandy soil. A touch confirms its bony nature, and a few finger scoops later a human skull emerges. Probing further, I find no vertebrae, no ribs, no other bones.

If I'm to have company, my guest must have a name. "Yorick" springs tritely to mind. Kneeling before the skull, I try to imagine its owner's past as "Yorick" becomes "Urok," which evolves into "Unok." A beret of lichen decorates Unok's brow. And given the remarkably slow growth of lichens, its maroon expanse reveals that Unok's skull has lain right here for at least two hundred years.

"Unok," I softly inquire, "Would you like to join me at one more campfire?" Hearing no response, I reverse our roles. Now Unok's the host and I'm the vacant skull. How would I respond to such an invitation? Yes, YES. Of course, YES!

With Unok's skull cradled in my hands, I return to my dwindling fire and blow the embers to life. Forcing a stick into the tundra, I brace it with rocks, then guide Unok's foramen magnum over the shaft so his skull stands upright, supported on a spinal cord of bone-dry spruce. Beneath a purpling sky, Unok and I commune.

How many generations, how many millennia, have passed since our ancestral kinfolk shared a fire, not knowing that some of their descendants would migrate north toward Scandinavia to become my ancestors, while others would travel east, perhaps eventually crossing the Bering Strait to become the first North Americans—each to invent and refine stories of how the Earth was formed and the universe was born?

Some North American tribes tell of a muskrat that dove to the bottom of an eternal ocean and returned with a trace of mud. For others, a deep-diving loon retrieved the first lump of clay. Tahitians also created an aquatic myth, believing that their islands had been pulled from the ocean floor by gods.

Letting my mind flow into the recesses of Unok's dead but omniscient skull, I find an African tale to brighten the darkening sky: Bushmen tell of a lovely girl who dipped her hands in a fire and threw the still-hot ashes into the sky to form the Milky Way. The sparks flew even farther, and now live on as stars.

As firelight flickers across Unok's brow and cheekbones, I have a brief qualm about moving his skull. As if in response, he fills my mind with a scene from ancient Egypt where skeletons have been seated beside feast tables as a reminder that the reward for life is death. "Live life while you can," whispers Unok. "Live wisely. Let judgment, not fear, be your guide."

With our fire reduced to embers, Unok and I search the sky for a few of the thousands of meteors that plunge into our atmosphere each minute, escaping notice by day and lighting flares at night. As we watch, one spark after another streaks across the sky, adding tiny bits of mass to the Earth in a process that began some 4 billion years ago.

When my neck begins to cramp from looking upward, I lie back, cradle my head in my hands — and smile. The northeastern sky has donned the aurora borealis, the "luminous negligee" of the night. Turning to Unok, I tilt him backward against a stabilizing mound of sand so that he, too, can enjoy the view.

Some of Unok's ancestors believed the aurora to be the spirits of dead elders playing with a walrus skull, while others reversed the tale, allowing walrus spirits to toy with human heads. One Inuit tribe described an enormous wedding, with the guests arriving on glowing sleds called komatiks, and though some whistled to bring the aurora close, others whistled to hold it at bay. Point Barrow Inuit, believing that the numinous lights could extend evil arms, kept their knives close at hand and threw dog excrement skyward to repel the ominous glow.

Unok and I, however, see wavering curtains set aglow by the solar wind. Stirred by the sun's exhalations, our ionosphere blushes a palette of nitrogen blues, hydrogen greens, oxygen yellows and reds. We also know that our evanescent skies are merely standard fare. Let the sun sneeze and its shimmering gusts can destroy communications, disrupt power transmission, induce electrical currents in pipelines, and, with ghostly humor, open your garage's remote control door.

As the Northern lights flare above our evergreen-fringed amphitheater, I listen for the crackling sounds that many claim to hear, but the skies have an antidote for eavesdroppers like me, and I soon succumb to sleep.

Later, awakened by the cooling night, I lift Unok from his wooden spine and with the aid of my flashlight return him to his bed of flowers. When he's properly ensconced with his lichen beret tilted jauntily to the south, I bid my friend goodnight.

While the aurora prances through the coal-black, arctic skies, I settle into my sleeping bag and soon drift off to sleep. Far above, the eyes of night follow skeins of migrating caribou, search the tundra for howling wolves, and squint in puzzlement at a Yukon beach that bears the name of Sally.

# Faith Healing — Death Dealing

from the Saint Paul Pioneer Press and others

Nearly three years have passed since Carolyn Hyatt rose to testify before the California legislature. Her riveting testimony would help scuttle exemptions that faith-healing religions get from being prosecuted for crimes of child endangerment and manslaughter. As she testified, the room quieted beyond the norm, for Carolyn was deaf, and with devastating detail, she "signed" her story.

Carolyn told of a long series of untreated illnesses that led to her loss of hearing when she was seven years old. She described the pain in her ears, how it grew day by day, while her Christian Science parents told her it was just a lack of faith that caused her pain — that it was her own fault! By the time Carolyn had finished, many of the legislators were in tears, and support for religious exemptions was in shambles. Unfortunately, Carolyn's suffering and disability are not unique, and stories like hers represent just a portion of disgraceful case reports that have often left me, like the California legislators, blinking back tears.

In January, 1990 it was South Dakota's turn.

Sioux Falls had become the home of End Time Ministries, a charismatic group that promoted "positive confession theology" and opposed medical care. Its leader, Rev. Charles Meade, came from the notorious Faith Assembly of Indiana, whose beliefs had caused more than one hundred unnecessary deaths. In South Dakota, End Time Ministries soon lost five babies during home deliveries that were not attended by licensed health care providers.

Unfortunately, South Dakota's exemptions, much like Minnesota's, prevented prosecution. South Dakotans, however, recognized the situation as intolerable, and introduced legislation to remove all exemptions from providing health care to sick children. The bill carried the endorsements of all the major social service, medical and religious organizations, and of CHILD Inc., (a Sioux City, Iowa organization headed by former Christian Scientists whose fifteen-month-old son died of meningitis.) Even more crucially, the bill had the support of Joni Eddy, one of the End Time mothers whose baby had died — and who courageously agreed to go public.

The Christian Science church, the largest and most powerful of the faith-healing sects, led the opposition. Believers try to justify the needless suffering, disability and death of defenseless children, as documented by CHILD Inc., as an extension of their religious rights. As in the past, they charged violations of freedom of religion and wrongly characterized the bill as an attempt to prevent the use of prayer. In fact, the bill merely set an even standard, requiring health care for all minors. Those who choose to pray in addition to providing medical care remained free to do so. South Dakotans, however, recognized the pre-eminence of a child's right to live, and the bill not only passed, it passed UNANIMOUSLY.

End Time Ministries moved to Florida, where two of their members were charged with felony child abuse of their son for withholding medical care for ailments that cost him a third of his body weight. Investigations showed that his feet were so severely infected that buckets had to be placed under them to catch the draining fluids.

The end to these abuses lies with the adoption of child protection laws like those of South Dakota, laws to protect children like the young Ian Lundmans of Minnesota, who died of untreated diabetes, and laws to prevent their prolonged suffering and disability that are far more common than their deaths.

In the meantime, faith healers will continue to claim to heal with prayer alone, ignoring the existence of the body's own defense and repair mechanisms. They provide no records, and their "evidence" is anecdotal. They argue that medicine also has its failures, which indeed it does, though these failures are dwarfed by mountains of success.

These arguments will soon be repeated in the Minnesota legislature. Once again, Minnesotans have the opportunity to make all of its citizens equal, exempting no one from the duty of providing health care to minor children.

Finally, an appeal: Our legislators will hear the arguments of established, well-organized groups like the Christian Scientists who will call, write and lobby their legislators. Unless we also make our feelings known, Minnesota children will continue to pay the price, and our exemptions in the child protection laws will continue to make accomplices of us all.

# Why Horses Laugh
from The Villages Daily Sun and the Mesabi Daily News

In the days of horse and buggy everyone knew what a feedbag was. When filled with oats, the bag was attached to the front of a horse, which converted the grain into energy — except for a few undigested oats that passed on through to enrich the Earth and a few appreciative sparrows.

Wealthy Republicans, appalled at the loss of a few grains of oats, and believing that nothing happens by chance, searched for a message in the offal oats. Like gypsies reading tea leaves, they scrutinized the stable floor, but the riddle of the rejected oats remained intact until it was called to the attention of the Republican National Committee, which concluded that therein lay the economic model of the future.

"The horse," they said, "represents the upper class. The more it is fed, the more undigested oats will pass through to benefit the sparrows, which are obviously unfit to feed directly from the bag. The oats that the horse leaves behind are the result of generosity, not waste. If the altruistic horse can display such concern for its fellow creatures, should we not reward these noble animals, and increase their rations to the benefit of all?"

Thus, in a burst of '80s double talk, "trickle-down economics" was conceived and sold to a gullible public and a Congress composed largely of horses. The chief salesman was a Reaganite named Stockman, who eventually admitted that his scheme was designed to enrich their already wealthy "friends."

In the years that followed, the horses gained weight, due not only to the extra grain, but because their ingenious guts devised new ways to trap the oats that had once slipped past, to be consumed by the hungry sparrows.

At election time, the magnificent horses have always advised the sparrows to be patient, because "these things take time." The naive sparrows, having also been told that oats must first pass through a horse to be useful, continued to nod their heads in submission as they settled down to wait.

Years passed, bringing Bush I and then Bush II, the great uniter and self-described war president who gets his orders from God — and now another election.

Perhaps, in 2008, the sparrows will finally realize that they outnumber the horses, as do their votes. Perhaps a few of the spunkier birds will decide that pre-horse oats might be even more nutritious than those the horses dispense, and decide that it's time to re-direct the oats. Others, however, will continue to gaze up at the huge, healthy beasts while denying that such impressive creatures could ever be wrong or, worse yet, greedy.

This November, ALL of the horses will once again vote for bigger, tighter feedbags for themselves and their corporate owners. Most of the sparrows will flock to the polls to vote for fresh, clean oats and for sparrows that are in touch with the working class. A few will waste their votes on a principled-but-unelectable owl at the nadir of his career. But others, conditioned by years of whinnies, snickers and chortles, will be much too busy to vote as they trail behind the horses, awaiting their "manu" from heaven — and getting little else.

# Will Work for Food or Gas
from the Minneapolis Star Tribune

He was standing at a stop light just north of I-94 when I pulled into the station for gas and a wash. The sign he held high, red crayon on cardboard, tugged at me: WILL WORK FOR FOOD OR GAS.

I watched him as I topped my tank, wondering at his life and circumstances. Then out with my Visa card and into the wash. Full tank, clean car, no mortgage and I was on my way to the Freethinkers picnic. Why not ask him to come along? I knew we would feed him and I was betting we'd fuel him, too.

A small, creased and weary looking man in his mid-forties, he looked like Willie Nelson with a Kenny Rogers beard.

"Where you from?" I asked.

"Been working up near Fargo," he replied.

"And where's home?

"Arkansas."

I had noticed a rust-gutted, Arkansas-plated Chevy van in the corner of the lot.

"That where you're heading?"

"Yessir. My brother's off working somewhere and when he gets back we're movin' on, 'less the Missus finds work too," he said, pointing to a wisp of a woman and two children across the street with a similar sign.

"Well," I said, "I'd really like to give you a hand but I don't have any work for you. I was about to invite you to a picnic where we'd fill you up, but I suppose you can't leave until you're back together, and who knows when that will be."

"That's real nice of you, sir, real nice. And thanks for comin' over.

Good of you to take the time."

The Phalen Park picnic was all that I expected: good people and great food, from the brats to the slaw, the salads and some truly unusual fortune cookies. But even as I enjoyed the laughs and lasagna, my mind was back beside I-94. I was troubled that we still have families who live from hand to mouth. I was angry that the Rolex/yacht/Ferrari/jet-set/tax-evading/family-value-trumpeting conservatives have the gall to carp about taxes and unemployment costs while seeking tax cuts that fatten the rich, but do little for the middle class and less for the rest.

When I returned they were still there, aiming their hand-lettered signs at the oncoming traffic. Once again I approached him.

"I'd really like to help you," I said, "so why not just pull up to the pumps and we'll fill your tank."

"No sir," he replied, firmly but politely. "I appreciate your offer, but I gotta work for it."

"Why not consider it a loan?" I continued, "A debt you owe to someone down the road when they need a hand." Once again he declined.

I headed home, determined to find a way to help them out, finally deciding I would return, bringing a pen, a spiral notebook and a large, stamped, self-addressed envelope. I would tell them I had a job for them; that I did some writing and was always on the lookout for stories; that I wanted them to write down everything that happened over the next several days and I'd pay them in advance. But by the time I returned, they were gone, having earned enough to move on to another intersection in yet another town.

I wonder what they think of America, of our breast-beating slogans and of trade policies that export jobs to other countries whose burgeoning populations provide very CHEAP labor. I wonder if they are resentful that for every job that migrates to Mexico or Asia or India, another American will be searching for cardboard and crayons? And I wonder if they see irony in the fact that the Land of Opportunity has come to mean that they, too, can pick out a corner, any corner, from which to raise a sign — WILL WORK FOR FOOD OR GAS.

# Why have a House chaplain?

So the speaker of the Minnesota House thinks that "being ecumenical is wonderful." Does his ecumenism extend to having Shintos, Buddhists, Humanists, Muslims or American Indian medicine men open the meetings of the House, or is this position reserved for Judeo-Christians only?

On a more important point, why are Minnesota taxpayers required to pay for such activities? Whatever happened to the separation of church and state? If one considers the substandard ethics of some recent and current members of the Legislature, it is obvious that such prayers are either useless or are ignored, both here and above.

George Erickson, president, the Humanists of Mpls. and St Paul.

# Defending Evolution
from the Minneapolis Star Tribune

Michael Gallagher's opinion piece disputing evolution demonstrates only that some people prefer a few verses from Genesis to taking time to understand the mutually supportive disciplines of science that have converted the theory of evolution into a virtual certainty. In addition, Mr. Gallagher, who seeks to have creationism taught as real science in our schools, arbitrarily rejects a multitude of creation stories from other religions, because only his biblical version is correct.

He argues that evolution has missing links, but considering that we only have access to a thin layer of the Earth's surface containing perhaps .001% of all fossils, it is amazing that the record is so good — and it's getting better. Given another century, the relatively young science of paleontology will undoubtedly continue to fill in the few small gaps that remain.

In asserting that fruit flies exposed to intense radiation have not produced a new, different or improved species, he minimizes one of nature's endless and sometimes subtle "mechanisms" that can influence a species over thousands of generations and millions of years. He states that "At no time is a human embryo a fish," implying that science has made such a claim, which it has not. Instead, science has noted that beginning human embryos display (and then modify) certain anatomical features common to lower forms, including fish and reptiles.

He claims that evolution violates the second law of thermodynamics, which states that energy always runs downhill and order tends toward disorder, but neglects to note, or is unaware, that the law applies to CLOSED systems. Furthermore, the second law refers to the overall energy level of a system and does not eliminate the existence of local, temporary exceptions. Seen as a billiard table strewn with colliding balls, entropy says they will eventually stop, but does not preclude that a few, struck by one or more balls, will accelerate. They are like planets that receive solar energy. Like Mr. Gallagher's fruit flies that are hammered with intense radiation, the planets that lie too close to the sun will probably not develop new (or any) species either. Others, more fortuitously located, could develop life that can resist entropy in a temporary way.

Mr. Gallagher's fundamentalist view is opposed by most of his fellow Christians, including Dr. Conrad Bonifazi, professor of philosophy and religion at the Pacific School of Religion in Berkeley, CA, who has stated, "... an extremely conservative wing of Christian sectarianism, which has little or no repute in the world of theological scholarship, adheres to a literal interpretation of the Bible ... Its belief in the 'infallibility' of the Bible does not even permit it to recognize that in Genesis itself there are two accounts of creation, each differing from the other in background and in content. It is also true that the major denominations of Protestantism and the Roman Catholic Church in the United States recognize and support the teaching of evolution in the disciplines of natural Science."

(For more information, please see "Voices for Evolution," a 140-page compilation of statements in support of evolution from religious and secular institutions. Write to the National Center for Science Education or Betty McCollister, 314 Woodbridge Ave., Iowa City, Iowa, 52245. The cost is $6.00 per copy.)

# A Fair Shake for Rational Views
from the Minneapolis Star Tribune

Martha Sawyer Allen's report on a creation "science" meeting at Bethel College was as biased and irrational as the meeting she attended, but when a number of us wrote to the editorial pages to protest the claims she presented as fact, none of our letters were published.

In the past 12 to 18 months, the commentary pages have also run opinion pieces that have attacked Hemlock Society goals and the "right to die" movement. Although the Star Tribune received at least three rebuttals, none were printed.

More recently, a local attorney wrote a commentary on behalf of fundamentalist efforts to teach creation "science" in the public schools. I know for a fact that you received several well written responses, but, again, none saw print.

American fundamentalists are becoming increasingly intolerant, strident and bold. The violence at and around Planned Parenthood clinics is a direct result of their preaching, and with their easy access to the religion pages and the editorial section, they have the press for a pulpit. While I do not argue with your right to air their views, I resent your policy of denying dissent. It would appear that the purpose of your "Counterpoint" section is to allow rebuttal to all issues except those promoted by the religious right.

In a recent edition that containing a large feature on religion, Molly Ivins lamented the fact that we no longer have Robert Ingersoll, who would have attacked the fundamentalist foolishness, and that we have lost H. L. Mencken, the critic of religious and political fraud and pomposity.

Yes, we have lost them, but others are out there, writing letters and making calls, competing for space in a news media determined to offer large doses of mind-numbing milk from the sacred cows of sports and conservative religion. Occasionally, if their responses are sufficiently timid and circumspect, they find print.

Like Martin Luther King, I, too, have a dream. I dream of news media that PROMOTE the free and open exchange of opinions, where voices on all sides of EVERY issue find equal space. Tell me, did the Reaganites so thoroughly scuttle the fairness doctrine that there is no hope for return?

George Erickson,

President, the Minnesota Humanists

# Defending Carl Sagan
## 1934—1996

1981 Humanist of the Year of the
American Humanist Association

Best known as the creator of the "Cosmos" series on the Public Broadcasting System and as a leader in the nuclear disarmament and environmental movements, Carl Sagan was born November 9, 1934, in New York City. He obtained a Ph.D. in astronomy and astrophysics at the University of Chicago in 1960. From 1962 to 1968, he worked at the Smithsonian Astrophysical Observatory, was associate director of the Center for Radio Physics and Space Sciences from 1972 to 1981, and was responsible for NASA Space Probes Pioneer 10 and 11 and Voyager I and II.

Up until his death, he was David Duncan Professor of Astronomy and Space Science at Cornell University. His numerous books include the Pulitzer Prize-winning "The Dragons of Eden: Intelligent Life in the Universe" as well as "Broca's Brain," and "Pale Blue Dot: A Vision of the Human Future in Space." In 1981 he was awarded the Humanist of the Year Award by the American Humanist Association in recognition of his work as an educator, skeptic, activist, and popularizer of science. The film version of his novel "Contact" was released in 1997.

"There are worlds on which life has never arisen. There are worlds that have been charred and ruined by cosmic catastrophes. We are fortunate: we are alive; we are powerful; the welfare of our civilization and our species is in our hands. If we do not speak for Earth, who will? If we are not committed to our own survival, who will be?" (Carl Sagan in "Cosmos," 1980.)

Missing from this memorial is mention of Sagan's last book, *Demon-Haunted World*, which was, in my view, his most important. In *Demon-Haunted World*, Sagan argued for the use of reason and logic, and against reliance on supernatural beliefs.

After seeing him looking well and talking optimistically about his prognosis on television, I emailed him, asking if he would consider doing a phone interview for The Humanist magazine, but although he defeated his cancer, pneumonia slipped in and took his life. Now we must be content to celebrate Carl Sagan's life through his books.

Two days after Dr. Sagan died, Eric Ringham, a Minneapolis Star Tribune editor, wrote admiringly about Sagan's intelligence, but nitpicked his nonreligious nature in a piece that used Sagan's death to push the very sort of thinking that Sagan opposed. Armed with his Sunday school religion, Ringham used Sagan's reluctance to embrace religion to push his own. Worse yet, a week later, D.J. Tice, in the St. Paul Pioneer Press, printed a bitter and slanderous piece.

When the Star Tribune printed my response to editor Eric Ringham — see first letter below — it did so under a subtly (perhaps inadvertently) biased headline, which prompted a private, not-for-release follow up letter — also printed below.

To the Mpls. Star Tribune,

How brave of Mr. Ringham to question, however sympathetically, Carl Sagan's philosophy, now that he cannot respond. In suggesting that Dr. Sagan, having died, might now share his indoctrinated beliefs, editor Ringham mirrors missionaries who planted crosses on the graves of Inuit who refused to convert, and perpetuates the smug, insulting myth that no matter how brilliant and productive humanists like Sagan are, they are somehow defective without a supernatural belief.

Mr. Ringham, a proponent of one of the world's many religions, notes that the Roman Catholic Church has finally apologized for threatening Sagan's colleague, Galileo, but he fails to mention the unacknowledged thousands who were tortured and died at the hands of the Church.

According to editor Ringham, none of Sagan's writings that he had read explains why Sagan thought subtlety and intricacy argued against the existence of the creator. Perhaps the editor needs to read more Sagan and include new authors. In addition, Sagan's alleged failure to argue against a mythology is hardly an argument for it, particularly since his livelihood was influenced by believers. Like Isaac Asimov and Gene Roddenberry, the creator of Star Trek (both secular humanists), Dr. Sagan knew how to measure his words. Tell me, If I believe that an undetectable vegetable causes the tides, should I take Mr. Ringham's silence for tacit assent?

Instead of proclaiming his distress that Sagan's "brilliant mind studied the universe and found no evidence of God," Mr. Ringham should deplore those who accept traditional beliefs without scrutiny, lacking sufficient interest or integrity to hold them up to the light. We should study ALL religions and philosophies, and then examine their fruits.

Unfortunately, under the current editors, whole pages of the Star Tribune have become forums for the uncritical thinking that Sagan deplored. Galileo would turn in his grave.

George Erickson, Vice President, the Humanist Association of Minneapolis and St. Paul

To the Star Tribune editors,
(Not for publishing)
Now that Carl Sagan's beliefs have been attacked and defended, I'd like you to consider a suggestion that some might call nitpicking, but I would call professional.

Over my response to Eric Ringham, which I appreciate you honoring your responsibility to print, you printed, "It's an insult to Sagan to lament his lack of faith." Most readers might find that headline innocuous, but it really isn't because of the baggage carried by the word "lack."

In common use, the word "lack" is usually followed by a word with positive attributes: He lacks courage, intelligence, integrity, good judgment, etc. In contrast, I've never heard anyone say that someone lacks brutality, dishonesty, measles or AIDS. To headline a supportive piece on Sagan by mentioning Sagan's "lack of faith" reveals either pro-religion bias or, I hope, a hurried, ill-considered choice of words. A more appropriate selection for Sagan would have been "It's an insult to Sagan to lament his rationality."

Let's consider the subject from a different perspective: In the unlikely event that one of your editors would have the poor taste to write (and you print) a similarly critical piece upon the death of the Pope, would you headline a Catholic Counterpoint submission "It's an insult to the Pope to lament his lack of rationality?" I would hope not.

Those of us who manage quite well without relying on supernatural beliefs do not feel we are lacking anything of value. In fact, we resent assertions or implications that operating without a supernatural belief makes us somehow defective. Like Carl Sagan and the majority of the Nobel laureates, we have taken the time to study the alternatives and are proud of our choice. In contrast, at least 3/4 of the populace acquire their religion by accident of birth or marriage. In what way is that superior? Aren't those who fail to make an educated choice, wherever it leads them, the ones who are lacking something?

In closing, please consider two points:

1. In fairness to those who write to you and your readers, headlines should reflect the intent of the letter writer.

2. This letter would not be necessary had Mr. Ringham restrained himself or if your headline writer had chosen "rationality" instead of "lack of faith."

George A Erickson


To the St. Paul Pioneer Press,

Having read editorials for forty years, I thought I'd already seen the epitome of tasteless journalism, but D.J. Tice has proved me wrong. After first excusing himself by proclaiming his reluctance to speak ill of the dead, Tice, who has rejected all of the world's many religions but one, picks over Carl Sagan's bones because the world-renowned astronomer rejected just one more than Mr. Tice. Instead of praising Sagan for opening the eyes of millions to the grandeur above, Tice castigates him for declining to ascribe those sights to any of this world's many mythologies.

While railing against Dr. Sagan for honestly responding to questions about his beliefs on television and for publishing his thoughts, Tice emulates Sen. Joe McCarthy. Though Tice claims that many of Sagan's fellow scientists "disdained his career as a popularizer of science," he offers no figures. What percentage is "many?" Ten, perhaps? And what does the purported jealousy of some of Sagan's coworkers have to do with his views on religion or his freedom to express them? Mr. Tice, having declined to cast the first stone, throws handfuls, all off target.

The world's Tices are rankled by those who disagree with their theology and especially by those who have the nerve to openly state their views. Perhaps it has not occurred to these religious conservatives that free speech means more than their freedom to preach and ours to listen. When targets like Carl Sagan are too popular to attack while alive, sages like Tice, who know the unknowable, simply wait until they're dead.

Dr. Sagan, like the hundreds of religious and nonreligious people I have known, was a fine, intelligent, ethical person who cared about his fellow humans and about our sheltering earth. It's a shame that his death has been marred by the rantings of a few self-anointed oracles who cannot abide dissent.

Would I censor these carrion feeders? Of course not. The public needs to know their views, just as they need to know the views of the Ku Klux Klan, the skinheads, and all those who, lacking proof, resort to anger when others disagree. Still, instead of listening to me or to Mr. Tice, I urge everyone to read Dr. Sagan's books, especially *Cosmos* and *The Demon-Haunted World*. Compare Dr. Sagan's life and accolades to those of Mr. Tice. Decide for yourselves.

George Erickson

Vice President, the Humanist Association of Minneapolis and St. Paul

# Pickin' on Perkins

To the manager and owners of Perkins Restaurant, Moundsview, MN

When I and a dozen friends stopped at your restaurant for supper last Tuesday before going to the caucuses and primaries, we were surprised to see a notice posted near your cash register that offered a 10% discount for those with church bulletins. None of us recalled seeing it when we recently stopped for lunch after cleaning our Adopt-A-Highway section of Interstate 35.

Your discount for church bulletins is discriminatory, and it displays a lack of tolerance or understanding of the many perfectly moral people who choose not to be involved in the Christian religion. Your sign, in effect, says that Christians get preferential treatment at your restaurant. It is a disservice to the Perkins chain of restaurants, a chain that has provided good food in pleasant surroundings for many years without relying on such tactics. Thoughtful, ethical Christians should recognize the bias that your sign represents, and should not accept the discount.

What is next? Discounts for people who share your nationality, or discounts for whites?

On behalf of our members and all non-Christians, our board of directors asks that this policy be discontinued. As a business practice, it is doubtful that it succeeds, for you not only lose 10% of the gross revenue from the few people who respond because of this sort of thing, you will lose 100% from the many Jews, Agnostics, Humanists, Hindus, Atheists, Muslims, etc. that your sign offends. Most, of course, never say anything. They'll just dine at Bonanza or Embers.

In writing to you, I am saying that I believe that you had not considered how this policy would be viewed by non-Christians and that you will consider changing it. I hope I am not mistaken. (They dropped it!)

# Privatize the Profit, but Socialize the Loss

from the Villages Daily Sun and the Mesabi Daily News

It began with Ronald Reagan and a "trickle-down" guy named Stockman who was indicted for fraud in 2007 and who has admitted that his trickle-down farce was a ruse to enrich his party's wealthy, upper crust friends.

At the same time that the Reagan Republicans were dismantling the banking and investment safeguards that were legislated after the Great Depression, several senators, including John McCain, met with his buddy Charles Keating to try to find a way to restrict inquiries into a growing scandal that ended with the failure of 747 savings and loan institutions, a prison sentence for Keating, a slap on the wrist for McCain — and a $1.4 trillion bill for U.S. taxpayers.

Deregulation and privatization delivered the Enron, Global Crossing and Arthur Anderson disasters. But the moguls of greed had an even bigger plan: pass a law designed not by Senator Dodd or Representative Franks, whom others have faulted, but by GOP Senator Phil Gramm, a law that prevented the Securities and Exchange Commission and the Commodities Futures Trading Commission from regulating institutions that dealt with hedge funds and derivatives.

Unsupervised, these institutions ran amok until the summer of 2008 converted Republicans into socialists. They'd have been happy to take their subprime mortgage profits, but now they cried for taxpayers to shoulder the losses incurred by Bear Stearns, IndyMac, Fannie Mae, Freddie Mac and Lehman Brothers, to name just a few.

Merrill Lynch, the bull that became a cow by getting itself leveraged 30 to 1, had to sell out to Bank of America just to save its hide. Shortly thereafter, the Federal Reserve "loaned" AIG 85 billion for 80% of the company — which then threw an expensive party for its executives.

"Don't meddle in business," cry the Republicans when the money rolls in, but when the ink turns red, even gurus like Greenspan, who cheered deregulation, beg taxpayers to cover their losses. "Save us," they plead — "These markets need regulation!"

# Beauty Meets the Energy Beasts

from *Back to the Barrens: On the Wing With da Vinci & Friends*

Lake Athabasca, a two hundred mile crescent of crystal-clear water, staples together two of Canada's Western provinces. The easternmost is known as Saskatchewan, and we call its neighbor Alberta.

On the southern shores of this Inland sea lie hundreds of miles of honey-hued dunes. Formed when melting glaciers carried immense amounts of sand to a low region south of the Athabasca Hills, the dunes were exposed when the icy barrier finally withdrew, and the lake's excesses could once again escape to the north, leaving behind the largest area of sand dunes in all of Canada.

When you fly across the lake, swirls of rippled sand rise up from its depths as the Athabasca dunes come into sight. On the horizon, barren, dune-strangled trees reach for the sky like the masts of foundering ships. To the east, the MacFarlane River limits the dunes' progress, trapping windblown sand, which it carries into the lake, but to the south and west lies a seemingly endless sea of sand.

Few of the dunes reach 100 feet. Walk through them and you'll pass dome-shaped dunes, ribbon-like dunes, and breaking-wave dunes. Like ocean waves trapped in mid-curl, they wait for the wind to shift their shapes. Moving on, you'll find dunes with herringbone patterns and trees with half of their roots suspended in air, exposed by forceful winds that carried away the sand. Between the wind blowouts, stunted pine and birch trees rise above patches of yellow-green tansy and sand heather. The dunes are home to fifty rare plants plus ten that grow nowhere else, which is why they were designated a Provincial Wilderness Park in 1993.

At the western end of the lake sits Fort Chipewyan, the oldest settlement in Alberta. Known in the 1800s as the "Athens of the West" because of Alexander Mackenzie's 2,000-volume library, the fort served as Mackenzie's base, from which he traveled north to the Arctic Ocean. A year later, he headed west to the Pacific, preceding Lewis and Clark to become the first person to cross North America.

Fort Chipewyan is located at the northern edge of the world's largest inland delta, a water-logged paradise for muskrats and mink fed by the convoluted channels of the Athabasca River. Vilhjalmur Stefansson, the Arctic explorer who rafted the Athabasca in 1920, noted " ... the smell of the tar, which here and there trickled down the banks of the river and soiled our clothes whenever we went ashore." Stefansson's tar, however, is no longer annoying because mining this Florida-sized expanse of oil-saturated sand has become a burgeoning business that brings Alberta $6 billion per year.

Below our plane's wings, an irregular patchwork of sprawling pits and angular settling ponds march outward from either side of the river. Some would call it a moonscape, but it's no different than any open pit operation — you remove what's in the way to get at what you need. More than a million barrels of oil are stripped from these sands every day, much of it destined for the United States, which relies on Canada for 18 percent of its oil — and is eager for more.

Centered in the tar sands sits Fort McMurray, a boom town whose population jumped from 10,000 to 60,000 in just a few decades when they began to mine the sands, which are reputed to contain the largest single oil deposit in the world. Covered by a thin layer of muskeg, the tar sands contain 1.7 to 2.5 *trillion* barrels of a heavy oil called bitumen, about one-fifth of which is recoverable with current techniques.

On the west side of the river, huge, 2,200 hp turbocharged excavators equipped with GPS displays and buckets that carve out fifty cubic yards per bite are dumping sand into grunge yellow, $3.5 million Caterpillar trucks with six $20,000 tires and rear axles that weigh 37 tons. Moving back and forth from pit to plant at up to 40 mph, each truck delivers 300 tons of bitumen containing 200 barrels of oil to processing plants each day. There, the sand is mixed with hot water to create a slurry that is pumped into settling vessels. The oil floats to the top, and the remainder goes back to the mined-out areas, which are covered with topsoil and replanted in a semi-successful attempt to restore the boreal forest.

Bitumen in the deeper deposits is removed by injecting steam to make it easier to pump to the surface. The molasses-like bitumen is then pumped to a refinery, emerging as sweet crude oil — the good stuff that all nations desire. This seems pretty rosy, but there's a hidden price to mining the sands, and any honest person would call it pollution.

Today, the once-pristine Athabasca River is tainted with high levels of arsenic, mercury and an assortment of hydrocarbons, all of which are blamed for the humpbacked walleye fish with pug faces and bulging eyes that the Fort Chipewyan natives are afraid to eat — and for human cancer rates that have risen to three times the national average.

While the plane is being fueled, I ask the dock hand to recommend a convenient hotel.

"The Podollan would be handy," he says, pointing toward a tall building not far from the base.

"Thanks," I reply, "and what should I be sure to see before I leave town?"

He thinks for a moment, then says, "I guess I'd take in the Tar Sands tour and the Heritage Park on King Street."

"Okay, but if I have to pick one, which do you recommend?"

"Well," he says with a nod to the plane, "You've probably seen more from your Cub than the tour can show you, so I guess I'd check out the park."

At the Podollan Pub, I order a quarter-pound burger with onions, fries and a strawberry shake. The burger is delicious, but the pub is crowded with oil conventioneers, and it's much too loud. By the time I finish, I'm having doubts about spending a night in noisy surroundings, so I put off registering. Maybe I'll stay, but I'm already envisioning the hundreds of quiet lakes lying not very far to the east.

The cabby in front of the Podollan puts down his copy of *Fort McMurray Today* and asks, "Where to?"

"Heritage Park."

As we head up Franklin Street, he asks, "Are you here for the convention?"

"No, I'm up from the States — just flying around in a seaplane enjoying your beautiful country."

"Oh," he says, his eyebrows rising in the rearview mirror. "So what do you think about Bush?"

"You mean our great 'decider,' King George? He should be impeached."

"So why don't you?" he asks. "How could you try to impeach Clinton for having zipper trouble, but do nothing about a guy who lies you into a war?"

"Wish I knew!"

I watch him in the mirror. His eyes reveal that he's smiling. I expect him to continue, but he switches to the price of housing, which he calls "obscene," then pauses and says, "Your guys and my guys aren't getting along very well these days!"

"How's that?" I ask, thinking that he means the war in Iraq.

"The paper says that Washington keeps ignoring NAFTA rulings that favor Canada on a bunch of disputes, one of them being subsidies to U.S. corn growers that hurt our farmers. That's not going to help you guys get more oil from us, you know, especially with China pushing for more every year. The oil guys say that China will be taking half of our oil by 2010. That's good for us, but not for you, eh?"

He's right, but it's also bad news for the environment. Processing the sand produces three times as much greenhouse gas as does pumping the same amount of oil from a well. That's bad enough, but there's more. Hidden within our rush for this expensive oil is an unspoken warning: The reason that sources like this have become desirable is that world oil production is already declining while demand is on the rise. We are taking the first steps toward scraping the bottom of the global oil barrel. Getting serious about alternate energy sources is long overdue.

We have enough oil for the very near future, but before that enormous barrel runs dry, every nation must invest in wind and solar power, and perhaps in a commodity that is plentiful in Saskatchewan, the province at the eastern end of glittering Lake Athabasca.

That mineral is uranium. Like the tar sands, uranium also has great potential for profit — and for delivering a new set of environmental hazards. It's found throughout the Athabasca basin, but the best is located at McArthur River, which sits atop the world's largest, high grade deposit of uranium — a modern "mother lode" that is said to contain more than

400 million pounds of uranium oxide. At Hatchet Lake, Cameco Ltd., the big dog in the uranium business, is developing a mine that will yield ore 100 times richer than ores from elsewhere around the globe.

If — or when — we finally say goodbye to oil and *again* say hello to uranium, it will largely replace the tar sands, and residents of small but mushrooming settlements like Key Lake, Cliff Lake and Rabbit Lake will be bragging about Saskatchewan's billion dollar surpluses — and complaining about the housing shortage, about pollution, and about prices they'll call obscene.

# Greed and Hypocrisy
from the Mesabi Daily News

To the editor,

The Tuesday, May 19, 2009 issue of the Mesabi Daily News was remarkable in two very different ways. The first was surprising; the other, outrageous.

In the first, George Will, in an amazing burst of rare candor admitted that "Greed grows when Republicans hold the presidency. They did so throughout the '80s [the Reagan/G. H. W. Bush years] and no less an authority on probity than American journalism named it the Decade of Greed. Furthermore, everyone knows that we are in our current economic pickle because greed, which slept through the Clinton administration, was awakened by the Bush administration's tax cuts and deregulation. ... Republicans will capture the presidency now and then, igniting greed revivals."

Wow! Was that a pig that just flew by?

If so, it's far superior to the outrageous, apparently home-brewed (unsigned) cartoon that "graced" the same page — a cartoon that depicted a person being water boarded in one frame and a Muslim beheading in the other.

Are we supposedly superior because we terrorize people with water boarding, which can be endlessly repeated and can and has caused death? Why aren't the people of this nation, many of whom claim to follow the Prince of Peace, at the forefront of protests against this practice, and why are only a few pressuring Congress to investigate and prosecute, if warranted, those who authorized these crimes? Can you spell h-y-p-o-c-r-i-s-y? How low we have sunk!

# The Atlantic's Top Twenty
# Influential Americans

To the editor,

In these days of politicians who specialize in Bible waving, it's refreshing to note that your top twenty influential Americans included at least eight deists or atheists who either avoided involvement with organized religion or condemned it. The eight include Lincoln, who, despite being incessantly pressured, never joined a church; Washington, whose references to God were deistic; Jefferson, who rewrote the Bible and called St Paul the great "corrupter"; Franklin, who wrote "I have found Christian dogma unintelligible"; Edison, whose "Religion is all bunk," has been censored from most texts; Grant, who urged taxation of the churches; Mark Twain, who frequently let his characters speak his mind — as in "Faith means believing what you know ain't true."; Madison, who railed against the sins of organized religion, and Thomas Paine, the patriot/backbone of the American Revolution whose "My mind is my church; my religion is to do good" and his seminal "Appeal to Reason" turned his bigoted countrymen against him.

In their place we have the self-proclaimed war president, G. W. Bush, the man who prior to his last "election," stated that no one would out-Christian him, and a hawkish vice president named Cheney who rose to power by avoiding military service with *five* deferments. How far we have fallen!

(They did not publish this letter.)

# Glenn Beck, Where Were You?

from the Villages Daily Sun, the Mesabi Daily News and others.

Glenn Beck, the inflammatory, 21st century version of Sinclair Lewis's super-patriot, Buzz Windrip, has been using images of marching Nazis to support his preposterous claim that President Obama will slide toward fascism — which the dictionary calls "A system of government that exercises a dictatorship of the extreme right, typically through the merging of state and business leadership, together with belligerent nationalism."

If Beck is such a defender of our rights, where was he during the reign of George W. Bush — a reign that employed most of fascism's tools? Let me list them:

1. Overt nationalism with constant use of patriotic mottos, symbols, flags and a "dissent is treason" mentality that curbs criticism by appealing to prejudice.

2. Government and religion entwined to garner votes and manipulate public opinion.

3. Disdain for human rights, evident in the suspension of habeas corpus. Legalization of torture and endless incarcerations.

4. Scapegoating of racial, ethnic or religious minorities: liberals, socialists, suspected "terrorists" and the 20 million Americans who reject supernatural beliefs.

5. A hugely expensive and glamorized military.

6. Homophobia and opposition to abortion and sex education in schools.

7. Obsession with national security.

8. Managing news by feeding compliant media "approved" material.

9. Allowing corporations to guide economic decision making.

10. Opposition to unions

11. Transfer of wealth from the middle class to the super-wealthy.

12. Contempt for intellectuals and the adulation of Joe Sixpack and Joe the Plumber.

13. Obsession with crime and punishment. Unlimited power of search, arrest and detainment via legislation with deceptive names like "the Patriot Act."

14. Deeply suspect elections.

15. Legalized invasion of privacy via warrantless eavesdropping.


Bush and company promised to restore decency and honor to government, but they trashed it instead. He promised to unite the nation, but split it in half. Bush said he'd balance the budget, but brought huge deficits, a fraudulent war and greatly expanded government.

While Bush and Cheney were marching on, Beck stayed silent. Where were you then, Glenn Beck?

# Fed Up With Palin

from the Villages Daily Sun, the Mesabi Daily News and others.

When John McCain extended his arms in triumph and, with an immense smile, offered up shiny Sarah Palin at the Republican National Convention, I was willing to cut her some slack. After all, dear John, who abandoned his crippled wife to pursue a willowy model named Cindy, has had an eye for beauty queens, so Sarah was nothing. However, a look at her record revealed that Sarah's glitter was hiding the dark side like that of Jekyll and Hyde.

As an Alley Oop creationist, she believes that humans and dinosaurs were contemporaneous. She disputes the fact of evolution, and has taken step one toward the banning of books. She claimed to have turned down the infamous bridge to nowhere, but later admitted having supported it, her switch to "opposition" coming after Congress had seen to its death. She disputed global warming, then softened a bit, but opposed the idea that humans were part of it, then later said — well maybe a little, but the cause doesn't matter.

Although she listed Ireland as a country she had visited, her "visit" amounted to nothing more than a fueling stop. She has approved the killing of mother black bears with cubs, put a bounty of $150 on wolf paws and spent $400,000 of taxpayer money to kill a bill that would have made it illegal to hunt exhausted wolves from airplanes. At the top of the Republican ticket we have Kill, Kill, Kill from Palin and Drill, Drill, Drill from McCain. Is this really the best that they can offer?

Palin initially welcomed an abuse-of-power investigation for allegedly using her office to take revenge against her former brother-in-law, but then fought the process with the aid of attorneys provided by

McCain. She's an End Timer who believes in rapture and the apocalypse, so I worry that she'd be willing to push the "button" to make her fantasies come true. After all, she claims that G. W.'s war in Iraq is "God's task for America."

If asked about foreign policy, she ducks the issue and repeats her refrain about oil. She pushes school choice and vouchers that harm our public schools. She opposes abortion, even in cases of rape and incest, opposes sex education in schools and supports abstinence-only "education," the effectiveness of which was displayed when her daughter became pregnant at age seventeen.

Though seething, I restrained myself until she babbled about polar bears because, as it happens, I've traveled the North extensively, have two books on the subject, and I'm loaded with facts about Nanook, the Lord of the Arctic, the peripatetic polar bear, which places me far above the governor of our only state that has them.

She admits that the ice pack is shrinking, but when she wrote in The New York Times that these "magnificent, cuddly, white bears are doing just fine and don't need our protection" and "If the ice melts, they'll adapt to living on land," she pushed me over the edge. Why? Because I have a great affinity for these fantastic animals. I have photographed them from less than eight feet and have learned the facts of their lives, which are NOT suited to surviving on land.

Polar bears make their living on the sea ice hunting seals. At the end of an average winter they come off the ice with enough fat to carry them through until fall, but a shrinking ice pack means less time to hunt, so the bears are now coming off the ice 10-15% lighter than before.

A well-fed polar bear can be an even-tempered bear, but a hungry bear is not. Although a healthy *ursus maritimus* — the water bear — can swim 100 miles to land, it cannot survive a 200-mile swim from the shrinking pack ice to shore. As a consequence, many of Palin's "cuddly white bears" are *drowning*. Does she know this? She should. Does she care? Why would she? They're only for shooting!

As the climate warms, wasps, robins and grizzly bears are slowly moving north. When polar bears begin to encounter grizzlies, which has already happened, the polar bears will die, for an underfed Nanook is no match for a healthy Griz.

In Palin's world, belief is what matters, ignorance is bliss, and anything goes in the search for power and profit. Palin talks about the 1000-mile gap between Anchorage and Russia as if the largest country in the world was right outside of her door. Perhaps she should also look to the east, where Alaska and Canada share a much longer border — and you know how war-like those Canadians are! Perhaps her witch-banning minister from Africa hasn't told her that the antichrist is lurking just north of Saskatoon.

In a few weeks, too many will vote for Palin and a belligerent man with a bad temper, a private jet and more homes than he can remember, who has nothing in common with ordinary folks. These working-class folks are the same people who must now make sure that the fear monger with simplistic answers is rejected and that the rapture-believer never gets close to the power that can destroy our civilization.

# Disputing a Limbaugh Clone

from The Villages Daily Sun

Joe Angione, in his January 6 column in The Villages Daily Sun about a "dumbed-down America," wrote that we once " aspired to think and act like intelligent people," and I agree, but his column went downhill from there. If the country has been dumbed down, why didn't he credit its most shining example — the self-proclaimed Decider, the one that many call the "Dunce-in-Chief?"

Angione warned us that "heartstrings are often manipulated by those whose humane-sounding objectives are driven by the lust for power." Oh, really? Does Dick Cheney spring to mind?

"There is no free lunch for America," wrote Angione, and there certainly isn't for the people I know, but golden parachutes still work quite well for conservative CEOs who've been dancing the trickle-down polka for 25 years while the rest of us paid the bills.

Moving on, he bemoaned the national debt, but failed to mention G. W.'s fraudulent, $3 trillion war, the $1.4 billion Keating/McCain savings and loan scandal — or Republican Phil Gramm's "Commodity Futures Modernization Act of 2000," which led to the collapse of Bear Stearns, IndyMac, Fannie Mae, Freddie Mac, AIG and Lehman Brothers, to name just a few.

Angione then argued that global warming is liberal nonsense, and that its proponents rely on "junk science." This from a person whose faith-based, abstinence-only president (his poster-girl lives in Alaska) has for eight years demoted the importance of science in virtually every federal department except, of course, the Defense Department, which had a whopping $800 billion budget for just 2008.

In fact, the consensus of reputable scientists — not "scientists" like those who were paid to assert that smoking was good for you — is that global warming is real. And if Mr. Angione can bring himself to tune out Limbaugh (who is trying to pin the recession on Obama by calling it "the Obama recession") even I have faith that a few sessions in the Villages' World Affairs Club — a hotbed of realist thinking — might persuade him to change his tune.

If he sticks with O'Reilly, Limbaugh and Beck, he'll doubtless be back, claiming that Jack Abramoff, Lee Atwater, Donald Segretti, Ollie North, G. Gordon Liddy, Spiro Agnew, Howard Hunt, Tom Noe, David Stockman, Richard Nixon, Mark Foley, Stephen White, James Trafficant, Paul Ingram, Bob Mathews, Charles McGee, Nicholas Elizondo, Jeff Habay, Bob Ney, Jim Gibbons, Curt Weldon, David Safavian, John Burns, Howard Scott Heldreth, Randall "Duke" Cunningham, Larry Craig, Ted Stevens and a host of others — all Republican, self-confessed liars and/or convicted criminals — are either saints in disguise or were led to their downfall by those dirty, scheming liberals.

# From Grand to Gross Goes the GOP
from several MN and FL newspapers

If the philandering Governor Mark Sanford has anything to be thankful for, it's the death of Michael Jackson, the event that removed him from the headlines and pushed him toward the trash bin, where he truly belongs, there to join the expanding pantheon of sanctimonious Republican liars, adulterers, cheats and crooks who love to talk about honesty and character — you know, wonderful folks like Senator Vitter, Rep. Newt Gingrich, Senator Ensign, Senator Craig, Richard Nixon and Vice President Agnew, who were quick to fault others while committing the same acts themselves or hiding other transgressions.

While covering up his own affair, Rep. Henry Hyde helped lead the charge to impeach Bill Clinton, and was quickly joined by a long list of Republican philanderers that included Rep. Bob Barr, Rep. Dan Burton, Rep. Bob Livingston, Rep. Don Sherwood, Rep. Vito Fossella Jr., Sen. John McCain and Rep. Helen Chenoweth, who told her constituents that God had pardoned her for her six-year extramarital affair.

Remember Mark Foley, the six-term congressman who resigned following revelations of a decade-long record of sending sexually explicit emails and text messages to underage boys? And how about Sen. Bob Packwood, who was forced to resign following charges of sexual abuse and assault by former staffers and lobbyists?

Add to these pillars of virtue Rep. Donald Lukens, who was convicted for having sex with a 16-year-old girl, and Rep. Robert E. Bauman, the homophobe who founded the American Conservative Union and admitted to soliciting sex with an underage male.

Even a partial list of Republican reprobates is long:

Lee Atwater — Reagan era operative who confessed on his deathbed to inventing lies about Democratic opponents.

Jack Abramoff — convicted of bribing congressman and defrauding native Americans.

Donald Segretti — convicted of forging campaign documents.

Oliver North — convicted in the Iran-Contra weapons-for-hostages scandal and pardoned by George H. W. Bush. Now a Republican columnist and frequent guest on neocon TV.

Rush Limbaugh — the talk show host, who was death on druggies until he became one — and then addiction became an unfortunate disease.

Sen. Strom Thurmond — the racist pedophile, who had a child with a sixteen-year-old black girl.

G. Gordon Liddy — convicted of conspiracy, burglary and wiretapping for Watergate. Now another right-wing media personality.

Howard Hunt — Republican operative of Nixon convicted of burglary.

Tom Noe — Republican fund raiser who was convicted of forgery, theft, money laundering and tampering with records.

David Stockman — inventor of "trickle-down" economics, the scam that he admits was designed to aid the wealthy at the expense of the underclass.

Rep. Bob Livingston — adultery.

Neal Horsley — Republican antiabortionist who confessed to having sex with a mule.

Gov. Bob Taft — pleaded no contest to charge that he broke state ethics laws.

Donald Rumsfeld — authorized the rape of children in Iraqi prisons in order to pressure their parents into providing information.

Nicholas Elizondo — director of the "Young Republican Federation," who was convicted for molesting his six-year-old daughter.

Republican Charles McGee — convicted of jamming Democratic and union phone lines on Election Day.

David Safavian — G. W. Bush's chief of staff at the General Services Administration who was convicted on four counts of lying and obstructing justice in the Abramoff scandal.

Sen. John Burns (MT) — Named one of the 20 Most Corrupt Members of Congress by the Citizens for Responsibility and Ethics in Washington.

Tom Delay — Resigned as G. W. B.'s "Hammer" after being indicted by a Texas grand jury on criminal charges that he had conspired to violate campaign finance laws.

Rep. Randall "Duke" Cunningham — convicted of taking bribes.

Governor Ryan — convicted on 18 felony charges including racketeering conspiracy, mail fraud and tax evasion.

Rep. Bob Ney — convicted in the Abramoff corruption investigation.

Republican Party leader Paul Ingram — pled guilty to raping his daughters.

Republican anti-abortion activist Howard Scott Heldreth — convicted child rapist.

This fine list of characters leads to a question: What about the Democrats? Are they so squeaky clean? Of course not, but they have resisted climbing onto the soapbox to proclaim their purity when others fail, leaving that display of hubris to the moralizers and pontificators of the "Moral Majority" and the "Family Values" crowds who, filled with right-wing indignation, know how everyone but themselves should always behave.

With their cumulative downfall — and there is more to come — these shining examples have given three rarely-used words vivid meaning — words like <u>duplicitous</u>, <u>sanctimonious</u> and above all, <u>hypocritical</u>.

George Erickson www.tundracub.com

# Single Payer Now!
from multiple FL and MN newspapers

Senator Paul Wellstone, who was widely known as the "the conscience of the Senate," wrote that he spent 85% of his time fighting Republican attacks on working families. Were Paul still alive, he'd be fighting for the thousands who die or are driven into bankruptcy every year due to a lack of health coverage — and he'd be fighting insurance and pharmaceutical companies that sponsor deceitful ads like the Harry and Louise videos of the '90s that torpedoed the Clinton health program.

Harry and Louise have lost their charm, so the health insurance companies, the pharmaceutical companies and the Republican Party have hired Rick Scott, a part owner with G. W. Bush of the Texas Rangers, to design and lead a disinformation campaign that is costing $1 million per day.

Rick Scott has an "interesting" past. He's the guy who started and headed the lucrative Columbia/HCA chain of for-profit hospitals that paid kickbacks to "cooperative" physicians and overbilled Medicare so egregiously that Columbia was forced to pay a record $1.7 billion in fines. Mr. Scott was given the boot, but he also received $10 million in severance pay and stock options worth $300 million. In a show of sympathy for the unemployed, the GOP gave him a job: to oversee an anti-Obama health plan campaign developed by the very same company that "swiftboated" Senator Kerry.

So why are these people so afraid of a Canada-style single-payer program, a plan that is far superior to our for-profit system? That system leaves 47 million Americans with no insurance and millions more with inadequate coverage due to policies that let the insurance companies decide which procedures will be allowed and which will be denied?

Here's why: health is a lucrative business. Medicare, a single-payer system that lets you choose your MD, has low overhead costs that run around 3%. In comparison, our much-vaunted private health care system admits to spending an average of 20% of your premium dollar on what they call "operating costs."

Those who run Medicare receive modest salaries, but in 2002, Norman Payson, the CEO of Oxford Health Plans took home $76 million. Leonard Schaeffer, CEO of WellPoint, received $21 million and D. Mark Weinberg, executive VP of WellPoint was forced to make do with a mere $14 million. That's per year!

In fact, the twenty highest-paid health insurance executives in 2002 received $237 million. Add another $1.1 **BILLION** in stock options (for a total $1.75 billion for **TWENTY** people) and it becomes obvious why these "for-profiteers" have no interest in change.

They don't care that the U.S. ranks 33rd in health care — just behind Castro's Cuba. They don't care that we have a higher infant mortality rate than single-payer countries like Canada, the UK, Australia, France, Germany, Japan and Sweden, and they don't care that we spend twice as much per person on health care (but live shorter lives) than citizens of those countries.

Under the for-profit system, insurance company employees are rewarded for finding loopholes in company policies that permit the denial of coverage, while single-payer systems exist to deliver health care, not deny it.

Currently, we Americans are saddled with a system that works very well if you are a member of Congress or if you are wealthy enough to pay for deluxe coverage, but for most of us, that's just a dream, as evidenced by the fact that more than 60% of all personal bankruptcy filings involve unaffordable health care costs.

What about Big Pharma? In single-payer countries, identical medications cost just half of what we pay! Could our drug costs be high because there is no competition? Could it be because drug companies spend millions on ads to persuade us to get our MDs to prescribe this drug or that? Could it be because, in 2002, the pharmaceutical companies paid a record $91 million to 700 lobbyists — and that was in <u>2002</u>!

How, I ask, can we believe Rick Scott & Co.'s lies and distortions about Canadian care after learning that Canadians, when asked to name the Greatest Canadian, gave that honor not to Alexander Mackenzie, who was Canada's Lewis and Clark, or to one of their national leaders, but to Tommy Douglas, the father of the Canadian Health care System?

Why aren't we ashamed that the BBC documentary "Panorama" revealed that a British medical team dedicated to providing care to poor people overseas ended up spending 60% of their time assisting poor AMERICANS, many of whom had risen at 4 a.m. and driven 100 miles to stand in line for a chance at medical care?

And what about cost? Yes, taxes go up, but premiums go down, and more of your money goes to patient care, not to pay a for-profit company's 20% overhead. In addition, those who currently lack insurance will have access to inexpensive preventive care, which drastically reduces trips to very expensive emergency rooms at taxpayer expense when things get out of hand.

We spend more money on defense than the rest of the world combined, some of which, according to the Pentagon, is used to staff and maintain 741 active military sites abroad. That's one reason that just a 15% cut in military spending could pay for 100% of the Obama health care plan or even a single-payer system without raising taxes.

As for the Republicans who support improving the current system instead of adopting a proven single-payer option, why should we trust the people who have opposed Social Security, minimum wages, unions, women's rights, animal rights, bank regulation and a host of other citizen-friendly advances? Why should we trust these Republicans who have already amended the Democratic Senate health bill nearly to death with more than 360 amendments?

Finally, how can we be so incensed over the deaths of 9-11, but ignore the fact that 23,000 Americans die every year for lack of medical care? Why aren't we rushing to establish a system that has proven efficient, effective and evenhanded in countries that have single-payer plans that broaden coverage while lowering per capita costs?

The rich don't care, and neither do many of our legislators, especially those who are in the pocket of Rick Scott, the insurance companies and Big Pharma. Call and email your legislators in support of the single-payer option. Watch how they vote — and remember it at the next election. That's what Wellstone would want you to do!

# Pushing Back I

from the *Minnesota Journal of Law and Politics*

The title of Stephen Young's article, "The Religiosity of Secular Religion," is oxymoronic. "Secular" means "pertaining to worldly things that are not religious or spiritual." "Religion" always includes one or more supernatural beliefs that require acceptance without evidence. The term "secular religion" was invented by those who are eager to intrude religion into the public schools, claiming that the ethics of humanism make it a religion, despite its rejection of supernatural beliefs.

Mr. Young's article arises from the unproven, egocentric assumption that there is a God that concerns itself with human affairs. Drilled into children by generations of God-fearing parents, it is a concept that is difficult to set aside, requiring education, a dedication to rational thinking and the willingness to risk rejection by superstitious friends and relatives.

Unfortunately, the body of Mr. Young's piece is as flawed as its title. First, his piece treats as FACT the assumption that HIS God exists and that HIS religion is good, forgetting pedophilic priests, fraudulent TV preachers and the oscillating horrors of religious conflict, including the warring Orthodox Catholics, Muslims and Roman Catholics in the former Yugoslavia, where, with few exceptions, our compliant press babbles about "ethnic cleansing," glossing over the reality of religious wars.

Second, he applauds the fact that a "student" Christian newspaper receives funding from a public university, which compels ALL taxpayers in that jurisdiction to support a religion with which many disagree.

Young says that "people, fallen as they are, need religion" and that "too much secularization and rationalism corrodes the structures of public faith and confidence." To the contrary, religions demand belief without evidence and make supernatural threats and promises that corrupt the mind, diverting it from ethics and rational thinking.

"Fallen" people need education, fair treatment, honesty, opportunity and the ability to determine the difference between a contract and a con. They need an ethical system that emphasizes caring, honest behavior as best for the individual, for society, and for our earthly environment, not one that promises rewards or punishment with the carrot and stick of heaven and hell.

If Mr. Young is right, and religion is so beneficial, why are 90% of Nobel laureates secular humanists and/or atheists, and why does the religious 85% of our population contribute 98% of its convicted criminals?

In advocating that public office is a trust that blends the "secular with the moral," Mr. Young needs to remember that religion is but one source of morality, and that ethics and morality have been taught by the secular world long before Christianity arrived. (Try Confucius.) In fact, the abuses of religion when combined with public office were well known to the Greek philosopher Seneca: "Religion is regarded by the common people as true, by the wise as false, and by the rulers (government) as useful."

Mr. Young writes of the "tolerance and freedoms provided for different religions," but I wonder if he expects them to be tolerant of those with different faiths and philosophies. If so, may I assume he opposes forcing the nonreligious to listen to the prayers of the religious in public schools?

In closing, Mr. Young turns to the "soul," a popular religious concept devised to avoid the fact of death, claiming that "What is needed then is … religious expression for the good of our souls." No, Mr. Young, what is needed is for conservative religions to realize that they have no right to force others to listen to their particular supernatural beliefs.

Finally, in response to the endless complaints of the religious right that they are restrained from promoting their views (tons of television time and reams of newspaper copy notwithstanding), I note that their lament appeared in the *Journal of Law and Politics* and I wonder, is *Popular Mechanics* next?

# Pushing Back II

In January 2008, when I was teaching a memoir writing class that I had taken over from an atheist/Unitarian friend who had just died, I received a group Email from one of my retirement community "students" (age 70) that denigrated atheists — to the obvious pleasure of the sender. The Email described a courtroom scenario in which an atheist was suing to have a special holiday created for atheists because Christians had Christmas and Easter. In response, the judge angrily told the plaintiff that there already was an atheist holiday — April Fools' Day — and dismissed the case.

Most freethinkers would probably let this pass, but I've had enough of this sort of thing, so I wrote back to my "student" as follows:

Gary,

The group Email you sent me was also sent to me about two years ago by a retired airline captain who was a <u>great fan</u> of my bestseller, *True North*. When the book came out in 2000, he told me it was the <u>best book he had ever read</u>, and agreed to be quoted on my promotional materials.

After I read his E mail, which was identical to yours, I replied with the following, which I now also tell you:

"I was a member and officer in several protestant churches in my earlier years. I later became the president of the Minnesota Humanists, and was subsequently elected to serve two terms on the board of the American Humanist Association.

"During those years in and out of churches I came to know hundreds of good people who were mildly to very religious or were mildly to very nonreligious, the only difference being that those who had a supernatural belief usually considered themselves better than those who lived equally good lives by relying on secular values and sources.

"I have known hundreds of marvelous, intelligent, charitable, thoughtful, responsible atheists, humanists, agnostics and freethinkers, and none of them would even think about acting like the fake "atheist" in your story. Incidentally, 90% of the nonreligious people I have known understand the content and the history of Christianity a lot better than the Christians who try to elevate themselves by putting freethinkers down.

"<u>Your story is an example of the straw man</u> argument in which a person is invented to do something foolish or criminal and then is knocked down for doing it. It is a fiction designed to denigrate someone who holds a different opinion.

"The judge in the story is a bigot. His judgment was not made on the basis of law. It was made because the defendant didn't share his religious views."

In an angry response, my former "friend" told me to never mention his support of my book again. What a fine "Christian" reaction, one might say.

Gary, you need to know that your former instructor, whom I knew quite well and who labored under great physical difficulty and declining health to help you folks in the memoir class, <u>had no use for religion</u> and neither do I. Your "joke" is an insult to the approximately 50 million Americans who have no use for <u>organized</u> religion, many of whom call themselves atheists.

At the end of this email I have included a <u>partial</u> list of the many atheists, humanists, agnostics and freethinkers who have advanced humanity, and who either never joined a church, or if they did join, changed their minds and left. If you are not willing to accept these names on faith, I can supply quotes to prove the point.

Were I made from the same mold as my airline captain, I'd be telling you that I don't want to see any more of your work, but I'm a better person then that, so I will continue to do my best for you because, like all of my friends, I prefer to set a good example in the hope that others will learn from it.

George

## Famous freethinkers

A partial list of agnostics, atheists, freethinkers, rationalists, secular humanists and a few deists at the end who have eased our way — with a few quotes inserted.

Steve Allen, Susan B. Anthony, Isaac Asimov, Margaret Atwood, Ingmar Bergman, Leonard Bernstein, Ambrose Bierce, Sir Richard Branson, Gautama Buddha, Luther Burbank, Robert Burns — "Why has a religious turn of mind always tended to narrow and harden the heart?" Helen Caldicott, Albert Camus, George Carlin, Andrew Carnegie, Arthur C. Clarke, Michael Crichton, Francis Crick, Marie Curie, Frédéric Joliot-Curie, Clarence Darrow, Charles Darwin, Richard Dawkins, Marlene Dietrich, Denis Diderot, Benjamin Disraeli, Phil Donahue, Frederick Douglass, Clint Eastwood, Thomas Edison — "Religion is all bunk!" Barbara Ehrenreich, Anne Ehrlich, Ralph Waldo Emerson, Richard Feynman, W.C. Fields, F. Scott Fitzgerald, Harrison Ford, Jodie Foster, Sigmund Freud, Betty Freidan, R. Buckminster Fuller, J.K. Galbraith, Bill Gates, John Gielgud, S.J. Gould, Mikhail Gorbachev, Sam Harris, Ernest Hemingway, Katherine Hepburn, Christopher Hitchens, Victor Hugo, Julian Huxley, Ibsen, R. Ingersoll, Helen Keller, Alfred Kinsey, Stanley Kubrick, Aldo Leopold, Longfellow, Bill Maher, John Malkovich, Karl Marx, Henri Matisse, H.L. Mencken, John Stuart Mill, Edna St. Vincent Millay, James Mitchener, Mozart, Taslima Nasrin, Nietzsche, Madalyn Murray O'Hair, George Orwell, Blaise Pascal, Linus Pauling, Penn & Teller, Brad Pitt, Ayn Rand, Tony Randall, James Randi, Sally Jesse Raphael, Nikolai Rimsky Korsakov, Tim Robbins, Gene Roddenberry, Andy Rooney, Salman Rushdie, Bertrand Russell — "Christianity has been and is the principal enemy of moral progress," Carl Sagan, Jonas Salk, Margaret Sanger, Susan Sarandon, Jean-Paul Sartre, Arthur Schopenhauer, Charles Schultz, George Seldes, Harlo Shapley, George Bernard Shaw, Percy Bysshe Shelley, Peter Singer, B.F. Skinner, Steven Soderbergh, George Soros, Benjamin Spock, Elizabeth Cady Stanton - "The Bible and the Church have been the greatest stumbling blocks against women's emancipation," Steinbeck, Gloria Steinem — "It [religion] is an incredible con job," Oliver Stone, Donald Sutherland, Julia Sweeney, Leo Szilard, Ted Turner, Mark Twain, —Peter Ustinov,

Alice Walker, James D. Watson, Steven Weinberg, H.G. Wells, Walt Whitman, Ted Williams, Gore Vidal, Voltaire, Kurt Vonnegut and **deists** Clara Barton and Oliver Wendell Holmes.

President Washington had no use for Christian dogma and Lincoln, though pressured, refused to join any church. Einstein, a deist at most, was angered by those who tried to make him sound conventionally religious, calling them liars.

In response to the often church-promoted lie that our founding fathers were Christians, you should know that Presidents James Madison, John Adams and Thomas Jefferson rejected the virgin birth, miracles and the trinity. Now add Thomas Paine, who wrote, "My mind is my church; my religion is to do good," and Ben Franklin's "I have found Christian dogma unintelligible. Lighthouses are more useful than churches."

# Decisions

Like most of our nation's 30 million freethinkers, humanists, agnostics, rationalists and atheists, my wife and I opposed the Bush, Cheney, Rumsfeld, Rice and Rove (Axis of Evil) war. And although we try to improve the lives of others with our time, our money and efforts, we are frequently denigrated by TV preachers and even by public officials.

Today, I face two of those efforts: The first, irritating, but easy to resolve, requires me to write a check to the IRS, part of which will go to pay for G. W.'s trumped-up war. The second is to evaluate thirty-eight applications to a scholarship I established at my local community college — applications that will mix pleasure with regret since my wife and I can only afford to fund three. I'll be seeking the three with acceptable grades, the greatest need and the probability that they'll use the training. The end will satisfy, but getting there is always an emotional task.

"Katie" has a 3.1 grade point average and lives with her mom. She wants to be a psychiatrist, but her need is marginal, so her application joins the rejected pleas of a diabetic vocational technical applicant, a 32-year-old waitress/nursing home worker with no husband and three kids who seeks a nursing degree, and a fundamentalist who seems to have all the answers but needs a degree.

As the applications fall to my feet, it occurs to me that the three trillion dollars consumed by the war on terror (or the millions in tax cuts G. W. Bush has handed the already-rich) could fund the education of all of these people — not just here, but across the nation — with money left over for national health care.

An hour passes. Twenty one applications lie spread across my floor, leaving seventeen for further review. One by one, I winnow them down, rejecting some despite glowing recommendations and great GPAs because they have no crushing financial need.

The seventeen dwindle to six as I reluctantly say no to a man of 32 who lost his job when the factory closed, to a bright high school senior who has been working since he was 12, to a girl on antidepressants with a father and brother in Iraq and a mother who can't quite cope, to a victim of rape, and to a twenty-three-year-old single mom who wants to give her child "all of the opportunities I missed while I was growing up."

The hard, and sometimes tearful, part is selecting the final three. In an attempt to isolate myself from their stories, I try to become an indifferent calculating machine, but every time, I fail. With regrets, I reject "Patricia," who received a nursing assistant certificate at age 45 after being abandoned by an abusive husband who called her "stupid," and having learned that she isn't, wants to return at age 58 for a two-year business degree.

"Richard," who has a fiancée, two kids and a part-time job, is also rejected. Why? Because his impressive recommendations imply that he'll probably work things out.

The last to fall is a freshman named "Cory," who admits that he "used to be a troublemaker. "I never finished high school, but now I've got my GED and last semester I even made the Dean's list. I don't like the stress of paying only the priority bills while going to school and worrying about the rest."

So here are the three I've chosen in my attempt to find the most needy and deserving students who will relentlessly persevere.

Twenty-eight-year-old "Jan," after graduating from the Job Corps, had been bartending and cooking until her arms required six surgeries. After a long list of low-paying, part-time jobs, "Jan" is now completing her first year at college (with great recommendations) and has made the Dean's list. I'll pay for year number two.

Ruth, who began her bio with Bon Jovi's "It's my life. It's now or never," is wheelchair-bound by scoliosis and spinal muscular atrophy. While still in high school, she enlisted Social Services to help her leave her alcoholic parents and live with her sister. Ruth's grades are barely acceptable, but her recommendations are strong, so we'll bend the rules to help Ruth attain an elementary education degree.

The third applicant, and the one that I'm least sure of, is Mary, who, despite miserable grades, graduated from high school thirty years ago because her teachers "took pity on me." Born with a cleft lip and palate, Mary has overcome drugs and alcohol and has worked as a nursing assistant for almost 20 years. She needs bifocals, and a computer wouldn't hurt. Now, while living in an adult foster home and taking medications for depression, she is completing her first year in college with acceptable grades and average recommendations — and hopes to return next fall. Her goal is to become "a self-sufficient, self-reliant nurse who doesn't need Social Security." I'll take a chance on Mary. Go for it, girl!

A year from now, I'll receive a similar stack of requests. When that time arrives, people like me will still be the target of religious bigots, and I suppose that I'll still be angry, knowing that all of the applications that have fallen at my feet could have been funded by the cost of just one Hellfire missile fired in a fraudulent war that was caused by a person who claims to follow the Prince of Peace.

# Dear John

The following letter was sent to a recipient of one of the college scholarships I fund who sent a thank you letter that made references to Jesus.

Dear John,

I hope you have Internet access because I would like you to visit my website, which is www.tundracub.com.

I am pleased that you appreciate our assistance. My father taught state and local government, history and philosophy at Mesabi Community College for more than 40 years, and he was very popular with both the faculty and the students. Like most people, he was raised in a mildly religious family, but after taking college courses in comparative religions, he came to be skeptical of all supernatural beliefs. As I grew up, I was free to attend church or not as I saw fit.

Because of his love for teaching and for working with young people, and because I have been successful and believe that the future of the country lies in education — not indoctrination — I decided to establish a scholarship in his name that would assist three individuals every year who might not otherwise be able to attend college for financial reasons.

After I graduated from college, I married a great gal who was a Presbyterian, so we were married in her church, where I eventually became an elder (We've had 53 great years together).

Most people acquire religion in one of two ways: they are born into it or they marry into it — neither one requiring critical thinking. However, as time went by and we both began to expand our education and our life experiences, we came to realize that the people we knew who never attended church were just as good as those who did. Furthermore, we discovered that many of the people who were in church were not as good as some of our nonreligious friends.

In time, we moved to the Unitarian church because it is the least doctrinal of the churches and it encourages critical thinking — as do their generally well-educated people. And although we still occasionally attend the Unitarian church, primarily to associate with our many friends there, we are no longer religious.

About 20 years ago, we became involved with the Humanist Association of Minnesota, a group that does all the good things that churches do but without supernatural threats and promises. Not long after joining, I became its president and later became a board member of the American Humanist Association, which is headquartered in Washington, DC.

Over the years, I have met and enjoyed thousands of moral, ethical, upstanding people who call themselves atheists, secular humanists or freethinkers, and I mention this primarily because many preachers and grandstanding politicians make it a point to put down or denigrate these good people, like myself, who now number at least 30 million in the U.S. alone.

They are all around you, but they rarely speak up because it is unpopular to reject the dominant religion in any country — and many know that if they were open about not being religious it would mean the end of their jobs.

I am pleased to help you get your life straightened out and if you needed religion to get you going, that's OK. Just remember the next time you hear someone criticizing atheists, that it was one of them who, believing in the importance of education, chose to assist you regardless of whether you did or did not have one of the many supernatural beliefs.

Finally, because the public is so ignorant of the contributions nonreligious people make, I have included the list of the many atheists and freethinkers who have improved our lives and helped us along the way. FYI, a deist — a few are mentioned — believes only in the god of nature or, one might say, of the Big Bang that set it all in motion. Many of these people were crusaders against slavery, against bigotry and against keeping blacks and women from voting.

You will not recognize many of these names because you have not yet had courses that reveal their contributions. You would be wise to look them up on the Internet.

By the way, the large, publicly-owned indoor tennis facility that you can see from highway 53 exists because of me. About six years ago, I established the committee to build the facility and chaired the committee for three years, during which we raised more than $700,000 toward the cost of that $1 million facility. Of that $700,000, I contributed a major chunk because I wanted to do something good for the citizens, young and old, religious and not, of the community I grew up in. We gave the city the $700,000 and the city paid the rest.

Good luck to you. However, please remember that in many cases we make our own luck by the actions we take and by thinking ahead. As you go through life, keep your mind and your *Eyes Wide Open*, which happens to be the title of my fourth book due out next year. The rest are listed on my website – www.tundracub.com.

Cheers
George Erickson

# The End?

*from True North: Exploring the Great Wilderness by Bush Plane*

Who hasn't watched a stream carry away the last leaves of summer without wondering what meanderings will take it to the sea? And who, while pondering the flow, has not sensed the metaphor of the stream of life. Another bend in the river rounded — another day slipping away.

Life is like an immense hourglass that is fixed to the Earth. We cannot turn it over. We cannot reverse the flow. Its upper half is opaque as night, so we cannot know how much sand remains. For some, the upper half is full at their birth, but for others it's almost empty. And as the grains stream down, we rarely stop to wonder how many have yet to fall. For many, especially the young, it would come as a shock to discover that only a few remain.

Though our lives begin with a cry of surprise,
and a question awaits at their close,
in between lie days filled with wonder
for all to slowly unfold.

In forest and canyon cathedrals,
in treasured libraries and halls,
welcome them, open them, savor them,
for after the question — who knows.